Growing Up Kennedy

Growing Up Kennedy

The Third Wave Comes of Age

Harrison Rainie *and* John Quinn
with exclusive photos by Brian Quigley

G. P. PUTNAM'S SONS
NEW YORK

Designed by Richard Oriolo

Library of Congress Cataloging in Publication Data

Rainie, Harrison.
Growing up Kennedy.

1. Kennedy family. I. Quinn, John. II. Quigley,
Brian. III. Title.
E843.R35   1983   973.922′092′2 [B]   83–9736
ISBN 0–399–12864–6

PRINTED IN THE UNITED STATES OF AMERICA
Fourth Impression

To my wife,
Linda Anderson Rainie, and my infant daughter Amanda,
who both saw to it that life was sweet enough and calm
enough for this book to be done.

H.R.

For Dookie.

J.Q.

Contents

CHILDREN OF JOHN F. KENNEDY AND JACQUELINE BOUVIER

Caroline Bouvier Kennedy Born 11/27/57; Concord Academy (1975), Harvard University (1979).

John Fitzgerald Kennedy, Jr. Born 11/25/60; Phillips Academy, Andover (1979), Brown University (1983).

CHILDREN OF ROBERT F. KENNEDY AND ETHEL SKAKEL

Kathleen Kennedy Townsend Born 7/4/51; Putney School (1969), Harvard University (1973), University of New Mexico Law School (1979); married David Townsend (1973); children—Meaghan (born 11/9/77), Maeve (born 11/1/79).

Joseph Patrick Kennedy II Born 9/24/52; Manter Hall School (1971), University of Massachusetts (1976); married Sheila Brewster Rauch (1978); children—twin sons, Joseph P. III and Matthew Rauch (born 10/4/80).

Robert Francis Kennedy, Jr. Born 1/17/54; Millbrook School (1972), Harvard University (1977), London School of Economics (1978), Virginia Law School (1982); married Emily Ruth Black (1982).

David Anthony Kennedy Born 6/15/55; Milton Academy (1973), enrolled at Harvard University.

Mary Courtney Kennedy Ruhe Born 9/9/56; Milton Academy (1974); married Jeffrey Ruhe (1980).

Michael LeMoyne Kennedy Born 2/27/58; St. Paul's School (1975), Harvard University (1979), enrolled at University of Virginia Law School; married Victoria Gifford (1981); children—Michael LeMoyne, Jr. (born 1/9/83).

Mary Kerry Kennedy Born 9/8/59; Putney School (1977), Brown University (1982).

Christopher George Kennedy Born 7/4/63; Georgetown Prep School (1982), enrolled at Boston College.

Matthew Maxwell Taylor Kennedy Born 1/11/65; Moses Brown School (1983).

Douglas Harriman Kennedy Born 3/24/67; enrolled at Potomac School.

Rory Elizabeth Kennedy Born 12/12/68; enrolled at Potomac School.

CHILDREN OF EDWARD MOORE KENNEDY AND JOAN BENNETT

Kara Anne Kennedy Born 2/27/60; National Cathedral School (1978), Tufts University (1983).

Edward Moore Kennedy, Jr. Born 9/26/61; St. Alban's School (1979), enrolled at Wesleyan University.

Patrick Joseph Kennedy Born 7/14/67; enrolled at Phillips Academy, Andover.

CHILDREN OF ROBERT SARGENT SHRIVER, JR. AND EUNICE KENNEDY

Robert Sargent Shriver III Born 4/28/54; Phillips Exeter Academy (1972), Yale University (1976), Yale Law School (1981).

Maria Owings Shriver Born 11/6/55; Stone Ridge School (1973), Georgetown University (1977).

Timothy Perry Shriver Born 8/29/59; St. Alban's School (1977), Yale University (1981).

Mark Kennedy Shriver Born 2/17/64; Georgetown Prep School (1982), enrolled at Holy Cross University.

Anthony Paul Kennedy Shriver Born 7/20/65; enrolled at Georgetown Prep School.

CHILDREN OF PETER LAWFORD AND PATRICIA KENNEDY

Christopher Kennedy Lawford Born 3/29/55; Middlesex Prep School (1972), Tufts University (1976), Boston College Law School (1983).

Sydney Lawford Born 8/25/56; Foxcroft School (1974), Toby Coburn Fashion Institute (1978); engaged to Peter McKelvey.

Victoria Francis Lawford Born 11/4/58; Lycée Français (1976), Mt. Vernon College (1980).

Robin Elizabeth Lawford Born 7/2/61; Unis School (1980); enrolled at Marymount College.

CHILDREN OF STEPHEN SMITH AND JEAN KENNEDY

Stephen Smith, Jr. Born 6/28/57; Collegiate School (1975), Harvard University (1979), enrolled at Columbia Law School.

William Smith Born 9/4/60; Salisbury School (1978), Duke University (1983).

Amanda Mary Smith Born 4/30/67; enrolled at Spence School.

Kym Maria Smith Born 11/29/72; enrolled at Marymount School.

Foreword

THE TWENTY-NINE GRANDCHILDREN OF JOSEPH P. AND ROSE Fitzgerald Kennedy have grown up at the center of the world's stage. They had no choice in the matter. They were thrust into instant notoriety by the election of John F. Kennedy as President and kept there by the feverish press of great and terrible events that followed.

No group of children has ever been reared in such a super-heated atmosphere, and no one has ever before examined what it is like to grow up not so much with television as on television. That is one purpose of this book. Another is to introduce the third wave of America's newest seigneurial family as the oldest of them, now more than a dozen strong, stake out public positions of their own.

What are they like? How do the six singular families—Shriver, Smith, and Lawford as well as the three surnamed Kennedy—differ? How are they similar? What do they feel now about the presidency of Jack and the careers of Robert and Ted, about their family's commitment to achievement and service? How have they measured up? Where have they failed? Will they carry on the tradition? Who are the likely candidates?

John Kennedy's brief but dramatic presidency that began with the Bay of Pigs and ended with his assassination; his brother Robert's effort to follow him into the White House, which seemed almost certain to succeed until it was abruptly halted with his own murder; the third brother, Ted's, fall from grace at Chappaquiddick and his long climb back to a presidential candidacy of his own, ending in unexpected defeat. All these events have had profound effects on the attitudes and behavior of the family's third wave.

Most of the older cousins are now in a period of uncertainty, torn in their mid-twenties or early thirties between a desire to lead normal lives and the certainty that their heritage probably will not allow it. "Kennedys cannot be on the sidelines," says young Teddy, speaking for them all. They believe this without question.

They are joined to one another and to a large proportion of the American and even the world public by the ties of tragedies endured together. They believe they are summoned by family and by destiny to finish important business begun by their fathers or uncles.

They are starting on this self-assigned task under vastly different circumstances from those under which John, Robert, and Edward began—changes brought about by the civil rights movement, feminism, the drug culture, the generation gap. John and Robert in particular helped initiate some of these changes, which makes the cousins' response to them all the more intriguing.

And they also set out under the protection of a secret and infallible weapon that no sorrow can efface, no law can abrogate: the family.

Senator Edward Kennedy alone among the parents greatly helped in the completion of this book, giving generously of his time and opening some of the family's personal papers. He and his staff, especially Bob Shrum and Melody Miller, patiently and courteously answered numerous requests for information and helped open literally more than a hundred vitally important doors.

Of the cousins themselves, Kathleen, Joe, Bobby Junior, Michael, Chris, and Kerry among the RFKs submitted to lengthy interviews and were extremely candid in their responses. Kara, Teddy Junior, and Patrick of the EMK home were similarly cooperative, as were Bobby, Maria and Tim Shriver, Steve Smith, Jr., and Chris and Victoria Lawford. The book would have been impossible without their help.

In addition, scores of friends of the family have left their fingerprints all over these pages. Among the busy people who kindly helped with information or anecdotes are:

Jamie Auchincloss, Bill Barry, Chris Bartle, Eric Breindel, Barbara Grant Briggs, Bob Brown, Richard Burke, Juan Cameron, Tom Caplan, Mary Gallagher Civetti, Ramsey Clark, Dick Clasby, Anne Coffey, Mary Alice Cook, Andy Cushner, Rita Dallas, Lorenzo di Bonaventura, Mary Ann Dolan, Dick Drayne, Peter Emerson, Father James English.

Theresa Fitzpatrick, Blake Fleetwood, John Florescu, Dick Gallagher, Akiva Goldsman, Tim Hanan, Dr. Tim Haydock, Theo Hayes, Claude Hooton, Dr. Larry Horowitz, Peter Kaplan, Andy Karsch, Abby Kaufman, the Kelleys (Karen, Pamela, Candy and Margaret), Tom Koutsoumpas, Ruth Kovnat, Angelique Lee, Richard Licata, Evelyn Lincoln, Melissa Ludtke.

Senator George McGovern, Robert McNamara, Father Richard McSorley, Sam Medalie, Maura Moynihan, Larry Newman, Neal Nordlinger, Angie Novello, Cindy O'Brien, Linda Potter, Adam Randolph, Richard Rougeau, John Seigenthaler, Linda Semans, John Sheridan, Doug Spooner, Sophie Spurr, Adam Walinsky, Jack Weeks, Oprah Winfrey, and Judy Zack.

Finally, Lila Karpf made many astute suggestions and was unfailingly supportive.

Harrison Rainie also wants to acknowledge the support he received from James Wieghart, editor of the *New York Daily News,* and Lars-Erik Nelson, Washington Bureau Chief of the *News,* both of whom encouraged this work and were extremely generous in helping bring it to life and tolerating the demands it placed on Rainie.

None of them is responsible for the results. Although they and the Kennedy family made the book possible, and much of the story is in their own words, neither family nor friends have controlled what we have written in any way. This evaluation of growing up Kennedy is ours alone and we are responsible for any mistakes.

The Third Wave

The Hinge Turns

IT WAS, APPROPRIATELY, A SHINING BLUE-AND-GOLD AUTUM-
nal day. A day for looking backward with pardonable tears. A
day for looking forward with a quickening of hope. Only one
of the 29 grandchildren of Joseph Patrick and Rose Kennedy
was missing—the oldest, Kathleen, who was due to give birth
to her second child that day. (With typical Kennedy orneriness,
baby Maeve was 11 days late.)

The other members of the third generation—Kennedy, Shriver,
Smith, and Lawford—arrived with available parents in a convoy
of limousines, each with a modest placard affixed to the right
front door saying *Kennedy Family*. They were there with 7000
others in the Boston suburb of Dorchester on October 20,
1979, for the dedication of the Kennedy Library, devoted to
the works and memory of John F. Kennedy and his brother
Robert—either father or uncle of each of the 28 gathered cousins. It was the only time that so many of them—from husky
Joseph P. Kennedy II, then 27, to tiny six-year-old Kym Smith—
had gathered in one public place.

Moments before noon they took their seats on the stage or
in the first five rows of audience facing I. M. Pei's abstract but
nautically suggestive white-concrete, dark-glass-and-steel struc-
ture that shimmered at the water's edge, a spectacular memorial
to men who loved the sea. Off to the side, the late President's
favorite sloop, the *Victura*, strained upon its mounts as though
tacking for a favorable breeze.

In a group famous for revels, everyone was on good behavior
as the elders took their places—the widows Jackie and Ethel,
Ted and Joan, Steve and Jean Smith, Sargent and Eunice Shriver,
Pat Lawford, joined by the celebrated older members of the
next generation, young Joe, Caroline, and John. Still, there

was a thrumming tension in the air, as there is on most occasions when Kennedys gather. Almost imperceptible at first, it gradually builds until it resolves in a powerful climax, often unexpected.

The tension began as President Jimmy Carter and his wife Rosalyn arrived and took their places alongside the family. Almost everyone present, including Carter, knew that Senator Ted Kennedy had decided to challenge the President's reelection in the Democratic primaries, and some, especially the hundreds of journalists there, were hoping for the crackle of political musketry between the two. That was not to be. Although Ted in part had based his decision on the conviction that Carter had betrayed the liberal legacy of his murdered brothers, he had postponed his announcement until this event, so important to the whole family, was securely behind him. He had no intention to mar the occasion with rancor or discourtesy.

Solemnly, President Carter ran the family gauntlet on the stage, forthrightly pumping each male hand, chastely pecking each female cheek—until he got to Jackie. There the presidential pucker almost went a-begging, as Jackie's stony face retreated and remained impassive as Carter planted his kiss. The crowd buzzed.

The Boston Pops Orchestra zipped through a lively medley—Beethoven's *Oberon* overture, Copland's "Fanfare for the Common Man," Bernstein's overture to his *Candide*, Sousa's "Stars and Stripes Forever"—and the crowd settled back into comfortable detachment as young John Kennedy, a dedicated and relatively accomplished amateur actor, was introduced by his sister Caroline and came forward to deliver a tribute to his father—a poem of Stephen Spender's, "I Think Continually of Those Who Were Truly Great."

The tribute was in accord with the reticence typical of John and Caroline and their mother. It was, that is, romantic and visionary and without any direct reference to Jack or to themselves. By their mother's design, the children of Jack Kennedy show nothing of themselves to the world, perhaps because, as a family, they had been so battered by worldly intrusion. Give them nothing to remember, the JFKs seemed to be saying, and maybe "they" will leave us alone.

Then it was Joe Kennedy's turn, and he was anything but diffident. Unlike Caroline and John, Joe does not shrink from telling the world what he thinks and how he feels. He is very much Robert Kennedy's son—direct, pugnacious, careless of proprieties.

Like his mother and other members of his own family, Joe was nettled by the relatively small portion of library exhibit space devoted to his father as opposed to the abundance accorded to Jack. "Daddy's not in that library," one RFK child later complained. Joe also wanted to shake a verbal fist in Carter's face—guest of honor or no guest of honor—and he knew Uncle Ted's respect for hospitality would not admit the message that he wanted Carter to hear. He wanted, in his way, to do what he knew his father would have done on such a state occasion—shake the place up.

He had trained for this day like a fighter. He had not been sure he would be picked to speak, so his first job was to be the best prepared. He assembled facts, drafted and redrafted the words. He read over his father's speeches and pondered how best to characterize the man. Finally he titled his speech "The Unfinished Business of Robert Kennedy."

When Ethel gathered her oldest children around her to decide who would speak about their father, Joe said that he had put "a little something" together. The others shrugged and gave him the honor. He told them nothing about his remarks. More importantly, he did not clear them with Uncle Ted. It was the first time any of the cousins had given such a highly visible and political performance without checking it first with the male head of the family. But Joe wanted no tampering with this speech. He told others later he was not even sure what tone he would take until he actually stood before the throng.

He began gently: "As I stand here and think about my father and what his life was all about, I have to admit to myself that there is only one kind of completely satisfactory memorial to him, and he, himself, tried to build it—a better, a much better, America."

He spoke of what his father meant to him and, so he believed, to the family and to the nation. "My father died waging a struggle. As I have grown up, I have come to appreciate what that struggle was about." Joe then cited the things his father had striven to do for migrant workers, blacks, Chicanos, Eskimos, ordinary working people everywhere. He tried, Joe said, to give voice to voices that were not heard.

"One day it may be different here," he went on, shifting to a higher emotional gear, "but only if we acquire what my father called 'moral courage.' " At this point elements in the crowd began to stir, some with apprehension (was Joe going to start something?), others with delight. "Moral courage" was an RFK family buzzword that started deeply programmed responses tolling in Kennedy consciences. Robert Kennedy had peppered his final speeches with "moral courage." It became his family's motto.

Fixing Jimmy Carter with a stare, Joe continued: "I hope and pray that my generation will work to bring about the decent and just world he so much wanted to see. We all know inflation bears down hardest on the poor. Now we're being told by the chairman of the Federal Reserve Board that the standard of living for the average American has to decline if inflation is to be reduced. Well, what about the standard of living of the people on the boards of the giant oil companies that are squeezing us so hard all the time, and who is stopping them?"

Now many of the older Kennedyites began to catch the drift of Joe's message and they were, in a word, appalled. They could do nothing, but their angry glances raked the young upstart who was, as they saw it, spilling gravy all over the day's neat white shirtfront. With furrowed brow, Senator Ted held his chin in his hand and fixedly examined the toe of his right oxford. Finding no dust, he pensively contemplated the space several feet above the heads in the crowd. Yet the RFK wing of the crowd, including the cousins, began to whoop and pound their thighs.

Joe, who soon would found a company to sell heating oil to the poor at lower than market prices, was now in overdrive. He lashed out next at two other favorite liberal targets, the coal barons and factory farmers. In conclusion, he quoted a famous speech his father had made on a visit to South Africa 13 years before: "The future does not belong to those who are content with today. Rather it will belong to those who blend vision, reason and courage in a personal commitment to the ideals and great enterprises of American society."

Galvanized, the cousins leaped to their feet to applaud their oldest male. Joe was calling them with the authentic Kennedy voice that had governed, even haunted, their childhoods. It was the kind of knock-their-socks-off speech for which Robert Kennedy was famous. Far more than Jack, Robert had been the family's defiant liberal advance guard, posing the issues that came to dominate their political thinking and exhorting them to get on with the job.

Then it was Jimmy Carter's moment, and even the fiercest

Kennedy partisans present later acknowledged that this was the President at his best. As a Cracker in Kennedyland, he no doubt expected a wall of hostility between himself and the audience, but he never acknowledged it. Instead, he beguiled them with an example of the late President's wit at Ted's expense. In March 1962, after he'd been in office a little over a year, Jack had been asked about some remarks of brother Ted. Ted had said that he didn't think he'd "ever be interested in being President" after he'd seen the toll it had taken of Jack. So the inquisitor put it to Jack: Would he do it over again? And would he recommend it to Ted? "Well," JFK had replied in his driest Yankee voice, "the answer to the first question is yes, and to the second question is no—at least for a while."

That is the message Carter wanted Ted to hear, too, and no one better appreciated Carter's jibe than Ted, who led the applause for the joke at his expense.

Then Carter grabbed the heart of the crowd by recollecting his personal reaction to the slaying of Jack Kennedy. Like many of his countrymen, he could summon in vivid detail exactly what he had been doing on that terrible day almost 16 years before:

"I remember that I climbed down from a tractor, unhooked a farm trailer and walked into my warehouse to weigh a load of grain. I was told by a group of farmers that the President had been shot. I went outside, knelt on the steps and began to pray. In a few minutes I learned that he had not lived. It was a grievous personal loss—my President. I wept openly for the first time in more than ten years—for the first time since my father had died."

The wall between Carter and the crowd was washed away in an instant by the tears that all could call forth when they remembered that day. Perhaps even Jackie was moved, but that was hard to say. When Jackie wears her masklike public face it is, for practical purposes, impenetrable.

Ted's own remarks were heavily weighted—as all Kennedy voices are on such occasions—with understandable nostalgia and elegy. He remembered his brothers as men and said of Jack's brief, eventful presidency: "We recall those years of grace, that time of hope. The spark still glows. The journey never ends. The dream shall never die."

On cue, as orchestrated by Steve Smith, the late President's voice then washed over the crowd in hauntingly realistic Dolby sound delivering excerpts from Jack's major speeches, beginning with the Inaugural Address. The only sound in the throng was soft weeping as that unmistakable voice and those familiar cadences hung in the air.

"I was thinking to myself that I knew all those speeches and all those words," Michael Kennedy (an RFK child) recalls. He and his siblings had been given leather-bound books by their Uncle Ted many years earlier called "Words Jack Loved." "I had read it many times," he says. "All the speeches were in that book. It really felt like he was there."

"It was eerie and ghostly," agrees Steve Smith, Jr. "The whole day reawakened something in you. Uncle Jack gave America the sense of collective possibility, and that day was our way to make contact again with something not present in contemporary American society."

As Jack's voice stilled, the crowd began to gather belongings and then slowly drift away.

Despite the misgivings of most of the elder Kennedys, young Joe's speech had gone almost entirely unreported and caused little stir in the outside world. The public, and hence the press, was preoccupied with the larger Kennedy drama of the coming campaign, and partisans looked eagerly for a return to the special leadership they believed the second generation of Kennedy brothers had brought to the nation. Young Bobby Kennedy, Steve Smith, Jr. and their friend Peter Kaplan sensed it when they fell in afterward in the parking lot with veteran liberal Allard Lowenstein. "We're coming back," Lowenstein had exulted. "The feeling was very tangible," Kaplan adds, "that the politics that had been buried since Robert Kennedy's death was returning."

Inside the Kennedy network, though, Joe's speech had been The Moment of the day—unforgettable and important as the next generation's call to arms. Its real significance was not fully apparent, however, until some time after the dedication ceremony. Knowingly or not, that day Joe, speaking for all the cousins, had taken up RFK's challenge and announced that the third wave of Kennedys had arrived. The hinge had turned.

Even Uncle Ted, who had been so embarrassed by the speech during its delivery, now says unreservedly, "It was the high point of the day."

First Blood

THREE WEEKS AFTER THE LIBRARY DEDICATION, TED KEN-
nedy, to no one's surprise, said that he would run for the presidency. Several factors had influenced him: the genetic Kennedy
drive to fight and to win, polls that showed him lathering Carter
two-to-one nationwide, and the pleas of Senate Democratic
colleagues who were afraid that the crippled President would
take them down with him.

Before he could declare himself, the senator had to resolve
questions about his wife and from his children. Simply put, Joan
was a reformed alcoholic. She had always had difficulty accom-
modating the Kennedy political and social imperatives and the
changes they brought to her life. At first she fought, then she
retreated. Finally she gave up.

Her spirit had been sapped by rumors about her husband's
behavior, and by the slayings of her two brothers-in-law. What
finally broke her was the Chappaquiddick affair, in which young
Mary Jo Kopechne had died in circumstances that at the very
least inculpated Ted. She had escaped into drink.

Many who came in contact with the family in the late 1960s
and early 1970s saw the toll that it all took on Joan. In her
home and in public she now acknowledged she was a sick woman.
A physician classmate of Ted's at Harvard recalls meeting them
at a reunion: "The senator came bounding in with his entourage,
tanned and radiant and full of smiles. Behind him came Mrs.
Kennedy with a vacant look in her eye, her hair awry and food
stains all over her blouse. It was impossible not to feel sorry
for her. Her face was bloated. Your heart went out to her."

Some inner urge to save herself eventually took hold. Joan
joined Alcoholics Anonymous and began the painful reversal
back to self-esteem and good health. By 1978 she had been

strong enough to leave the family home and establish herself in Boston, where she resumed the college-level study of music.

For her husband the questions before the campaign were: Could she stand the rigors of the campaign? Would she? After extensive discussion, the doctors said yes to the first question. Joan said yes to the second. That left the children.

With Kara, Teddy Junior, and Patrick, the issue crystallized into a single four-letter word—fear. They, like the pundits, had no doubt whatever that Ted would win. The polls confirmed it and they believed the nation yearned for it. What plagued them was their terror that what had happened to Jack and Bobby could happen to their father. It was so deeply rooted and pervasive that they could not, would not, talk with him about it.

Ted, sensing this, dispatched his old friend and counselor Larry Horowitz to help Kara and young Teddy through the critical passage. Horowitz went over the security precautions with them in great detail and tried to convince them that the violence of the past had been tempered. Patrick, the youngest, was so resistant and inconsolable, however, that Ted dealt with the boy himself.

All through the summer of 1979 the discussions went on, in pairs or in groups, while out sailing, while walking the beach, while just sitting on the porch. Never once in any of the talks was the unmentionable—that Ted might be shot—mentioned. But eventually the children capitulated. Teddy Junior explains: "It was something he'd devoted his whole life to. I really could not deny him that chance. I didn't want him to have any regrets."

The campaign was on.

The older cousins speedily enrolled. "In this family," says Joe Kennedy, "when you're called, you go." Steve Smith, Jr., gives a more detailed explanation: "First, we all love Teddy, especially those to whom he was a father after their own fathers were gone. The other thing is that you should be a part because everyone in the family is a part."

They began the great adventure in high confidence. In Manchester, New Hampshire, the state that holds the first presidential primary, a jolly Uncle Ted produced some of the cousins for a curious, not unfriendly gathering:

"I just want to introduce you to a few members of the family. Heeeeere's my son Patrick! Say hello, Patrick." The 12-year-old rose shyly and waved his hand with eyes bowed. And then there's my daughter Kara! All right, Kara!" She was up and back in her chair in a flash, blushing. "Then my niece, Maria! Okay, Maria!" The attractive brunette of the family Shriver acknowledged some whistles.

"And here's one who has been around quite a lot—my nephew, Joe! Now, just because he ran my Senate campaign in 1976 and is doing a lot of work for me now, Joe certainly doesn't want to run for public office—in Massachusetts or anywhere else. Right, Joe?" Joe smiled and shook his head "no."

"There are a lot of Kennedys and you'll see most of them before we finish in New Hampshire. And you'll be seeing them all long after that! There are more Kennedys coming!"

The reception from the electorate was not nearly as enthusiastic. The once mighty plurality in the polls evaporated, and the first voters to have their say confirmed the reversal. Ted lost in quick succession in Iowa, Maine, New Hampshire, Florida, and Illinois.

In the process, the third wave quickly learned that many of their countrymen did not love Ted or their family at all, but were feverishly hostile to both. Kara was particularly affected by the virulence of some of the attacks, according to her friend John Florescu, in part because she was just coming out of her adolescent shell when the worst of the assault came. Florescu remembers escorting Kara to a church in suburban Philadelphia before the Pennsylvania primary, where about 200 people watched open-mouthed as the priest who was supposed to introduce her launched instead into a broadside attack on her father: "I disagree with everything her father stands for," ranted the priest. "He does not deserve to be President." Stunned, Kara tried to interrupt, but the priest shouted her down and Kara rushed, sobbing, from the hall.

Another time, as she distributed leaflets outside the Pan Am Building on New York's East Side, some passersby recognized Kara and hurled savage epithets. "Your father's a killer!" was one of the milder ones. Later, on another Manhattan corner, a man walked up to her and said to her calmly: "You know, your father killed a young woman your age."

Whoever said "Names will never hurt you" was wrong. Kara still feels the pain, says Florescu, but that pain had the tonic effect of drawing her closer to her father. "This shy, reticent woman was forced to make a choice. Either she could retreat or she could stand up to it." She stood up. So did her cousins.

For veteran campaigner Joe it was easier. In Des Moines one

afternoon a young woman wanted to know how Ted had "the nerve" to run after what had happened at Chappaquiddick. Joe's response was deft: "You either give up and say that life is not worth living, or you can try to get up off the mat and do the best you can and work as hard as you can for the things you believe in. And I think that's what Ted Kennedy has done for the past ten years."

As the campaign wore on the senator began to win a few— New York, Connecticut, Pennsylvania. Still, some of the cousins were learning new and disturbing things about their family's standing in the nation. Though it is hard to believe, some of them had not seriously encountered concern about their own or their uncle's safety until the campaign.

Victoria Lawford recalls greeting voters outside a Detroit polling place. She smiled at an elderly man garnished with Carter buttons and asked: "Would you think about voting for my Uncle Ted?"

"I can't," he replied. "I don't want anything to happen to him—or to you."

Taken aback, Victoria rallied with: "Don't worry about us. We are all together and we're all behind him."

When the man left several minutes later after voting, he flipped over his lapel to cover up the Carter buttons and whispered to Victoria: "I voted for Ted. Now, please, take care."

"It made me proud of what Ted was risking," she said later, "and I felt good, too, because I had made a convert."

But eventually it became clear that Ted might lose, and the mood on planes and in hotel rooms changed from buoyant to blah, even sour. "No one foresaw what was going to happen," says Patrick. "All of a sudden things started to go wrong."

Many of the young campaigners found themselves for the first time having to defend themselves against angry charges of presuming upon their wealth and privilege: "There was a great deal of animosity toward me and my money," Michael Kennedy wonderingly recalls, "which is a laugh, because my family at least does not have much."

They were in demand, however, and the need, even compulsion, to use the Kennedy prerogative was there. Kathleen sometimes had difficulty getting phone calls returned when she used her married name, Mrs. Townsend. But when she was Kathleen Kennedy, the ringing never stopped. "Many privileges go with the name," Kathleen admits somewhat ruefully.

On the stump, the cousins quickly developed idiosyncratic styles. Kathleen, for example, hit hard on women's and environmental issues. She did not mind such notoriety as she occasioned, but she grew to hate the interest groups who openly sought to barter votes for a pledge of support. Although log-rolling is a practice long honored in American politics, Kathleen recoiled from it as somehow unclean, and her experience prompted her to begin a study of the spiritual decline in American society during the 1970s and early 1980s.

Down in Dixie, her brother Bobby ladled on a mixture of Boston blarney laced with Southern charm in accents reminiscent of the engaging backwoods characters he met while he was writing a book in Alabama in the late 1970s. He was the perfect surrogate for Ted, except for a tendency not to let facts undercut a convincing argument.

Joe, as usual, was ambiguous about his place in the process. He was commissioned to work hard in the beginning, but then was woefully underused in the latter stages of the campaign. No one regrets his underemployment more than his uncle, who later asked why Joe's advice from the field was not taken more seriously. As a stump performer Joe is both tense and engaging. He will shake a hand with the best of campaigners, but there is a part of him that does not enjoy it.

As for the others, Maria Shriver was earnestly convincing in a way that suggested her mother, Eunice; and Michael Kennedy was serious, thoughtful and correct—and, like many of the others, came into his own after the worst of the abuses had receded. They still talk about the time he and Teddy Junior danced an afternoon away in a Slavic neighborhood in Chicago to keep a restive crowd happy while Senator Kennedy's plane circled a closed airport.

Young Steve Smith joined his father in the back room, where he scrupulously monitored the action in New York and helped orchestrate the biggest win of the failed campaign. Of all the cousins, Steve probably benefited most from the experience, coming away without bitterness, but instead with an invigorated taste for politics.

Caroline and John dutifully prospected in remote stretches of Vermont and Maine, playing on memories and often doing the most drudging volunteer work. Sometimes the nostalgia went both ways. Lorenzo di Bonaventura, a friend, remembers the day he went with Caroline to an Orthodox synagogue outside Boston, where the rabbi proceeded to wind a skein of tender and rollicking recollections of a young politician named John Kennedy.

At the beginning of the event none of the male congregants had shaken Caroline's hand, which she found unsettling even though it accords with the Orthodox tradition of keeping women, especially a stranger, at arm's length. But when the rabbi had finished, many in the congregation, men included, came up to embrace Caroline, who was so overcome she hardly said a word.

Atypically, Tim Shriver hated campaigning, yet served dutifully and with as much grace as he could muster. "I just don't like going to teas with people and have them stare at you because you're the Nephew," he explains—" 'Isn't it wonderful that he looks like them.'—It's so much of a fishbowl."

Before it was over, most of the cousins had been more affected than any of them might have imagined that day less than a year before when they had jumped exultantly to their feet after Joe's "Library Speech." He had let the world know that the third wave of Kennedys was coming and they had learned on their own the pitfalls of such a buildup.

Kathleen was at first bemused, then irked because "she could not get her message across," reports her friend Ruth Kovnat. Young Teddy rankled under similar frustrations: "People really didn't care about the real issues," he complains. His cousin, Maria Shriver, agrees: "Nineteen-eighty had a profound impact. All of us believed in the campaign very strongly, and the hostility to it was very difficult to understand. We all love Teddy deeply, so our jobs were not only to convince people of a certain system of beliefs that we thought would be good for the country, but also about a man who was very close to us. After a while, it was hard to keep your head on straight."

"For some of them it was the first time they had the worst of the sycophants and the worst of being surrogates," comments Jack Weeks, a friend who worked in the campaign. "On the one side were those who wanted to suck up to them—touch the hem of their garments. On another side were the professional political people whose attitude was, 'Oh my God, we have to find something for these surrogates to do. Why do we have to deal with this?' Then there were the just plain haters. All in all, it was the first time some of them ever were treated like meat."

For still others, the real shock of failure and defeat did not come until the contest was formally over on the night that Ted, seeing that he'd lost a crucial rules fight at the covention, publicly conceded. Until that very moment, some of the cousins still believed in and hoped for another Kennedy miracle of the sort that had propelled Jack into the White House and had been looming for RFK until that fatal night in Los Angeles. They really were not psychically attuned to defeat.

In the solitude of the family's suite at the Waldorf Towers, Teddy Junior went into the bathroom and wept—but not for long. As Teddy's friend and college roommate, Akiva Goldsman, tells it, soon Teddy was back out in the living room with his father and friends laughing and joking as if nothing much had happened. "That family," says Goldsman, "has the super-Irish capacity to laugh its way through anything."

Besides, for the family, Ted's defeat had certain salutary effects. Joan's ability to withstand the campaign, some friends suggest, gave her the courage soon after to question her marriage and begin the first really open discussions with Ted about their future. In the end they both had learned enough to agree to end a marriage that had long been unsatisfying.

Throughout the campaign there had been obvious signs of her growth in poise. After all those years she was coming into her own. "Whether we win or lose, I win," she told reporter Myra MacPherson. She said the campaign had been "the best thing in the world next to getting sober. I feel as though I had been let out of jail. Whatever happens, whether it's the White House or not, I will be okay." And she is.

For the children and cousins, there were also great strides toward maturity. Kara and Patrick overcame their fear, and even came in some ways to enjoy campaigning. Kara lost 20 pounds and emerged poised and lovely—a veritable beauty. Steve Smith, Jr., has become one of the real forces of his generation. His elders now regularly seek his counsel, recognizing that a surprisingly old and wise political head resides there on a pair of very youthful shoulders.

In an even broader sense, the loss removed probably forever the Superman cloak that idolators had draped upon a not altogether unwilling family. The cousins were certainly angry, chagrined, and chastened by the party's rejection of what seemed to them so clearly to be a national need. They were disconsolate for a time, but far from destroyed, and they quickly turned to other concerns.

When it was over, Ted Junior said: "I've got lots of goals for myself apart from public service and I'll try to meet them before I think about what the rest of my life will be like." Chris Lawford added: "A lot of us are just discovering things now that were assumptions we built into our lives—like love and careers and families. People think that we're supposed to have all those 'normal' things and then move on to greater heights. Well, those 'normal' things provide their own rewards and satisfactions."

The aftermath has become a time of reflection and readjustment to a new Kennedy reality. "A lot of them entered nineteen-eighty with a sense of infallibility," says Andy Karsch, a friend of several of the older cousins and a campaign worker. "It almost seemed like a divine purpose. For so many reasons, some explicable, some seemingly not, suddenly things changed. It was their awakening to a new order and a new way of thinking about the family."

They had to accommodate the fact that for the first time a Kennedy had suffered a major defeat. It dawned on them that John Kennedy's inauguration had been 19 years before and much had happened since. Manifest destiny had become manifest uncertainty. The effect had been sobering.

It is fitting that Uncle Ted, not as young as he used to be and graying at the temples, should deliver the last, sagacious evaluation of the effect of the campaign on the third wave:

"They saw from it that just being a Kennedy has its obvious advantages, but it also brings some expectations as well. They developed some understanding and appreciation that Kennedys—perhaps more than others—have to meet those expectations."

Fame and Family

Once a Kennedy

YOUNG TEDDY KENNEDY TELLS THE FOLLOWING STORY, A crucial part of family lore that he learned from his father:

It was June 1961, and President John Kennedy was getting ready to travel to Vienna to meet Soviet Premier Nikita Khrushchev. The weekend before, Jack went to relax at the already famous family retreat in Hyannis Port on Cape Cod. It was a typical Kennedy family summer weekend: sailing, touch football, horseplay, and lots of blunt talk about the tactics and strategy of politics—international and national.

As dusk fell that Saturday evening, family members and guests, the latter mainly from JFK's administration, began to gather for cocktails on the verandah of Joseph P. Kennedy's house within the huge estate. The President and a few aides were among the stragglers. Unsmiling, Joe watched from the porch as they hurried across the lawn. He did not like tardiness.

Three-year-old Caroline ran in tears to confide to her father some grave matter that had arisen between her and a playmate. Just then, an assistant called out to the President that he had an important phone call. "I'll be with you in a minute," JFK told his daughter abruptly, and went to take the call.

Joe Kennedy held his peace until everyone was in place at dinner. Then he spoke to the President of the United States. "I know you're worried about the trip and Khrushchev," he said evenly, although everyone in the room was aware of the weight he gave to each word, "but let me tell you, there's nothing you can do as President that is more important than how Caroline develops."

Jack accepted the rebuke without comment, and the meal proceeded with holiday good spirits.

Teddy Junior finds deep meaning in the story: "My father

tells it quite a bit. He clearly was impressed by many things my grandfather told him, but I don't think anything made a more lasting impression than that statement about the importance of children in the family.

"My father and my aunts and uncles have tried to live up to my grandfather's wish," Teddy goes on. "Our lives could have been overwhelmed by a lot of things—the press, the public, the so-called glamour of the family name, the power we supposedly have—all of those things. One of the reasons I don't think we were bowled over is that we knew we had a special place in our homes. We had pretty much everything we wanted right there."

Jacqueline Kennedy agreed with her father-in-law, but her tone was more desperate. "My major effort must be devoted to my children," she told interviewer Ruth Montgomery shortly after she entered the White House. "If Caroline and John turn out badly, nothing I could do in the public eye would have any meaning."

The source of their concerns was obvious. The whole world was watching them. Jack Kennedy was the first President of the Video Age, an age that many people equated with the man. With his father's money and savvy and the unstinting efforts of a supply of handsome and voluble brothers and sisters, Jack had finally consummated the momentous marriage of television to politics. The Republic would never be the same. The Kennedys were stars, and like all stars, they had to put on a show, and the show had to go on no matter what. The disruptions, the intrusions, the endless demands for a grand gesture—all these had a profound effect on the third generation.

The Kennedy era differed from other periods in American history primarily in the manner in which it capitalized on youth. Jack Kennedy was America's first dazzling young leader since Teddy Roosevelt. The generation that had fought World War II had come of age. They were tired of frumpiness at home and humiliation abroad, and they wanted one of their own to lead them.

Jack's timing was perfect, and if timing is not all, it is still vital. To emphasize dramatically his break with the immediate past, the President played the youth card as trump in every aspect of his spectacular, if short, years of power. He and his family—boisterous, jovial, incandescent with healthy good looks and glamour—artfully exploited the unspoken message with the eager cooperation of television. Still, they were no doubt true believers. "He was not just the President of one nation," his brother Robert said after Jack's murder. "He was President of young people around the world."

John Kennedy's presidency was a thousand days gleaming with youth and beauty. John and Caroline were the first small children of the White House since Alice Roosevelt in the early years of the century. An endless number of photographs recorded them in almost infinite detail for a public that seemed incapable of satiety. Elegance was in, and seemed to satisfy a long-suppressed national craving. Jack Kennedy had had a heroic war. He was regally slim, dashing, well tailored, graceful of speech, witty, apparently well read, yet no bookworm. He loved sports, and if his bad back did not allow him to be flamboyantly competitive, this lack was more than made up for by his other brothers. Americans gorged on the accompanying graphics.

And they loved it when Jackie—at astonishing cost—adorned herself with the latest fashions from a bewildering variety of exotic designers. So what if she rode to hounds and frequented art galleries? So did the Queen of England. Subconsciously Americans were looking for a royal family of their own. The Kennedys filled that bill in virtually every respect—right down to the imperial touch of a poet laureate, Robert Frost, celebrating Jack's inauguration.

It was the JFKs, then, who fueled the extraordinary growth of interest in the family, but they had a large and accomplished cast of co-stars: Robert and Ethel, Ted and Joan, Jean and Steve Smith, Patricia and Peter Lawford, Eunice and Sargent Shriver. Moreover, the family resemblance among Jack and his brothers and sisters replicated itself in most of their children, who began to come along, in RFK's case in particular, with breathtaking rapidity.

The telltale smile, toothy, full, sparkling; the shaggy hair, abundant and rich, chestnut and black. For the men, long hard bodies, unbent from the physical punishment they inflict on themselves. For the women, high-cheeked natural beauty in slender frames. For both, piercing eyes of aqua, emerald, and brown in square, open, expressive faces. Better-looking bearers of the great American dreams—fame, power, wealth, benignity, glory—could not be imagined.

Although the capture of the presidency had been old Joe's idea, Jack's follow-through had been deft and resourceful.

When he made his bid he had been far from brilliant as a senator—legislative routine bored him. Nevertheless, he was candidly aware of his two other liabilities: his Catholicism, still not comfortable for many Americans, and his father's past and sometimes questionable politics (his break with FDR, his isolationist beliefs, and his romance with Senator Joe McCarthy were anathema to liberals). Yet, in Jack's mind at least, the pluses tipped the scale. First—and crucially—the media agreed. And then the public.

When old Joe saw at length what the consequences might be, he made his last decisive act as head of the family, and he picked his son, the President, as target. In reproaching Jack, he clearly was reminding them all that the family came before the glory and the children were its future. At least that's how Teddy Junior interprets the little drama that was enacted on a June evening in 1961.

Despite the warning and the precautions all the families took, Grandpa Joe's worst fears were quickly realized. Rita Dallas, who nursed Grandpa after his crippling stroke, wrote that RFK's young son Joe told her when he was a young teenager that he could get a date with any girl he wanted just because he was Joe Kennedy. "I don't like it at all," said Joe. "It either comes too easy to get what you want, or it comes too hard. But I guess I'd better learn to get used to it. Once a Kennedy, always a Kennedy."

Another time, one of Kara's teachers at Cathedral School pulled Kara's friend Cindy O'Brien aside after the class had visited the White House and chastised her for being Kara's chum: "I know why you like her and want to be seen with her," the teacher hectored little Cindy. "She's a Kennedy. You're out to take advantage of who she is."

Each of the Kennedy cousins has a collection of similar anecdotes that illustrate the difference that a little over 100,000 votes can make—the margin by which their Uncle Jack slipped past Richard Nixon and into the White House in 1960.

The arrival of the Kennedys as a family of consequence was a textbook example of what immigrants to America could achieve. The Kennedy story is well known: The perilous crossing of Patrick Joseph Kennedy in the midst of the Irish potato famine. The rise of his son, Patrick Joseph and of John "Honey Fitz" Fitzgerald, who charmed his way through the wards of Boston into Congress and then the mayor's office. The marriage of

Fitzgerald's daughter Rose to Joe Kennedy, Patrick's entrepreneurial son, and Joe's climb to national and, as ambassador to England, world recognition. Along the way, Joe accumulated great wealth and a large and precocious family, from whom he demanded high achievement. Finally, there was the war heroism and political derring-do of John Fitzgerald Kennedy.

It was only when Jack won the presidency, however, that the full glare of notoriety—magnified by the distorting lens of television—was concentrated on an entire generation of young Kennedys, Shrivers, Lawfords, and Smiths in a potentially destructive way. The family had never faced anything like it before. As Senator Ted Kennedy noted: "Our lives were relatively free of the spotlight. That is totally different for my children's generation. Even before they've had a chance to make important achievements and accomplishments in their lives, they have been public figures." In fact, no family had ever faced such a test—anywhere, ever.

Lacking the distance that class and custom allow Brisith royalty, for example, to put between themselves and the curious, the younger Kennedys were almost instantly the targets of the most pitiless and pervasive publicity hounding in all history. In many ways it has shaped what they have become today. Young Joe, obviously, was disturbed by it. Caroline came especially to resent it, and still avoids it whenever she can, with an intensity comparable to her mother's.

Immediately after Jack's election, parental barricades were thrown up to dissuade the intruders. Jacqueline Kennedy was the most resistant and her sister-in-law Ethel the most pliant. "Don't put them on a pedestal," Steve Smith would admonish those who were interested in his children and their cousins. "They are children just like any other children." Ted's wife Joan was soon driven frantic, but unlike Jackie she seemed unable to fight back successfully: "There is such a tendency to make my children freaks," she complained to a friend. "I wish we could be left alone—all of us."

That was an impossible dream. Once Jack was President, there was no way that any Kennedy of the following generation would ever have a "normal" life, no matter how often or how intensely the various sets of parents would invoke that word.

Sometimes, all protestations aside, the Kennedys courted the publicity. They loved having their children with them, and they were well aware of the political magic a throng of attractive youngsters can make. But much to the frustration of some of the elders, and some of the children, the sword resolutely insisted on cutting both ways.

"When they were young it was especially hard to describe it to them," relates Angelique Lee, formerly Ted Kennedy's personal secretary. "Eventually they just assimilated it, and it's probably now what they have come to expect."

There always was—there always is—someone at the door who adamantly and persistently wants something that he or she expects the sovereign touch of a Kennedy to grant. Worse, there were those who loathed them simply because of their genes. They were pursued as legitimate objects of curiosity by many of their fellow citizens even before anyone had the vaguest notion of whether they were exceptional—and worthy of the attention. "You don't wake up one day and realize there's something strange about you," notes Chris Kennedy. "But as a Kennedy you generate more interest than somebody else. People expect something from you. Everybody seems to have known your parents, your aunts, your uncles. It's strange when you don't know anything about them."

Kara Kennedy says she meets three kinds of persons—those who are especially nice, those who are especially mean and those who are normal. "Most everyone is one of the extremes," she explains. "They act like they love you or they hate you when they don't even know you. I've had strange people just come up to me and try to kiss or hug me. After that, you learn to prize the ones who act normally."

Many of them feel as if they are forever onstage. Perhaps to compensate, several of them have turned to the stage. Teddy, John, Bobby, Robin Lawford, and William Smith all have been involved in acting or directing stage or film productions. The family's long romance with the entertainment industry began when Grandpa Joe made a small fortune from movies in the early days of talkies.

Certainly some things came easily for the cousins, but they feel they have paid a price. They are under constant suspicion about their motives. Much of the world believes that the fix is always in for the Kennedys, and the cousins have a hard time dissuading cynics.

"I think I have to work twice as hard as others would because I'm a Kennedy," says Teddy Junior. "I think people think, 'Well, he just got this job because he's a Kennedy.' That is not so.

But after you've proved you can do the work and don't have to rely on your name, people will treat you better. The pressure has gotten greater as I grew older. People expect you to make something important of your life. Kennedys really can't be on the sidelines."

In such circumstances, it is almost a reflex to suspect the motives of outsiders—even of friends. Was that person genuinely nice—or just looking for something? Was the interest real or sycophantic—or, as it often is, both? "I just can't tell," says Patrick with a sigh. "There are groupies around all the time and I need my friends to tell me who is being genuine and who isn't. Sometimes you can't tell until it's too late."

The immediate surroundings were only a small part of the problem, though, because the whole world is watching. Unwinking cameras and snooping reporters are everywhere, which soon taught Jackie Kennedy to combat publicity with all the energy and guile she could command. "I feel as though I had just turned into a piece of public property," she complained shortly after entering the White House, and from the first she saw it as her principal duty to protect the children from the attentions of television and the press. The attention was all bad, in Jackie's eyes, because it heightened the interest in the children, and no good could come of that.

"Jackie had a deathly fear that she and the children were being packaged and sold like some dime-store trinket," commented one friend who sympathized with her. "She wanted everyone to stop paying attention—to stop watching with slobber on their chins and leers in their eyes. That was how she viewed it."

Jackie was so adamant that the world not be allowed to peer into her home that she had affidavits drawn up for the White House staff to sign, enjoining them never to write or reveal a word about the family. Evelyn Lincoln, JFK's own secretary, showed the copy she got to the boss and asked him what to do about it. "He laughed and shrugged and told me to throw it out," she recalled. "His basic feeling was that the whole world ought to be able to enjoy his kids—within limits. The Kennedy children were the nation's children."

When the affidavit story got around there was the predictable outcry about Jackie and her "loyalty oaths." (Oddly, no one who signed it has ever broken it.)

If Jackie's quixotic longing for privacy as the wife of a public figure ever had a chance to prevail, it was crushed when she prematurely gave birth to John right after Jack's election. The wave of publicity that followed engulfed her protestations. The dramatic circumstances of the birth served only to enhance the effect. Jack, flying to Florida, got the news upon his arrival and immediately jumped aboard the accompanying press plane for a return flight. The whole world was soon awash in television and photographic records of JFK's race to be with his new young son and his beautiful wife and daughter.

Young John's birth touched off a worldwide Kennedy mania that has yet to subside. In frantic imitation, thousands of parents named their children John, Caroline, and Jacqueline. The President-elect happily reaped the rewards of this emotional outpouring and was mobbed in the days immediately following John's birth as he walked hand in hand with Caroline to church from their Georgetown home, or to visit his new son, carrying her obligatory stuffed animal with ostentatious informality.

Jackie's insistent rejection of publicity occasionally forced Jack into subterfuge to get it when he wanted it. Had it been up to him alone, the President would have let the world enjoy his children the way he did. He was not only pleased with them, but he knew that the extraordinary public interest in them helped fix the image of his administration in the world's eyes as one focused on the future and offering hope to the young.

Thus, when need be, he waited for the right moment to let the public get a view of his family. For instance, not until Jackie had left the country for a therapeutic trip following the death of their infant son Patrick Bouvier Kennedy in August 1963 did he invite *Look* magazine photographer Stanley Tretick into the Oval Office to snap pictures of him and little John playing together.

"As soon as she [Jackie] snuck out, I snuck in," Tretick recalls. "The President was rather candid about it. He said, 'You know, we better get this out of the way pretty quick. Things get pretty sticky when Jackie's around.'"

Tretick was already well aware of this. Another time, when he had gotten some pictures of Caroline at Hyannis Port that were incidental to a story he was shooting about Sargent Shriver, Jackie succeeded, with brother-in-law RFK's help, in having them all quashed. They never appeared anywhere. It was one of Jackie's few total victories.

Tretick also remembers that Jack could turn the faucet off,

too, when it suited him. He refused, for example, to allow photographers to shoot in the White House during one particular period—the several months when, for whatever reason, obdurate two-year-old John could not tolerate being around his father and cried every time the President came near him.

So the characteristically Kennedy clash between the appetite for public esteem and the desire for privacy was most pronounced at 1600 Pennsylvania Avenue—and least evident at Hickory Hill, where Robert and Ethel generally followed an open-door policy.

Despite their mixed feelings about publicity, all the Kennedys, even before the assassinations, were extremely attentive to the safety of the children. Although RFK basked in publicity, he always took precautions. In his long investigations of the Teamsters and their president, Jimmy Hoffa, for example, word got back to him that Hoffa had threatened to have some of his children blinded. Preposterous as the threat might have seemed, RFK took no chances. From this peculiar circumstance began his family's long-running affair with large dogs.

In time the growing band of cousins learned to be wary not only of the journalists and photographers, but also of anyone outside their own immediate circle. They were often victims of reverse discrimination. Kara, for example, was once accused of having her father's Senate staff prepare one of her term papers, a false charge. It was also laughable to the Kennedy staff because they knew the first one to pull such a stunt to curry favor with the boss's child would have been fired. On another level, Victoria Lawford once spent what seemed to her a mythic 18 months on a job hunt, the reason apparently being that no Kennedy could seriously be looking for ordinary work.

Similarly, when Victoria's brother Chris applied at a Los Angeles law firm, he was told that everyone knew the Kennedys were destined for political careers and there was no need for them to waste their time on him since he would fly off at the first opportunity to run for office. "They didn't want to take the chance on me because they figured I'd run off to my real love—politics—at the first opportunity. Well, politics isn't my real love. I want to be a lawyer."

Still, sometimes being Kennedy was fun, especially at Hyannis Port during the summer, when the publicity was less intense or could be diffused by sailing, tennis, touch football, or just playing around. The compound itself was sprawling, spectacular, and laid out with exuberant recreation in mind. Visitors walked through high privet hedges off Scudder Avenue and looked directly at the RFK home, glanced left to "The President's" home and then walked toward the beach to get to "The Ambassador's" home. Beyond that on the left stood the home that for a while the Smiths owned until they got rid of it in the late 1960s in favor of their own place in Bridgehampton, Long Island.

In all, it was about ten acres of playground. A huge open lawn stood between the Ambassador's home and the beach grasses that eventually gave way to sand. The lawn was like a huge playing field, and that is exactly its function. To the side stands a volleyball court, tennis courts, and tucked behind them is the swimming pool. The homes themselves are open and airy, favoring extensive porches and grand vistas of the sea. Inside each home are anywhere from ten to twenty rooms—full and formal dining rooms, huge kitchens, living rooms decorated with memorabilia of family triumphs, sitting rooms and sun rooms.

When they were young and he was still alive, Jack Kennedy saw himself as sort of a summer-solstice Santa there. Neighbor Larry Newman remembers the President bouncing out of his helicopter on weekends with sacks of gifts, which he took great delight in bestowing on son and daughter and nieces, nephews and playmates, saying that each had been especially selected for the recipient. Jack also organized regular expeditions on the "Toonerville Trolley"—a large buslike golf cart—to the five-and-dime for candy and trinkets or to the local ice cream parlor.

Nobody is perfect, however. Karen Kelley, daughter of a family that has figured heavily in Kennedy lives, remembers one summer when the cousins and their friends built a kind of store in the compound—"A shack really. We decided we were going to do something to benefit humanity. I think it was Ethel's idea. It wasn't for the tourists—it was just for those who lived in the area and could get easily to the compound. We would go to the News Shop and buy penny candies and come back to the Kennedy store and sell them for a couple of cents more. All the proceeds went to the Nazareth Hall for the Retarded. The worst shock came when we went around asking for collections. The President gave us the pocket change he had. Not even a dollar bill!" Karen learned early how inevitable it is to see idols fall.

Looking back, it is hard to see why some of the Kennedys, especially Jackie, feared the publicity the children received. It was mostly harmless and often appealing. There was little Caroline with, as George Plimpton noted, "the bridge of freckles across her nose" linking her two bright blue eyes, clomping up to some newsmen at the Kennedy Palm Beach home in a pair of her mother's shoes. What was her father doing, the men asked. "Sitting upstairs with his shoes and socks off not doing anything," she replied. Or Caroline asking totally bald House Speaker Sam Rayburn, "Why haven't you got any hair?" The publication of such anecdotes could hardly have damaged anyone.

Yet Jackie even insisted that Plimpton, a friend from childhood, delete his affectionate description of Caroline from an article he was writing, even though, Plimpton remembers, "the President was very fond of the passages."

In the end, the cousins accepted their strange life because they knew no other. "It was never all that conscious a thing for me and most of my cousins," said Steve Smith, Jr. "I remember reading Henry Adams' autobiography, the part where he tells about going to the White House when his grandfather was there. He said he didn't think it was an odd thing for a boy to do because it was the only kind of a life he knew. Same for us. You don't know how privileged you are until much later in life when people bring it up to you."

It is a given, says Chris Lawford, that Kennedys live under extremely abnormal circumstances: "Normal things are very precious to us and notoriety is nothing special."

By whatever conscious or subconscious process, the Kennedy cousins learned quickly the inevitability of their special rank and found ways to accommodate it and even enjoy it—to sometimes treat it with happy indifference. "All of us were pretty aware early on that we could go to the White House and that people were interested in what we, as kids, were doing," recalls Michael Kennedy. "It wasn't that great a thing because our house was more fun than the White House anyway. The same people showed up in both places, and we didn't have to dress up in those stupid shorts if we stayed at our house."

War Games and Special Olympics

AS A BOSTON IRISHMAN, OLD JOE KENNEDY KNEW THAT THE only way out—to anywhere at all—was to fight, usually through very tough competition. Joe Kennedy was different from a lot of the Boston Irish when he was young. He was relatively well-to-do and he embarked early on a meteoric business career that was to make him a wealthy man. Yet he suffered the same social affronts that all the Irish experience in Brahmin New England and it made him a bitter man. The patriarch knew from his own experience and his ancestral experience that winning was the only thing, and he reared his children accordingly. His children's children are another story.

Eunice Kennedy Shriver once said of her father: "Even when we were six and seven years old, Daddy always entered us in public swimming races, in the different age categories so we didn't have to swim against each other. And he did the same thing in sailing races. The important thing was win—don't come in second or third—that doesn't count—but win, win, win."

That is not what Eunice told her son Tim, however. "The best way to describe it," Tim says, "is that you are expected to push, push, push and do your best."

And that is not what Steve Smith, Jr. heard from his mother, Eunice's sister Jean. "My mother never told me that her father insisted that they win when they were young," Steve says. "She said his basic message was: Do your best and then the hell with it. That's what she tried to instill in us."

In the RFK home there was the lazy summer day when the elder Robert Kennedy and a friend were sitting on the porch in Hyannis Port. As Anne Taylor Flemming tells the story, one of Robert's sons came in after a boat race—although none of them owns up to having been the one.

"How did you do?" asked Bobby.

"I came in fourth."

Robert turned to his guest and said: "That's the difference between them—my children—and us. If we didn't win, we were sent to bed without dinner."

Ted Kennedy went out of his way to tell his children that the admonition they heard from others—that Kennedys had to be the best—was not so. "All my parents said was, 'Listen, try and do your best,' " says Teddy Junior. "At the school where I went they graded you on effort as well as the quality of your work. They gave you a one for little effort and a three for great effort. And my father said, 'As long as I see threes on your report card, I don't care what grade you get.' "

So Grandpa Joe's message without question has been filtered and softened. Winning is terribly important, but no longer compulsory. Or, put another way, the competition, with certain exceptions, is now of a different kind.

For the cousins, and for their parents as well, much of the game has become the pure adventure of overcoming a solitary challenge. "Winning" comes when the rapids are shot, the mountain climbed, or the slope skied. The elder Robert himself inaugurated the new era when he climbed Mount Kennedy, renamed for Jack, shortly after his brother's murder.

As young Joe sees it: "I like clinging to the side of a mountain, sailing across the ocean, or fighting an angry bull. Some people don't like the feeling. I happen to love it. These are exciting things. They give a person a feeling of accomplishment—of self-confidence."

Another virtue of solitary adventure is that it keeps the crowds down. Then, too, ordinary sports have become so professionalized that no one can excel in one without devoting full time to it, which runs counter to the Kennedy Renaissance-man penchant for doing everything.

Even the challenge can be unique nowadays—such as the one Eunice has taken up with her Special Olympics, a competition for the mentally retarded. The idea for it grew out of Eunice's lifelong involvement with her sister Rosemary, who is retarded. At the Special Olympics every competitor is a "winner" for having participated. Competing and finishing are their own rewards. In their way, the Special Olympics are the institutional antithesis of the winner-take-all standard Grandpa Joe imposed on his children. One longtime family friend suggested that the change in emphasis was sanctioned by Grandpa Joe himself after his own distress over Rosemary's handicap.

"He never said it, but I think he was in pain some of the time wondering whether he had been too hard on them, especially Rosemary," says the friend. He notes that the youngest children of Joseph and Rose Kennedy—Ted Senior and Jean—were reared in a far more tolerant atmosphere than the oldest children—Joe Junior, Jack, and Eunice. "There was a real softening that stemmed in part from his being around them more and his struggle in coming to terms with having a retarded daughter."

This new set of Kennedy parents substantially relaxed their father's iron rule because, as their friend, historian Arthur Schlesinger, Jr., explains it, "Apparently there must be more mercy for those who come later in the pack."

It could be rugged, though, at Kennedy homesteads. Karen Kelley of Hyannis Port, friend and neighbor to the cousins, reports that the civilizing process often bent and sometimes broke. "All of us fought, fist fights and stuff. There'd be a softball game and somebody would be called out, then Joe would say he was safe, then Bobby would say he was out and there'd be a fight. Sandy Eiler [master of sports at the compound] always had to break things up. He was as much a referee as a swimming coach."

All the cousins have trained in and played competitive sports—swimming, sailing, tennis, skiing, football, soccer. John and Michael, Chris Lawford, Tim and Mark Shriver all played competitive rugby at college, and Stevie Smith is a good amateur middleweight. The legendary touch football games, although less frequent, are still played, and still for keeps.

Like their parents, these younger Kennedys are driven people. Yet they are still able to laugh at each other when their combat becomes ridiculously contorted. Once young Joe was partnering Chris Lawford in a canoe race. They started out fine, but Chris was overcome during the race with a violently upset stomach and had to stop paddling. The canoe carrying Bobby Junior and his friend Doug Spooner overtook them. "Dammit, Chris, start paddling," Joe shouted. Chris could not. Even some canoes crewed by women passed them, and they finished dead last. The only consolation: Bobby and Spooner were so busy laughing at Joe's discomfort that they finished next to last. Nowadays when family gatherings turn, as they always do, to story-telling and ribbing, that is the one most often trotted out against Joe. It is the classic family tale about competition going over-board.

For young Bobby Kennedy that is an important factor in the equation—humor: "It was important for my father to teach us how to take a joke and how to be laughed at. A lot of people think that is just part of the 'spoiled Kennedys'—pushing people in swimming pools and the like. But it was important not to take yourself too seriously. If you look at the kind of humor that Jack and my father and Teddy are known for, it is self-deprecating, and that comes naturally to us."

If Grandpa Joe's insistence on winning was toned down, the demand that everyone must play to win was not, and this ac-counts for the cousins' obsession with competition. Virtually everyone who encounters them on their turf becomes a player in their games. Participation is essential. Spectating is heresy. Some select friends get a special pass on this insistence, but no Kennedy does. They do not allow one of their own to loll around.

Barbara Grant, a college friend of Kathleen's, remembers that Kathleen and her siblings never were idle. "If you weren't reading a book or having a discussion, you were involved in sports," with one important exception: "You weren't supposed to be cleaning your room. There were more important things to do."

To this day, no one has ever been able to catch an RFK child red-handed making a bed.

If fear was the enemy, courage and daring were the antidotes. The cousins have always been told that there were no limits to the heights that raw courage could help them scale. So fear was to be killed at birth, especially in the RFK home. All the RFK children remember their father swinging them higher and higher on the backyard swing. "Let's see if we can set a record," he would call out. "A Kennedy cannot be scared."

One who has watched them regularly attempt the unthinkable or the foolhardy guesses that their inner sense of worth is tied up with their dares—that they believed if they backed off from any challenge, no matter what it was, something inside them would be destroyed. Bobby Junior once observed, "Life is competition. People who run away from competition don't survive."

He later elaborated: "There were two elements to our competition. The first is the standard thing any child feels about wanting to win. The second is more complicated. It is a drive to expose yourself to danger. We were a large family, and doing dangerous things was a way of getting attention. If you wanted to get out of the shadow of an older brother, you jumped off the roof."

The central lesson was that the effort was the thing. Robert Kennedy often quoted Theodore Roosevelt to his children: "The credit belongs to the man who is actually in the arena, whose face is marred by dust and sweat and blood, who at the best knows in the end the triumph or high achievement and who at worst if he fails at least fails while daring greatly."

They believed that if something was hard or hurt them, it was probably good for them. This was the first family commandment. The second, at least for RFKs, was "Kennedys don't cry." Robert declaimed that on any number of occasions. "Daddy couldn't stand seeing a job half done," says Bobby Junior. "If we went out for a pass and slowed down, we would always hear him say, 'Don't ever give up!' "

Tim Haydock, a friend of young Joe's at Milton Academy, recalls the first time he played touch football with the RFKs. New to the house and a mere 17-year-old, he didn't know the seriousness of the matter. He drew the unenviable job of guarding Robert Kennedy, Senior, and it soon became apparent that the fleet Haydock was not going all out. RFK stopped the game and pulled Haydock aside. "If you are not going to play to win, then get out of here," he said, barely controlling his anger. "We don't need that here. If you don't try on every point, then don't play."

Not surprisingly, it is the RFK children—and the cousins who tried to emulate them—who excel at breathtaking stunts. For sheer dare-the-devil doings, Michael Kennedy and Stevie Smith, the sidekick who tried to keep up with him, stand out in a score of achievers. Steve laughs about Michael, but with admiration: "He and I were always competing. I would generally do what he did because I didn't want to be behind him. It exposed me to a lot of danger, though."

In the Andes once Michael and Steve outbrassed the entire Argentine Olympic ski team, who called the Yanquis *"los locos"*— "the nut cases." One time they pointed Michael toward a rocky overhang. What lay beyond it could not be seen. Michael plunged ahead anyway, and the last thing Steve and the others heard was his yelp as he became airborne and saw nothing remotely resembling a trail on the other side.

"It was typical Michael," says Steve. "We pulled him out of five feet of powder"—fortunately with few injuries.

None of the males is especially shy. Bobby Kennedy is fearless and Joe is similarly undaunted by any physical challenge, as is Chris Lawford. Chris's friend Jack Weeks remembers how Chris once impressed some *ganga*-smoking Jamaicans by first jumping, then diving, then swan-diving from a 50-foot cliff into a sea cove. John Kennedy, Junior, began to work out with weights in college, surprising those who remembered that he was the least enthusiastic participant in many of the family competitions. He will now take on challenges that did not appeal to him when he was younger.

Robert and Ethel drove home two other rules of behavior to their children—not to tattle and not to be sore losers. The great moral lessons of their lives were related in major ways to the manner in which they played with and against each other. As Kerry sees it: "People have the idea that competition is bad because it represents raw aggression. It was not that way in our home. It was my parents' way of teaching us to get along and do things together."

Her mother, Ethel, also had a carefully articulated view of the tonic effects of competition and adventure. "I think children should be encouraged to learn things young," Ethel once said. "It's hard, but you have to let them take those risks. Gosh, if they're going to develop independence, they have to do it when they're young." Learn they did, often by breaking limbs.

Pressing on regardless can be overdone, though. Mary Alice Cook remembers when her horse threw her into a jump when, as a teenager, she was riding with her friend Kathleen. Mary Alice broke several ribs. Ethel, who was riding with them, could not have known that, of course. Her concern was that the incident might cause the youngster to fear to remount, and so Ethel made her do it immediately and finish the ride.

The casual Kennedy attitude toward physical danger or harm can be disconcerting for an outsider. "They were crazy, all of them," recalls Candy Kelley, who was close to Kerry and Michael. "They'd do things no one else dreamed of doing—jumping or climbing. They would make you feel bad if you were scared, but God, you couldn't keep up with them." Lorenzo di Bonaventura, Michael's friend, agrees that "they do act sometimes as if they don't believe they can be hurt." But he notes that in Michael's case that risk is carefully weighed. Once the decision to forge ahead is made, there is no turning back, because Michael believes that hesitation then becomes the danger.

Several other family rules governing competition never changed. First, it was always Kennedys against the world. RFK arranged it so that his family would frequently contest others in the touch football games. "Kennedy rules" always prevailed, and the rules would often change as Robert Kennedy saw fit. There were special family rules for every sport. In football, each child down to the smallest would have a special play, and everyone participated. Even when it was time for just the older boys or the adults to play, the girls were arrayed in competent cheerleading crews to encourage "Daddy's team." Kerry, as is her wont, adopted the family's habit of rooting for itself to her own purposes when she was young. "Mary Kerry is great! Mary Kerry is great! Hip, hip, hooray!" she would shout endlessly some days.

When they were young they also trained for competition. The family hired Sandy Eiler, a former Olympic swimmer, as coach and games master at Hyannis Port, and all the families used him in one way or another. While the children of other families were hanging out at the beach or the yacht club, Eiler had the Kennedys doing time trials or dives or different strokes. It got so bad once that 12-year-old Karen Kelley and Mary Gallagher Civetti extensively plotted and achieved a great coup when Karen grabbed Kathleen Kennedy's leg "accidentally" during a torrid 50-yard freestyle race so that Mary could—at least once—beat Kathleen. Eventually the local authorities banned the Kennedys from at least one meet a year at the swim club so that some of the other children could win a ribbon.

So with the new crop of Kennedys as with the old, family involvement seems essential to incite aboriginal Kennedy drives. Just as JFK had battled with his brother Joe Junior before the latter was killed in World War II, so the third generation also saw combativeness at the top. "We tended to win against outsiders, so the competition was always better and more aggressive between us," says Bobby Shriver. "The important thing was whether Bobby Shriver could swim faster than Bobby Kennedy. I was the best tennis player, but that gave me not a dime's worth of standing in sailing or football. It kind of set the tone for the way we dealt with each other." As a family friend and frequent competitor put it: "When outsiders play with them, they are props. It's all in the family—Joe versus Stevie, Bobby versus David, Michael versus Chris."

That is because, according to EMK's friend Richard Clasby; "What the outside world thought didn't matter. It was what they thought of each other that was most important."

Another of the Kelley girls, Pamela, remembers that the Kennedy kids were spookily similar in their need to do well. "It was a much more important thing for them than for the rest of us. They didn't have to be told. It was subconscious, and the spooky thing was that there were so many of them thinking exactly the same way. The worst competitions they had were among themselves. That's when it really mattered."

The playing fields, then, were where the pecking order was established. When tragedy and divorce removed three fathers from the family, the competition moved into other realms. As Chris Lawford explains, there were 29 children who were taught to love and stand by each other through any circumstance. They created their own airtight universe and the arbiters of that universe were their parents. As all parents do, they bestowed precious rewards on the children—love, attention, status, and security.

When three fathers were gone, there was a feverish struggle among the oldest boys for the rewards and affection of the remaining parents and important surrogates such as longtime family friend LeMoyne Billings. Yet there were so few arbiters and so many children pressing demands that it was impossible for everyone to get everything he or she needed.

"I really feel I have twenty-eight brothers and sisters," says Chris. "I always knew I could count on any of them—especially after all we've been through. That's how it felt to be altar boy with some of my cousins at Uncle Bobby's funeral. It was 'us,' and all of us had to stick together. At the same time, it was very competitive. We had a depleted group of adults from whom we were seeking all the things kids want and compete for. I mean Uncle Teddy can only give each of the children so much of his time. It's a distorting thing when so much happens when you're so young, and then twenty-nine of you are left trying to grow up. Outside pressures always seemed to be robbing us of something."

Over the long haul, those contests—physical, mental, and emotional—are still being waged among the oldest male cousins.

A favorite childhood game was called "War." It involved

opposing teams racing around the compound, almost literally, it seemed, trying to do one another in. There were times when the place resembled the state of nature. "Survival of the fittest" was the hallmark.

Other times it was formal combat. Boxing matches between the older boys were in fashion for a while, with Sandy Eiler in charge of training and refereeing. Bobby Kennedy routinely bested Bobby Shriver, who took some comfort in routing Bobby K at tennis. The important point was that they were always squaring off against each other in one way or another, and it still characterizes their dealings with each other down to this day—at school, in social gatherings, even in career accomplishments. It is so much a part of their nature that at times it will not be stopped even if it can be hurtful. Bobby Kennedy once determined that he would swipe one of Bobby Shriver's dates, and did. Next time they were at a party together, Bobby Shriver never let his girl off his arm, it is said. Those two have gone through periods when they will not talk to each other, although to outsiders they always speak reverently of each other.

The other boxing pairing that everyone remembers pitted big Chris Lawford against the slighter David Kennedy. The bout got quite a buildup. RFK enlisted a special trainer, Secret Serviceman Jack Walsh, to prepare David. A fierce but inconclusive battle ensued. Chris believes he would have won on the cards, but he says David was the real winner because he lasted the match and never retreated.

The jousting between Joe and Bobby Junior merits special attention and they tell it best in their own words:

When Joe got married in 1979, Bobby toasted them, but warned Joe's bride, Sheila Brewster Rauch: "Sheila, you are now going to become a roommate of Joe's. I used to be a roommate, and I understand what it will be like for you. Not good. My roommate once killed my turtles for no reason." He went on to attribute a number of other destructive or mean-spirited actions to Joe.

Three years later on Bobby's wedding day, Joe struck back with sardonic references to Bobby's teenage wildness. "It will be hard living with Bobby," Joe cautioned his brother's new wife, Emily Black. "I can remember all the times when we were young and there was bed check and he wasn't there."

"I don't know how Joe knows this," Bobby stuck in. "He couldn't even spell. It was difficult being the younger brother when the older brother was always wrong, but you couldn't correct him for fear of physical violence." This was a reference to the time when they were teenagers and the muscular, short-tempered Joe had been wrestled to a fall by the puzzlements of his mother tongue.

"How do you spell 'which'?" he yelled downstairs to a governess who would soon be quitting. The governess wondered whether he meant the kind that rode a broomstick or the kind that stood in for a noun. That was too much for Joe. Several inconclusive exchanges made it clear to Bobby in the room next to Joe's that it was the pronoun that was meant.

"It's w-h-i-c-h, you jerk," Bobby finally shouted in exasperation.

"The next thing I heard was BOOM!" Bobby recalls. "Joe knocked the hinges off my door and came after me. He threw me against the wall and beat the hell out of me."

The differences in approach between Joe and Bobby grew wider as they grew older. Joe never used his name to gain a social advantage, and avoided it altogether when being introduced to women. Bobby, on the other hand, traded on it like a broker with a hot stock.

The intrafamilial jockeying is essential Kennedy, but no one else may do or say to them what they do or say to each other. After having battled without quarter, they close ranks against everyone else. Select outsiders are accorded the special place of giving and receiving barbs, but for the most part they present a unified front to the rest of the world. Grandpa Joe had taught them that if they stood together, there was little that could defeat them.

"They fought with each other more fiercely than any other family I've ever seen," says a former aide to EMK. "The insults are more cutting and the putdowns more withering. Yet they'll wipe out an outsider who tries to do the same, who dares to seek intimacy without their permission. They are tough, tough people."

They revel in their toughness, in fact. "They are bullies when you first meet them," says Jack Weeks of the older males. "They want to test how far they can go with you and they push you around getting there." Weeks, a former national Golden Gloves boxing champion, found himself squaring off several times with some of them before the Kennedys got the message that he was just as tough as they were. Men like Secret Service agent

Joe Foster remember that even as a preteenager young Joe would push and shove his way around the playing fields, one time shoving Foster into a hedgerow. They liked to assert themselves.

The original point to the large family and the tribal hazing was to ensure that there would always be a tough guy ready to take over. It was proved when Joe Junior was lost and Jack stepped right in. When Jack was killed, there was Bobby. And when Bobby was slain, Ted moved up.

The third wave still lives by these loyalties. And they never forget. Kerry Kennedy is not old enough to have firsthand knowledge of the publicized clashes between her father and Roy Cohn in the 1950s when they both worked for the Senate investigations subcommittee run by Senator Joseph McCarthy. (Cohn is now a prominent New York lawyer.) Yet Kerry has acquired the knowledge and lives by it. Not long ago at a party, someone who had professed to like her told her that he liked Roy Cohn too. "You can't have both," Kerry declared, and left.

Another time, one friend instantly became an ex-friend when he stopped dating one of the female cousins for reasons that were not acceptable to the men.

Yet the network embraces true friends like family. Bobby Kennedy's friend Chris Bartle remembers the time Lem Billings—the all-purpose Kennedy friend—was thrown off the side of a raft in churning rapids. Bobby, Michael Kennedy, and Chris Lawford instantly dove into the roaring waves to help their endangered friend. "It was the most impressive reaction I'd ever seen—absolute pure loyalty," says Bartle. "Lem was a friend and they helped their friends. That's all they needed to know in order to risk their lives."

In the other families, competition was a good deal less volatile, especially among the JFKs and the EMKs. At the JFKs', both before his death and after, Jackie's reserved personality governed Caroline's and John's responses. At the EMKs', Joan tried to keep up with the Kennedy absorption in sweat and strain, but eventually fell back exasperated. In addition, the men of the family were all incapacitated in one way or another.

The Smiths and Shrivers and Chris Lawford are more in the fevered RFK camp, and tend to measure themselves against the RFK men.

Finally, what comes through in all of them is the jaunty Kennedy mien. They love to play. More, though, they love to win.

Growing Up Catholic

IT IS BEDTIME AT THE HICKORY HILL, VIRGINIA, HOME OF Robert and Ethel Kennedy. The children gather in a loose circle around their parents' huge bed. They are ready for bed and reasonably well scrubbed and pink-faced. There is a certain amount of tittering and nudging, and Joe lands a really hard one right in the middle of Bobby Junior's right bicep. Bobby winces. But the children know that prayer is serious business. Bottoms have been paddled before and will be again.

Prayers begin with everyone saying the Rosary, each child who is capable of it leading in a decade. This can take rather a long time, and can induce a bit of squirming in the small ones, but only very rarely is anyone excused, and a look from Ethel usually is enough to dampen revolt. A look from Robert is almost never required. Then one of the older children—it was usually Kathleen or Michael—reads a passage from the Bible, before the whole family corporately recites, "Now I lay me down to sleep . . ." And so to bed.

"When we were growing up," Maria Shriver remembers, "religion was a sort of given. You said the Rosary every night. Your brothers were altar boys. Later in life, just like most of my friends, I began to question it more. Now I'm not as much a practicing Catholic as I'd like to be. But it is still very important in my life. It's an Irish thing—God is going to take care of you in all you do."

Kerry Kennedy adds: "Religion is an important foundation for us all. It's an essential place to turn and in many ways has helped us through some hard times."

During his presidential campaign, Jack Kennedy strode onto a platform in Dallas, Texas, to speak to leaders of the Southern Baptist Convention. As a Roman Catholic, Jack was to them a representative of their ancient enemy, the Whore of Babylon. How could they accept him as President? Yet their predominantly Baptist state was vital to Jack's chances. What would he say to them? He looked straight at them and explained himself: "I am what I am, and I will be what I am." He carried the state—and, of course, the nation.

For Jack and Bobby and their father before them, probably much more pervasively than for their children or the other cousins after them, growing up Kennedy meant growing up Catholic. This had a great deal to do, of course, with growing up Boston-Irish. "No Irish need apply" was the standard warning in Boston newspaper want ads when Jack's grandfather "Honey Fitz" was a rising young politician. The Irish were second-class citizens, and the only way they could challenge their Brahmin overseers was through skill, cunning, and strong cooperative action.

The one unthinkable thing was to forswear the faith. Instead, it was militantly integrated into every aspect of life, social and economic as well as domestic and religious. It was the condition of survival. The family of Joseph Kennedy epitomized this very aggressive, if not necessarily pious, Catholicism. Church and Family were the poles between which the Kennedy psyche operated and the Kennedy character was formed—so much so that it was often difficult to see where family left off and church began.

For Rose—and it is usually the wife and mother who defines the norms of religious observance in any Catholic household—there was no bickering duality here: the family was inconceivable without the church, and the church without the family. Rose's piety is garden-of-the-soul variety. It is genuine, strong, and simple. By her teaching and example, she formed her children's and in some ways her grandchildren's views on religion, just as her husband had fired them with a will to win. "God has created me to do Him some definite service," she frequently quoted to the grandchildren from Cardinal Newman. "He has committed some work to me which He has not committed to another. I have my mission—I may never know it in this life, but I shall be told it in the next. I am a link in a chain, a bond of connection between persons. He has not created me for naught. I shall do good, I shall do His work."

"There is an immense amount of faith in that family and it comes from Rose," as Claude Hooton, a friend of Senator Ted, sees it. "Rose once told me that I should live every day as if it were the last—not in the sense that I should blast off and have a helluva time. It was in the sense that I should be a pretty good guy."

Stick to the fundamentals, state them clearly, promote them powerfully, execute them faithfully. That is Rose's Catholicism. With God, all things are possible, but only one thing really matters—whether one's soul was saved or not. So Catholics, at least Catholics like Rose, can take what seems to the secular world an amazingly composed view of the most terrible personal tragedies and trials. She and everyone around her have cited her bedrock faith as the source of her strength. "They believe in the most basic and heartfelt way in redemption and heaven and that has been the thing that pulled them through," says a friend of the cousins.

"People wonder how the Kennedys managed to cope with all that happened to them," says Angelique Lee, Ted Kennedy's onetime secretary. "It's not that hard to grasp. They were taught that they should accept the will of God. It was not any wickedness on their part that brought them trouble. And they were encouraged to be strong because that would help others be strong. They always knew they had an example to set."

Yet Kennedy fatalism is neither passive nor dour, but positive and daring. "They know the worst could happen," comments Bill Barry, an old friend of the RFKs, "but they'll take the risk anyway." Optimistic fatalism, in other words.

For the Kennedy cousins, the Shrivers have set the family standard on spiritual matters. The other parents in their ways have shown considerable fealty to the church, but it is by reason of temperament and fervor and age that the Shrivers are the standard bearers. Individually and as a couple, Eunice and Sargent are strongly dedicated to the church and its teachings, sacraments, rituals, and services. In addition, they fervently try to bring the church's teachings to secular life. They are, for example, the prime movers behind the Kennedy Center for the Study of Bioethics at Georgetown University, an organization with the goal of reconciling the apparent clash between scientific progress and traditional morality. It takes a considerable amount of their time.

Sargent's approach to the matter of faith is thoughtful, curious, sympathetic. As he put it in a speech back in 1958, he sees religious conviction as necessary to human happiness: "The only genuine elite in this world or the next is the elite of those men and women who have given their lives to justice and to charity. Without the love that St. Paul envisaged, the world is a clashing of object against object, class against class, tyrant against tyrant, race against race. With St. Paul's type of love, we are persons—deep calling deep, the human heart speaking to the human heart."

Eunice's manner is more like Rose's—direct and uncomplicated. She knows in the marrow of her bones, for instance, that abortion is murder. After considerable soul-searching and serious study of the question of how far religious beliefs ought to impinge on Constitutional law, she has also decided that public funding for abortions is wrong, as well. In this belief she differs from her brother Ted, who has taken the so-called pro-choice position on the flammable topic.

"My mother is like Dorothy Day and my father is the kind of person who likes to read Hans Kung," is how their son Tim describes the difference between his parents on the matter of religion.

Their influence is strong and telling. In 1973 Maria and her friends, Theo Hayes and others, created quite a stir in Washington after they read reports in the local press that physicians at the National Institutes of Health were hoping to do experiments on live aborted fetuses. As they discussed their outrage at such a thing at lunch one day with Eunice, she asked them why they did not do anything about it.

Authorities at NIH first refused to meet with them. So 300 girls from Stone Ridge, Maria's school, threatened a silent vigil outside the institutes. Once news outlets learned of Maria's involvement, the cameramen began to hover—and NIH officials suddenly wanted a meeting very badly.

The girls then started phoning physicians sympathetic to their protest and devised hard technical questions to ask the physicians who were seeking the experimental privileges. Under such a barrage, the embarrassed brass at NIH soon scrapped the whole idea.

The attitudes of the 29 cousins toward their faith vary broadly between devotion (the Shrivers, Kathleen, Kerry, Courtney) and toleration (the Lawfords, Michael, Kara, the JFKs) with a number of them more or less in the middle. Hot or cold, however, for all of them the same basic identification of faith with family remains undiluted, just as it has with Rose.

Politically, they still see themselves consolidating the new age of Catholic emancipation begun by Uncle Jack. Even now when the cousins tour the heavily Catholic areas of South and Central America they are treated regally. "It's traveling with a god," said friend Andy Karsch.

Maria Shriver, while she was studying at Georgetown University, thoughtfully and reverently explicated the family's connection to its religion. In her thesis on Jack's presidential campaign, especially the West Virginia primary, she pointed out that Jack did not correspond to the stereotype of the Catholic politician, having been rich, attractive, and self-assured. "He was not the son of immigrants, but of a wealthy, well-known family," she wrote. "He had a dream not only for himself but for all those who had found they had always come a little bit short of being real Americans . . . Thanks to John Kennedy's endurance, every Catholic could stand tall because his victory enabled a race to shed the stigma of second-class citizenship."

She attributes his win in part to his deft leap over the issue of faith by his identification of himself with America's "civic religion"—that mix of ceremonies, holidays, and beliefs, particularly the strong advocacy of separation of church and state. "He knew people were concerned about his faith and his youth and he sought to dispel both by displaying a brilliant knowledge of what all Americans should and did believe in, and by showing that he was first an American like everyone else and only second a Catholic."

So, in some respects, it was faith in the family rather than the family's faith that triggered piety in the Kennedy homes. The cousins would often memorize the more affecting utterances of family members just as they did verses from the Bible, particularly when there was spiritual content. As young Joe quoted so trenchantly from his father at the Kennedy Library dedication, so young Steve Smith will similarly quote Uncle Bobby's extemporaneous eulogy in Indianapolis the night Martin Luther King, Jr., was slain: "What we need in the United States is love and wisdom and compassion toward one another. . . . Aeschylus wrote: 'In our sleep, pain that cannot forget falls drop by drop upon the heart and in our own despair, against our will, comes wisdom through the awful grace of God.'"

As far as formal adherence to Catholic doctrine is concerned, Kathleen, the oldest, and emeritus regular bedtime Bible reader, is the one who has struggled most with what her spiritual life means. A feminist, she perhaps found the church's traditionalism respecting the role of women suffocating. But that's not all: "In Catholic school they give you too many straight answers all the time," she complained once to reporter Barbara Kevles. "The other day I went to a sermon in church and the priest was saying we should obey the policeman on the authority of God. I just couldn't believe it! That's the problem with parts of the Catholic church."

Kathleen also rejected "the uniforms and the rules and the exclusive focus on 'the right' way of religious thinking" in Catholic schools. "Everyone came from the same social background. You always got the Catholic point of view, pro or against something. I kept arguing in religious class. Once I got six D's—in courtesy, neatness, discipline—all the things they valued and that didn't make that much difference to me. I didn't like girls' school. Everybody spent a lot of time dressing up and putting on makeup for the special times they got to see boys. I figured if they were that important you might as well see them all the time."

That is why she switched to the Putney School in Vermont, where "there were hardly any Catholics, the school was co-ed and the kids came from all over the country. It was full of radicals—the children of writers and professors and all. It was a great new challenge."

At Putney, in her late teens, she stopped going to Mass regularly. She said at the time that trying to answer questions with "simple faith" was not adequate. "I decided not to rely wholly on Catholicism, though it's deeply ingrained in me," she told one interviewer. "I want to think things through for myself."

Her grandmother, perhaps with eyes rolled heavenward, embraced Kathleen's quest to find things out for herself, but could not resist a dig or two. "Someday you're going to inherit some money," Grandma Rose once told her. "If you're honest in your objections to the system, why not return that money or give it away?" Kathleen said she would think about it, but noted wryly that she kept coming back to her big, comfortable house, so the depth of her disenchantment was not that great.

In fact, at Putney she claims her deepest spiritual connections to her church were nourished. "I usually ended up giving the Catholic point of view in our discussions, or my family's point of view," she said. "Many of the other students had never heard of a Catholic that believed in what she was taught—and I did. I ended up still holding onto my religion."

Kathleen has gradually gravitated back to Ethel and Grandma's side, if not exactly their position, thanks to a thoughtful and still continuing inquiry into her faith. She is now considered one of the most pious cousins.

Kathleen's brother Bobby tells an anecdote illustrating how powerful a pull religion still exercises on him: Two years ago his grandmother, whose robust health was legend, was noticeably failing and required hospitalization at one point. "It was very difficult for us," Bobby relates. "Dougie came to me and asked me to go with him to another place and pray with him. It was very moving, really. I felt like a kid again." That is very typical of sensitive Dougie. His older friend, Tom Koutsoumpas, says Dougie would call him every day during the period when Tom's aunt was dying of cancer to tell him that prayers were being said. "It wasn't just an idle comment to Dougie," says Koutsoumpas. "He really does pray seriously. It is very unusual for a teenage boy."

For all his worldliness, Bobby Kennedy has a thoughtful explanation why the church still has a powerful sway over his generation of the family. "It is difficult sometimes to keep your bow to the wind, and the church is something that can help you hold your course. It's something you can retreat into. And it's one of the main things that brings our family together."

Bobby can get quite eloquent about the church: "Everybody can find something in the Catholic church, find some kind of refuge. It's not really an 'absolute' institution. God meant us to ask questions, and the Catholic church is the place where we are challenged to ask questions about our own lives. Religion is the place that speaks to the greatest sentiments in people— charity and love and hope. It is a tool to run your life by. It is the only place that addresses true altruism and it gives you justification other than the IRS to be charitable."

The root of the RFKs' feeling about the church was the abiding piety of Ethel. She is extremely devout and at one point considered being a nun—a consideration that gave Robert Kennedy difficulty. "I'll compete with anyone, but how can I compete with God?" he asked at the time. His own spiritual life was far less formal than his wife's. Robert Kennedy, according to Bobby, was "interested in the humanist side of religion."

In the EMK home, the family was quietly involved in many

of the critical stages in establishing a parish in McLean, Virginia. The senator was on the first lay parish board, and Joan opened their home for several years to church school organization meetings, recalls family priest James English: "Theirs is a very simple faith—we believe in God and He will do the rest," noted the priest.

Still, it is the Shrivers who keep the family abreast of church matters. "They are always open to us any time we want," reports Bobby Kennedy. "They were the ones who were most interested in Emily's [his wife's] conversion to Catholicism."

"Religion is an important defining characteristic for all of us," says Tim Shriver, "and deeds are only part of what you can do. That's important, but we were taught that you have to be a loving, caring, Christian person to make it worthwhile. I realized that to make up for what my family has and to pay for it, one does other things to help people one way or another."

In a neat, characteristically Celtic as well as Kennedy way, Teddy Junior sums up best what might be taken as the definitive attitude of the older cousins toward the faith of their fathers— serious but jovial, and emotionally strong: "I don't go to church that much when I'm at college, but it is important to me and I will make it an important part of my children's lives." He cocks his head to the sky, squints and smiles: "I have a guardian angel up there, you know, and I have a lot to be thankful for."

What? Me Rich?

"LISTENING TO A KENNEDY TALK ABOUT MONEY IS LIKE LIS-
tening to a nun talk about sex," Jack Kennedy's college pal
Chuck Spalding observed almost 25 years ago.

With this generation of Kennedys not much has changed.
"They've got it, but they sure as hell don't flaunt it," complains
a friend of one of the older RFKs who on occasion has had to
plumb his own wallet because a Kennedy just did not happen
to have enough cash with him. Uncle Jack Kennedy, too, was
always "borrowing" small amounts from less well-to-do com-
panions.

"Money is not important," old Joe Kennedy had said. "The
measure of a man's success in life is not the money he's made—
it's the kind of family he has raised." So, although he had spent
an enormous amount of time and energy to heap up a treasure
that has never been fully told—the best estimates are that Grandpa
Joe made $500 million by the time he died in 1969—the pa-
triarch never talked about money at home, and Rose still does
not know the full extent of her holdings. She learned of them
in outline by reading a magazine article in 1957.

The 29 younger Kennedys eventually discovered that their
grandfather was indeed a very rich man, but that he viewed
money merely as a means to free its holder to do far more
important things, like helping others. Someone, usually Grandma
Rose, was always reminding them about the responsibility that
goes with the money, except that she usually forgot to mention
the money. That may be why most Kennedys do not connect
their privileges with their money. Rose would quote St. Luke
to them: "To whom much has been given, much will be required," debiting them with a social mortgage that they had to
redeem.

Their own family amply corroborated the belief that money was not everything. According to Ted Kennedy, his sister Rosemary, who is retarded, was living evidence to all of them of "the importance of reaching out to others not as fortunate." He told his own children that wealth and power did not prevent Rosemary's handicap and that it is "essential for everyone to be treated with respect and love," and that "there is no way to insulate yourself from the needs of the world."

When he worked for the RFK family, doing everything from monitoring homework to teaching religion, the peace-activist priest Richard McSorley once told Ethel that her children would have two great obstacles in their lives—their wealth and their prestige. He believes that she shrugged off his warning, but it was clear from the way the cousins were trained that all the parents believed that St. Luke's message somehow would get through. They do not see any contradiction in being rich while also serving the poor.

Irrespective of family, as youngsters the cousins got little pocket money, friends soon learned. Ted and Joan were fanatic about it, and for Jackie, if not Jack, it was an article of faith, as it was for the Shrivers, Smiths, RFKs, and Pat Lawford. They believed that unlimited resources deform reality. In the EMK home there was also considerable emphasis on generosity. It got a bit out of hand once, though, when ten-year-old Patrick, after hearing for the uncounted time his father's stories about deprivation in Bangladesh, urged his older brother, Teddy, to ship some uneaten toast and jam to "the poor people in Bangladesh." Appropriately, Teddy threw the toast at Patrick.

While they were still in high chairs this new crop of Kennedys was taught, just as their parents had been, that the only gift worth giving was of oneself. That applied both to the immediate family and the world at large.

Expensive presents might reflect openhandedness, but they gave no evidence of personal concern. Kennedys were urged to make their own presents, and they did: Poems and speeches were drafted, photographs snapped, pictures painted, mobiles constructed, essays composed, needlework stitched. Scrapbooks were always in fashion, as Grandma found out. She now has hundreds of them.

In turn, the cousins got from their parents maps that described their travels, for example, and after the assassinations, remembrances of things past. Jackie has spent considerable time and attention in distributing some of Jack's mementoes, items such as his personal notes about important events such as the Cuban Missile Crisis, or the pens he used to sign the Test Ban Treaty.

Even more urgently, the cousins were exhorted not to view their wealth as a vehicle for escape, but as a means of doing good for others. Every cousin has vivid memories of how vital this notion was. It was drilled into them the way other parents drill their offspring in good manners. The "catechism," as Tim Shriver describes it, was: You have a special station and you should use it for the betterment of others.

"We saw the trappings of responsibility all around us," says Michael Kennedy. "We knew that our position brought responsibility." Or as Kathleen put it: "We're not going to sit back and enjoy what has been given us, because that's not what life's about. You've got to work at it, you've got to give of yourself, you've got to enter into the whole of life. It's just not enough to do something to gratify your own pleasures."

"Some people might call this noblesse oblige," suggests Bobby Kennedy, "but that implies the efforts of nobility to perpetuate the system that keeps them in power. That is not what we were taught. It was that the only important thing to do in our position was to work to help others. And we want to change the system, not keep it intact."

And they have responded. Virtually all the older cousins did social service projects during summers and in school. They worked with Indians, migrant farm workers, the retarded, runaway teenagers, prisoners, Eskimos, hurricane and flood victims in Guatemala, riot victims in England, Appalachian miners, poor rural and urban blacks, South Asian refugees, oppressed South African blacks.

Unlike other children of privilege who grew up in the 1960s and 1970s, they never considered rejecting their wealth. "We were taught that we've got advantages, and it is unfair that everyone does not have the same advantages," says Christopher Kennedy. "The important thing was to use our advantages in a way that makes it fairer for others."

Although dutifully practiced, all this selflessness has had its cost, and some of the cousins sometimes resent it, seeing it as diluting the family fortune. "We have spent so much of our money on others, and we don't really know how to take care of ourselves," one of them complained to another. The remark represented a touch of bitterness at the suggestion that Kennedys were devoting so much of themselves to doing good for others.

Maria Shriver sees the family fortune as consisting of more than wealth. It is, she says, "all the things the family had. I never thought, 'Oh wow, we're rich!' We were never treated like some rich kids—Rolls-Royces and things like that. You never thought about yourself as having a lot of money. It was important to the family that we not flaunt it."

The cousins are not ostentatious, and usually dress in the uniform of the day, be it jeans for college or relaxation or three-piece suits for business wear. Still, they are rich and there are ample signs of it in their lives. Several drive BMW sports cars. They take regular and spectacular vacations, which they arrange simply by calling a number at the Park Agency, in effect a private family bank managed by the elder Steve Smith. A self-proclaimed "mother hen" named Gertrude Ball at the Park Agency arranges their comings and goings upon request, hands them their tickets and points them to their destinations. Last-minute concert and theater tickets are simple to arrange with the proper phone call to the proper authority. When they want to splurge, the supportive resources are ample.

Like many of her cousins, Maria discovered that she was "different" not from her family but from her friends and from her reading. "People would tell me, 'You've got a lot of money. Your family has big bucks.' And at first I didn't believe them."

A former staff worker in the EMK office swears that Teddy Junior found out about his own wealth from a 1976 newspaper that mentioned he would inherit a fortune. The 14-year-old Teddy did not understand what "inherit" meant and had to ask his friends to explain it.

Michael Kennedy was like Maria—he did not believe the good news when he was told it. "So much else written about my grandfather was wrong," he explains, "that there was no real reason to think this was an exception—I mean, the notion that we had millions and millions and millions was a joke to me. It took a long while to sink in. But nobody in the family ever talked about it."

It all came as a surprise to Sydney Lawford, too, when she started collecting her full share of the proceeds at 21. She went right away to tell sister Victoria, two years younger, who told

Sydney to stop kidding her. "Money was not a big issue in our house," says Victoria. "We never talked about it."

The evidence is overwhelming that the cousins' naiveté about money is family policy, root and branch. Except for Jackie, Steve Smith, and Sargent Shriver, their parents never thought much about money. But all of a sudden it is beginning to have meaning for the cousins, and in the past few years the older ones have begun asking pointed questions, which have been skillfully parried.

The financial-disclosure statement required in 1976 of Uncle Ted as a senator told the children more about Kennedy finances than they had ever been able to dig out themselves. Armed with this, some of the older ones confronted Uncle Steve Smith, who manages the family trusts and parcels out individual payments through the Park Agency. Only then did Steve give details—grudgingly.

Yet the crafty RFKs by then were already onto a good thing. They had long since discovered that the agency, whatever its mysteries, always managed to take care of them if all else failed. When they were shortchanged at home—or denied their allowance because of some infraction—they could still run up a tab someplace and have the bill shipped to Uncle Steve's outfit. When Teddy Junior had unraveled the secret of inheritance, they clued him in to their buy-now, pay-later system. But at the more tightly policed EMK home, inspection of the bills was inevitable. Eventually the reckonings wound up with the senator and, says Teddy, "He always sends me the bill to find out what I'm up to."

The cousins' share of the family fortune has been diluted by their numbers, of course. They collect mostly from a separate trust for the grandchildren independent of the three major family funds. For those in the RFK and JFK homes, where the blood Kennedy parent was killed, each offspring gets an equal share of the estate along with the surviving parent.

Although there is a deliberate effort to obscure rather than reveal the extent and disposition of family funds, the following summary, based on available information, is probably near the mark.

Upon reaching 18, each grandchild begins receiving between $15,000 and $20,000 a year. The full inheritance income begins at age 21, when each grandchild collects up to $30,000 a year.

Each cousin's personal capital is said to be about $300,000. Some also share in their parents' portions, and Caroline and John have separate incomes from earnings on their mother's $20-million share from the estate of Aristotle Onassis. A major advantage of the trust arrangement is that the Park Agency pays the taxes, so that each cousin gets spendable income, equivalent to a taxable salary of at least $50,000. None of them lives exclusively on this allotment. Because all the RFKs help support the huge family homes in McLean and in Hyannis Port, and because their shares have been split twelve ways, they especially feel a pinch, or say they do.

"We really need to work—both of us," Kathleen says of herself and husband David Townsend. "I need a job just like anybody else," adds her brother Bobby Junior. "We're not rolling in money. If we didn't work, we'd starve."

The sense of a need to make money extends to others in the family as well. "I'm going to have to make some money in my life," says Teddy Junior. "There's not as much money for this generation as people think. My grandfather was a very shrewd businessman, but he couldn't foresee the impact of inflation and the size of our generation."

So the negligent Kennedy attitude respecting money of any kind, especially their own, is less persistent now. For some, like Joe (who gives himself a $50,000 salary from his oil company) and Tim Shriver (who makes only $20,000 from his two social service jobs) and Maria (who will not say), it is a matter of principle that they live off their wages. During his late adolescence, Joe's friends noticed that he became particularly concerned that he was being taken for a ride by others who wanted to get at all his "Kennedy money." Among the cousins, he is especially protective of his holdings now.

For others, Bobby Shriver especially, acquisition of capital is becoming a vogue. Bobby anticipates spending at least some time "making a lot of money," and he scored a respectable stock killing last year. He developed the interest in making money—and broke down the learned inhibitions about it—after formal study of his grandfather's life and fortune-making talents. "Bobby admires Grandpa so much—that's why he's interested in making money," says sister Maria. As always, the major motives Kennedys ascribe to each other are based on their connection to the family rather than their intrinsic worthiness.

"Wealth is a given to them," says Father English. "The question the family asks is, what are they going to do with it?" Kathleen first realized what the family's money and power could do when she worked with Indians in the summer she turned 17. "To get to the reservation, you had to go along this road—it might have been sixteen miles—that was totally unpaved," she recalls. "It was an awful ride. So I called Mummy and told her, and I think she called the Secretary of the Interior, and the road eventually was paved. I realized then that an awful lot of good could be done if you used your name and your advantages wisely."

English thinks that the emphasis on service so predominated in the Kennedy homes he knew that there was not much time devoted to discussion about the role and nature of money. "The radicals in the next generation are the ones who will want to make money," he believes.

On that basis the emerging radical is young Chris Kennedy, who developed a thriving sailboat-rental business in Hyannis Port in recent summers—staffed by pals. Its slogan is: "Get Blown Off Shore on Breakwater Boats." Chris goes straight to the heart of the matter, obviously more intrigued by the gospel according to Grandpa Joe than the one propounded by Grandma Rose: "Money gives you clear evidence of winning and losing," says Chris. "You either make money or you don't, and it's clear right then and there. It is fun." Chris has already started investing his newly arrived assets and is constantly on the prowl for venturesome and potentially lucrative projects.

For all his acquisitive zeal, though, Chris is also drawn by the family's notion of service. During several years in high school—which he hated—Chris spent afternoons and evenings in a suburban center for runaway children. He operated a crisis hotline telephone and helped counsel those who ended up at the center for want of anywhere else to go. Sometimes he would take the runaways home and would lend them money to get home. He was considered one of the most able and helpful counselors in the center.

There is no emerging candidate yet in this generation to take over the family business. Some guess that Joe might want it, that talented Bobby Shriver might be urged to take it, or that Steve Smith, Jr., might be the logical choice because of his father's connection to it already. If enthusiasm and entrepreneurial vigor are any gauge, young Chris might be the best bet.

As they have grown up, the Kennedy cousins have been urged

to live comfortably with their riches and live in comfort with whatever contradictions the wealth might raise in their consciences. Still, there is surely a tension between wealth and commitment to service, and the cousins have seemingly crossed that hurdle without difficulty. Sometimes, though, the ironies themselves are rich.

In the same summer she learned about the benefits power can bestow on the Indians, Kathleen and her friend, Sophie Spurr, lived the two extremes of Kennedy life. It was 1968 and they worked at a Navaho reservation in Globe, Arizona. It was truly in the wilds. They slept in either a makeshift dorm or sleeping bags in tents in nearby mountains. About a month into the project they were invited to the Pierre Salingers' home near Beverly Hills. A private jet was dispatched to pick them up, and they spent the next week at a series of lavish celebrity parties.

"The contrast was boggling," Sophie remembers. "One day we were living in a primitive village in the mountains, and working with shepherds. The next day we were were eating incredible food, meeting movie moguls and living this unbelievably affluent life."

One of the nicest things about growing up Kennedy is that the perks are pretty good and, if necessary, there are always opportunities to jet away from it all.

The Women's Movement

THE SUNRISE CASTS LONG, DISTORTED SHADOWS ACROSS THE empty desert when the dance begins. All through the sun-drenched afternoon, the centuries-old rite of passage proceeds, elaborate and hypnotic—the men like bronze peacocks with their flaring feathers, the women reserved, serenely feminine, supremely assured of their central role as source and nurturer of life. For the Apache, a matriarchal society, it is the most important thing they will ever do—ushering their maidens into womanhood. They are now ready for motherhood, the most vital business of the tribe and the race.

Kara Kennedy was there—about two hours' drive from Globe, Arizona—two years ago. "They told me no other white woman had ever been there," says Kara. They had asked her father, but he could not go because of other business.

To her astonishment, they asked her to dance—the first non-Indian they had ever permitted such an honor, they told her. For four days she danced from dawn to dusk. "It was incredible. We danced for hours," she said. Her brother Teddy and cousin William Smith were there too, "but they were not part of the scene at all. It gave them a taste of what it was like. I loved it!"

Kara spoke to an issue that still occupies the attention of this generation of Kennedy women: how they should define their role in a family widely perceived to be one of the great patriarchies of the age. All the cousins will agree, there is a difference between the men and the women. In their mothers' generation that was plainly obvious. The men ran for office or managed the family enterprises and the women did what was important to support them in those roles. That, in effect, is what JFK told reporter Marianne Means in the earliest days of his administration: "A First Lady must fulfill the responsibility common to any woman. Her first duty is to her husband and her children." He said he appreciated that Jackie's domestic interests were different from the public issues he addressed and that she did not have him rehash his political battles over dinner. His brother RFK summed this up: "She'd never greet him at the door at night by asking, 'What's new in Laos?'"

Grandpa Joe reared his daughters to be community-spirited in a broad sense. He embraced the traditional charitable efforts of his wife and daughters Pat and Jean as well as Eunice's much more expansive commitment to social betterment.

For the third wave, women and men, the role of women is a big issue. The cousins have given the matter a lot of thought, and the women obviously live in quite a different way from their mothers—but they have arrived at no final decisions about tradition versus liberation in their own lives. Some, especially Maria, are torn by the desire to have it all—career and family. Maria seems to be playing for time while she struggles with the decision. Others, notably Courtney, have obviously chosen tradition—at least for now. And Kathleen warily balances the two worlds of career and motherhood. Most of the female cousins are uneasily undecided.

The other thing that separates this generation from its predecessor is the public stature of its women. No Kennedy male is better known than Caroline, although the recognition stems more from her parents than from herself. But Maria's face lights up thousands of TV screens most nights as a Hollywood-based commentator on Westinghouse Broadcasting's "PM Magazine," and her celebrity is due to her own achievement, not to any family link. Still, the expectations of some of the parents and certainly of those outside the family are pinned to the men, just as they were in Grandpa Joe's day.

Given their position in the youngest generation of a notably patriarchal family, the women no doubt feel the strain keenly, which would partly explain Kara's delight in Teddy's virtual exclusion from the dramatic Indian coming-of-age ceremony. Then again, she just might have wanted to get back at him for his countless tricks on her. Certainly, feminist concerns have not eluded the female cousins. They are women of their own time.

First grandchild Kathleen has been the principal pathbreaker in her generation. It began when, as a teenager, she and her father, Robert Kennedy, agreed that she should quit the very traditional all-girl Sacred Heart Academy in Washington in favor of ultraliberal Putney. Once she had broken customary Kennedy practice in educating females, Kathleen has made a virtual career of overturning family stereotypes about their women.

Politics is the most obvious one. Kathleen sees herself as far more than a decorative adjunct to some man's campaign or public office, as her mother, her aunt Jackie, and her aunt Joan were. Kathleen is a keen and accomplished political operative. She helped manage Uncle Ted's 1982 senatorial campaign, even as brother Joe had run the 1976 edition, and her results were every bit as decisive, although her style was her own. "Joe is a bulldozer, Kathleen is a thinker and a persuader. They got to the same destination by different routes," says someone who critically evaluated both in action.

Although she prefers to use the name of her husband, David Townsend, Kathleen has been deliberately unconventional in the matter of childbearing, having given birth to both her daughters at home. While the Townsends were living in New Mexico, where Kathleen went to law school while David taught at St. John's College, Kathleen bore her first child, Meaghan, aided by a midwife and David—a circumstance that raised Ethel's eyebrows several notches but won Kathleen points with the third wave. "A friend told me about having babies at home," she says. "It sounded so wonderful." It also sounded very much like David. His long battle with arthritis in his legs has left him with a healthy disrespect for conventional medicine.

She created an even greater furor in Maeve's case, largely growing out of her insistence on again using a midwife. They were in New Haven at the time finishing law school. When they turned to Yale-New Haven Hospital for help, they discovered that it had a midwife program, but insisted that all its midwives perform in the hospital and not in home deliveries. Any midwife from the area who participated in a home delivery would be denied hospital privileges, and therefore be out of a job. Kathleen and David protested this arrangement to no avail. Not even Uncle Ted's intervention could help.

Denied access to any midwife in the area, they hunted statewide and finally located one at the far end of Connecticut—a long drive away. Not surprisingly, the midwife did not make it in time when Maeve, having dawdled for days, finally decided on an express arrival. So David had to deliver Maeve all by himself with the help of a police emergency manual.

Everything would have been fine except that "The police manual did not cover the emergency we had," Kathleen reports. "Maeve was born in the amniotic sac—Meaghan had been, too. It was hard to find a place to cut through the sac. The doctor in Santa Fe had a tool, but we didn't have anything. We finally had to bite through it. The police manual did cover that, however, and David massaged her the way they said to, and everything was fine." Both parents were "hysterical," says Kathleen, when the newborn did not breathe for 45 seconds after delivery, but that problem was cured too by David's ministrations. All the while their other child, two-year-old Meaghan, was in the next room, screaming, according to Kathleen, for a dabbing of Desitin. The whole effort was "exhilarating," Kathleen concluded.

Kathleen is a zealous mother—she couldn't be Ethel's daughter and not be—but does not see her role as exclusively domestic. Early this year she took a job as a policy analyst with the Massachusetts Human Services Administration, her first assignment being the plight of the homeless. It is a full-time job that takes her out of the home, now in Weston, Massachusetts, outside Boston. She took it only after long reflection. "At this point, my family comes first. But my concentration on them won't rule out my interest in a lot of other things," she insists.

Yet, like many an achiever, Kathleen has a craving for an active career and this raises questions in her mind about its impact on her family. She worries about her daughters. "They draw sunnier pictures—with faces that have smiles on them—when I'm around a lot," she acknowledges. She is clearly ambivalent about it all. In fact, she once raved so much about her children that one of Boston's best law firms turned her down for a job. They thought she would not be sufficiently committed to lawyering.

While she now works, and while she helped Uncle Teddy get reelected, David and an au pair look after the children. "He's writing the great American novel," Kathleen says of her talented husband. "He stays home. Basically, that's why I can work."

Kathleen rejects the suggestion that the Kennedy family still puts males first in public affairs, saying that "The basic problem is society's—not the family's." It is true that Robert Kennedy treated all his children with equal affection and urged them all to the greatest possible achievement. In Kathleen's case, achievement took the form of toppling sex barriers. "She truly believed that she shouldn't look at any activity anywhere and assume that women were not capable," says her friend Anne Coffey. "You may find out later that you don't want to do it, but she is not daunted by anything."

Coffey recalls that it was a point of honor for Kathleen to go on the same ski trails or ride the same horse trails her brothers tackled—until she was very badly injured in a riding accident.

Actually, there was no open inequality of treatment, but there were subtle indications that even Robert Kennedy believed that boys were different from girls and had different needs. He obviously did not require his girls to be as athletically competitive as the boys, for instance. Boys really needed tough competition to develop well, he believed. That is why he sent the boys to secular prep schools, just as his father had. "The sports aren't good enough at Catholic schools," RFK complained, "and the boys need to knock around a bit if they're going to learn anything." When the local bishop challenged him on this point, Kennedy stood by his judgment, but told him that Catholic schools were all right for girls. RFK later led a drive to finance a playing field at the local parish school, but that still did not satisfy Robert that his boys could get all they needed from religious school, so he packed them off to prep schools when the time came.

This different emphasis on competition for boys and girls has helped produce an interesting division in the way these young adult Kennedy men and women deal with each other now. When they were growing up, the women had the same training in swimming and sailing, and are still fiercely aggressive when the circumstances warrant. Yet long-term relationships were not settled on the playing fields, as they were for the boys. At some point in early adolescence the girls began to take a detached view of those pursuits and decided that there were other less combative ways to decide things. So the males still like to have at it with each other even now, while the women (particularly the older group consisting of Maria, Caroline, Courtney, and Sydney) are especially close and especially free from rancor.

"In our house it was all female after Chris went away to school, and it doesn't seem to me that we were running around trying to kill each other the way the boys were," says Victoria Lawford. A friend of one of the other women cousins asserts that the starkest difference between the sexes emerges when they are all in the same room together. "The males are usually strutting around and posturing, trading wise cracks and trying to be the center of attention, while many of the females swear off that kind of behavior," the friend notes. "Some of this probably comes from the fact that they were brought up to act demurely, but some of it is that they don't look at the other women and say, 'That's my rival in this family. I have to ace her out.' The men are doing that all the time."

At the end of the process, it was understood that it was entirely acceptable if the girls led unobtrusive lives. "Their futures were not nearly the focus of as much attention as the boys' careers—either inside the family or outside it," says one female friend of the female cousins. "They were always encouraged to do important things for others and to make an impact for the better on the world. The basic difference between the girls and the boys was that the boys were kind of expected to do it in a grander and more public way. They were supposed to be the ones out front"—that is, in politics or competitive public affairs.

In the EMK house, the jokes—only half in jest—center on what congressional district Teddy will pick. Rahway? Norwalk? Barnstable? "It's a very subtle kind of thing that doesn't say, 'Kara—you can't do it!' " notes a friend. "It says something like, "Teddy, you've gotta think about stuff like this, and Kara, you don't unless you want to.' "

That kind of reference, which also stemmed from Ted Kennedy's wish to make his cancer-stricken son feel a normal part of the family mainstream, has markedly diminished since Ted and Joan's breakup. Joan then started to think about feminist issues, and now regularly urges Kara not to accept uncritically the idea that marrying well and living a domestic life should be her exclusive goals. "I don't want her to make the same mistakes I did," she told one old family friend. "She has to learn to be happy with herself—and I don't see how that is possible if you just live for your man."

To a considerable extent, the gender issues that occupy the cousins' thoughts arise from the outside world. Maria Shriver, who along with Kathleen is the most outspoken on these matters and has done her best to break down the barriers, has this to say:

"When everybody thinks of the Kennedys, they just think of the Kennedy men. It is really too bad that my mother and my aunts and my grandmother have been overshadowed by the men of the family, because they are impressive women who made the men what they are. There was no better 'public servant' than Grandma, and no one who has helped or inspired more people."

Be that as it may, the parity that women of the third wave have achieved has been gained by struggle. One family intimate says that the parents wanted the daughters to be "accomplished"—that is, to have classic liberal arts training. But Maria remembers a parity of pressure in her home. "My mother made sure I was asked the same tough questions as the boys," and her father worried just as much about her studies as theirs. "It would not be enough," he told her, "to have others think, 'She's pretty.' They'd want to know if you had a brain and what you read."

Maria did not have far to turn to find encouragement. Her mother, Eunice, is probably the model most of the female cousins think of when they wrangle with this convulsive question of how to be feminine and motherly today and yet act decisively in the world at large. They know that Eunice virtually single-handedly established the Special Olympics for retarded children, and that her energy and lively intelligence have influenced any number of large public issues.

At 26 Eunice ran a juvenile agency out of the Justice Department while many of her contemporaries were setting up house. Later, to get a firsthand view of prisoners' lives, she lived in a West Virginia prison where she worked. She welcomed prisoners on work release into her home, and continued to do so even after one of them robbed the house.

A friend once asked Eunice if it was hard to open doors. "You cannot get anything in this world unless you are aggressive," Eunice replied. "You have to be aggressive."

"Eunice wants everything for herself and her children," says the friend. "She wants them to go to good schools, be good athletes, marry great spouses, and go into good businesses."

Not surprisingly, Maria is rent by the conflicting choices. "I love my work and want to stay at it, but I am insanely jealous of my friends who are married and have children," she says. "When you grow up as I have with the family being everything, you have to want that for your own life." Her friend Oprah Winfrey remarks that Maria wants to join the Peace Corps when she sees a beggar, she wants to be Barbara Walters after watching a good broadcast interview and she wants to be a mother when she's been around friends who have families. Spoiled for choice, she wants it all, and all at once, but it is hard to squeeze it all in.

Although Eunice may be the feminine exemplification of the Kennedy will to achieve, all the Kennedy women emerge as particularly strong personalities. Bobby Kennedy may wish that Aunt Eunice had gone into politics, but Eunice has long been on record about her personal convictions on the role of women:

"I believe in motherhood as the nourishment of life," she wrote in a 1967 magazine article. "It is the most wonderful, satisfying thing we could possibly do." In her view, Eunice had vastly more important things to do than politics. They are named Bobby, Maria, Tim, Mark, and Anthony.

On this most volatile issue, Eunice's certainty exactly mirrors that of her mother. Her daughter and her nieces do not disagree, but, like women of their time, they are wrestling more with the modern insistence that they can have it all. They and others note that Eunice has already bridged that gulf. If it is a choice between family and career, then for a Kennedy woman—for any woman, Eunice and Rose would argue—there is no choice. First, last, and always, they believe the family is a woman's first duty and final satisfaction. The women of the next generation want to accommodate other duties and satisfactions. They, like other women of their day, are asking themselves: How can we do it all?

The Play's the Thing

TOM KOUTSOUMPAS, A YOUNG MAN WHO HELPED AROUND Hickory Hill after Robert Kennedy died, became great pals with some of his younger children. They liked him so much that they decided to do something for him. "I got a call from young Chris," Koutsoumpas remembers. "They wanted to take me to Hyannis Port for the weekend. Ordinarily, I'd have been glad to go, but that weekend I was busy." He declined and thought no more about it.

Later there was another call from Chris's little brother, Max. Could Tom get a couple of pairs of handcuffs? Tom obliged, but, "When I brought them over to the house, they asked me to drive them to the airport to the plane they chartered to get them to the Cape. I did, but when I helped them carry some stuff onto the plane, they grabbed me, put a kerchief in my mouth, threw me into the plane's bathroom and handcuffed my hands and feet. I thought it was a joke until the plane took off. It turns out they had called my office and asked for them to give me a week off. They snuck into my home and packed a bag and had it all arranged."

Another time, a friend of Bobby Junior's begged off one of those white-water trips to which the entire family seems addicted. Bobby and some friends simply lashed the fellow to the deck—with a bottle of spirits within his mouth's reach—until they were under way.

Kennedy humor is not subtle. It is repetitive. It is usually loud, but on the whole it is good-natured—an Irish version of the British music hall, somewhat more imaginative than the exploding cigar and the whoopee cushion, but in that league.

Sometimes, particularly at the RFKs', what was fun for them was enraging to others. Food fights were a favorite pastime at

Hickory Hill, and when RFK's youngsters were in full career, mashed potatoes and string beans hurtled at high velocity around the dining room, distempering the walls and driving domestics to cover. "It was pandemonium at mealtime in that place," a friend recalls, not in admiration. It is said that some of the older RFKs still patronize only restaurants where nobody minds if half the spaghetti winds up on the furniture.

The general lack of discipline at the RFKs' no doubt contributed to the amazing staff turnover—some hapless servants did not make it through the first day. One unfortunate, upon being introduced to the group in the kitchen at Hickory Hill, was greeted this way by ten-year-old Michael: "Hiya. You're our eleventh governess. How long ya think you'll last?"

A rambunctious four-year-old Kerry once pelted a governess with one too many handfuls of oatmeal and was rewarded with an upturned bowl of the stuff over her head—courtesy of a family friend. The governess was already heading for the door.

After the situation got almost entirely out of hand, Ethel decided that a "governor" might get more respect than a governess. One was picked and on his first day discovered his charges placidly reading around the swimming pool. Before he could clear his throat to introduce himself, they had pounced and flung him into the pool. He was gone by dusk.

Those staffers who lasted any length of time were sometimes enlisted in the family flings—like driving slowly through Georgetown or downtown McLean while the RFKs pelted pedestrians with spare fruit and vegetables. A favorite projectile was the ice cream cone that usually had just been bought.

Esther Newberg, one of RFK's ardent campaign workers, cites a typical incident: RFK brought Chris and Max, then a toddler, to his office. Max immediately appropriated Miss Newberg's lap and typewriter, over which he promptly strewed crumbs from the crackers he was munching. "Show the lady how you learned to whistle," brother Chris prompted. "All over a brand new suit," Miss Newberg recalls. "Crackers everywhere! It was just a mess. The senator thought it was amusing. I wanted to slap the kid, but it really was kind of cute."

Max and Chris have been at it for much of the time since. They even formed a club called "The Blue Meanies" with humor columnist Art Buchwald as the leader. Club membership was given according to the dastardliness of one's deeds, and it was stripped away if one of the members was caught being too charitable.

The Ted Kennedys were more sedate. They liked to play "wakey-wakey" with guests. This involved deputizing an available child to invade a guest's room at the earliest possible hour and, without warning, to flick on the lights, pull the covers off the unsuspecting wretch and screech as loudly as possible into her or his ear.

The Shrivers, by comparison, were positively dour. The best they could muster were house-wide shaving cream and water fights, according to Maria's pal, Theo Hayes.

A favorite pastime, especially for the RFKs, was to fleece the tourists who flocked to Hyannis Port on summer pilgrimage:

"God, the tourists were gullible and would buy anything—I mean anything," recalls Karen Kelley, the neighbor child who was the seminal entrepreneur and who quickly enlisted the help of the Kennedys. "We sold 'Kennedy grass' and 'Kennedy sand' and 'Kennedy information.' The Kennedy grass started as tufts of grass we'd take from the compound, but then we just took any old grass clippings, stuck it in a Baggie and then sold it for a dollar. It was the same for the 'Kennedy sand.' First we started getting handfuls of sand from right in front of the compound, and then we decided we could go to any old beach and get the sand we needed. We sold that for a dollar a bag, too. People really loved the stuff.

"On the 'Kennedy information,' we'd answer three questions about the Kennedys for a quarter. The tourists always wanted to know when they swam and where the best place was to get a glimpse of them. They'd also ask the dumbest things, though. Like, 'What does Jackie like to eat for breakfast?' and 'What time do they usually eat dinner?' If they got greedy, we'd get greedy. After the third question, if it was clear that they wanted to go on, we'd say, 'Now, we'll tell you something really good about the Kennedys if you give us a buck.' They always paid, and we usually gave them bad information. There are probably a lot of people in the world who believe to this day that Jackie's favorite color is yellow. We just told 'em that. We had no idea what the real answer was."

The Kennedy children were quick to recognize the possibilities of this dodge, and were soon out there hawking Kennedy grass and sand themselves. More from Karen: "People would ask them, 'Are you sure this came from the Kennedy property?'

and the kids would say, 'I guarantee it,' even if it was the fake stuff. And when the tourists would ask the way to the Kennedy place, they were the ones who sent them all over the map. Sometimes, one of them would tell the tourists that he was a Kennedy. Then they'd look at us, and we'd deny it: 'That's not a Kennedy. He just wishes he was.' "

Caroline even got into the spirit of the thing, according to Hyannis Port local Richard Rougeau, a summertime cop who helped at the compound. While Rougeau was moving traffic away from the Kennedy houses, Caroline would saunter up to the rear windows of the cars and gab with the kids in the back seat as the adults in front were begging Rougeau for a peek inside the hedges in hopes of seeing Caroline or John. At Palm Beach when her father was still alive, Caroline and her cousins sold Kennedy Kool Aid to photo-snapping tourists and when they ran out of the powder mix, they simply sold water—Kennedy water—until JFK caught them and ended it.

John, too, at age five specialized in slipping out his bedroom window after curfew and helping Rougeau direct traffic in his Dr. Dentons.

There really was no end to the entrepreneurial gambits the cousins could parlay with their names. One summer, Ethel commissioned the building of a small shack on the grounds of the Hyannis Port compound that could be used by the children to sell trinkets to raise money for charity. The children had a charity, too—themselves. Karen Kelley, who appears to have total recall, sets the scene: "Bobby Junior and my brother, John, and some other guys started a little store out in front of the post office. They would go to the News Shop and buy an ashtray for $1 and sell it for $2 by calling it a 'Kennedy ashtray.' They also did a booming business in 'Kennedy grass' and 'Kennedy sand.' Later they jacked up the price to $5, and the tourists still paid for it. They would pay for anything and they would pay any price if they thought it was connected to the Kennedys. Well, the word got out that the Kennedys themselves were involved in this. The family found out pretty quickly and put a stop to it. But they made some money on it."

Another sure money maker had only a brief history. The Joseph Kennedy home at the compound had a movie theater, courtesy of the days when he ran his own production company and enjoyed watching his own films in his home. The practice of getting first-run movies to show in the family theater continues to this day. One summer, some of the cousins sold tickets for a couple of bucks to a first-run movie that supposedly would be shown in the Kennedy house—a true double attraction. "There was almost a riot in Hyannis Port," Claude Hooton remembers, "because they invited everybody, and I think they took everybody's money." There was never any movie, but nobody remembers what happened to the money.

When money was not the goal, hoodwinking the curious was. Karen Kelley also exposes the reporters who clustered at the compound during the summer like crows around a cornfield: "They were as easy as anybody else to fool. We told them all sorts of outrageous stories about the Kennedys and some of them got printed. You could also tell the difference between them and the tourists—they asked the sleaziest questions. They never got good stories, but we usually ended up with our dollars."

The Kennedy children got in on gulling the crows, too. Bobby Junior and a date hitched a ride from a reporter one day and Bobby served him up some nonsense about how he wanted to become a sanitation engineer and marry the girl who was with him. The story was duly printed.

For added measure, the obnoxious reporters often got a rotten egg under their car seats—a ripe old treat in summer—or a potato jammed into the exhaust pipe.

The Kennedys were always breaking one limb or another, so that there was always a surplus of crutches at the compound. These were used to play "miracle." According to Karen, miracle was played by starting to cross the street on crutches, then stopping in the middle, throwing the crutches down and screaming: "A miracle! A miracle!"

The Hickory Hill version of this was more madcap. A cousin would lurk in the bushes awaiting tourists. As drivers slowed to get a look at the Civil War mansion, the child would leap from cover, smack a hand on the trunk of the car and fall to the ground writhing as though in pain as others would scream, "You killed a Kennedy! You killed a Kennedy!"

Karen's sister Pam remembers the night they ragged the cop in Hyannis Port. The temporary summer police force in the summer community consists largely of college youths. One night some young Kennedys noticed a cop passed out from drink in the guard shack near the compound. They got busy and quickly painted the white shack bright red. Then they called headquarters with a distress call at the Kennedy compound. As expected, almost the whole of the Hyannis Port and neighboring police departments converged on the scene and on the hapless cop.

Another, less vulnerable victim was Tim Haydock, who loved the ribaldry: "It was really like guerrilla warfare. That is the best way to describe their interactions. You'd never know what to expect. Pails of water would come flying off the top of doors. Anything, just anything, could happen." Haydock once made the mistake of maybe drinking a bit too much and woke up to find that they had smeared ripe bananas all over his exposed body.

They are "opportunistic pathogens" laughs Haydock, now a physician.

That is probably how young Teddy's friend Sam Medalie felt about some of his dealings with Teddy. When they were traveling in Ireland, after his cancer operation, Teddy played his "Godfather" trick on Sam, having just seen the movie. Teddy's favorite scene was when the movie mogul found the bloody head of his champion stallion in bed with him. Teddy had to adapt. He planted the front half of the biggest fish he could buy at the local market under the covers of Sam's bed. Sam's scream was heard in County Mayo, across the lake from Galway.

Kara, too, dosed out a good share of mischief in her day. She and her friends Linda Semans and Cindy O'Brien were the class cutups for most of their high school careers at the National Cathedral School for Girls in Washington. They spent considerable time concocting ways to get out of class and stay out of class. A favorite was that Linda would "lose" her precious contact lens. This produced general dismay and perhaps a score of girls and the teacher would stop their class work to scour the floor searching for it for several minutes before one of the trio would "find" it—usually it was hidden in a closed palm. Then Linda, shaken from the ordeal, would ask if Kara and Cindy could please come to the bathroom with her to fix the errant lens. When the ruse worked, they had the rest of the period off for move devilry. Water fights were sometimes the aftermath.

Eventually some teachers caught on. Cindy describes how one of them chanced upon the three girls on one of the rare instances when they were innocent of mischief. "I swear I'll see you girls thirty years from now and you'll still look like you did something wrong," the teacher told them.

Sometimes the fun was not funny. Once when Kara was getting obscene phone calls, young Ted called the house, knowing that his parents were out and that Kara was there alone with a girl friend. He announced himself as the dreaded caller and said he was coming over. An hour later, he and some pals found the girls cowering in a closet. The girls did not laugh.

Bobby Kennedy, Jr., in his early teens, pulled a similar joke on one of the string of unlucky RFK governesses. He phoned the boyfriend of the governess, telling him that his beloved had just died, according to Father McSorley. "The children locked her in a closet and forgot about her and she suffocated," Bobby announced as he affected an adult's basso. The boyfriend was not convinced, but he called the house back just to be sure. Bobby, who was standing next to the phone awaiting the call, picked it up and said, "She's still dead!" The caller was assured only when he heard his girl friend's shrieks in the background, demanding to know what Bobby had done.

Bobby's interest in animals and his Hickory Hill zoo also was the source of much fun. There were, of course, the great dogs that jumped and slobbered and caused great commotion at even the most stately affairs or when RFK took them to his office. There was also the renegade sea lion that terrorized the neighborhood and escaped into the center of McLean before he was captured and turned over to the National Zoo. The deeds of his hawks and falcons were also legion—some of them scary and some funny.

McSorley has some additions for that category. Once he took Bobby to a McLean pet shop where the boy bought a thousand locusts and some mice to feed to his predators. During the ride back home, McSorley wondered why Bobby, an animal lover, would submit the locusts and mice to such a fate. That night McSorley got a frantic call from Hickory Hill. Bobby had released the intended victims, and there were hundreds of locusts and dozens of mice running through the house.

Another time McSorley walked into the bathroom next to Bobby's bedroom and came face to face with a falcon glaring at him from the shower curtain rod over a bathtub full of raw meat. The priest got out of there fast.

Through it all at Hickory Hill, the fitful attempts to impose discipline were not very successful. The parents did not allow the staff to punish the children, but only to make reports to RFK. This proved unworkable because Robert often was away, and the time lag between infraction and punishment destroyed the purpose of the discipline. Finally RFK ruled that the staff could chastise on its own, but Ethel would not have it. So it was often chaotic.

Theoretically at least, there was a schedule to be kept at Hyannis Port, which imposed the discipline of time if nothing else. This seems to have been the only discipline ever imposed on the RFKs. It was posted on the kitchen door: swimming, 8:30 A.M. to 9:30, sailing and picnic at 11 A.M., baseball at 3:30 P.M., reading, 4:30 to 5:30 P.M., dinner at 6:00.

Rules are made to be broken, of course, and that was part of the fun of summer. Everybody sneaked out of the house after curfew. The children were supposed to be in by 9 or 10 P.M., and they would dutifully say good night and go off to bed—or, more correctly, to their bedrooms. Then they would immediately exit by rope through the windows. After "sneaking"—as it was called—they would "hang out" with other "sneakers" at the News Shop, by the swimming pool, perhaps at the marina.

Barriers, they believed, were meant to be overcome more than honored. Pamela Kelley says the group had the local hospital in an uproar one summer while Pam was recuperating from a riding accident. In the middle of the night, in the middle of the day—anytime that suited them—the Kennedys and others would scale the three stories of the hospital to get to her room. They sometimes would invade other patients' rooms if the climbing got tough. If they made it to the top they would lift off the screen, hop in and present Pam with any number of small gifts and candies. "It was one long party—for us . . . not the hospital," says Pam.

Hanging out was an end in itself, with perhaps a forbidden cigarette as lagniappe. Later, hanging out expanded into making out with a summer date. A prime spot for teenage trysts was "the President's house." Jackie and family were rarely there after Jack was killed and there were plenty of rooms and couches for privacy.

It was also at the President's house that Kathleen made the only known attempt by a Kennedy to bug a Kennedy. Again, Karen Kelley, the Hedda Hopper of her time and place: "The Kennedys always got a lot of toys sent to them before they were on the market. They got a doll one year that had a microphone in its neck. You could talk into it and it would repeat what you said back to you. Kathleen and a bunch of us took this doll to the President's house. We propped it up on a couch and turned on the microphone. We got a lot of voices, but we couldn't make out anything anybody said."

The Great Hyannis Port Hair-Pull

KARA KENNEDY TELLS OF THE SUMMER AT HYANNIS PORT when her cousins Kerry Kennedy and Victoria Lawford, each then about 12, got into a fight, about what nobody can remember. Those two were always scrapping. So it wasn't the fight that was important, and the only casualties were a few hanks of hair; the reddish-blonde was Kerry's, the dark brown Victoria's.

What was important, Kara believes, was "how Ethel's kids cheered for Kerry, the Lawfords for Vicky and the rest of us either split or just watched." Kara will not reveal how they split or even for whom she was rooting. But she found it "interesting to see how the family broke down—very interesting." The point is that the 29 cousins are not only the grandchildren of Joe and Rose, but before anything else, the children of six different sets of parents, only half of whom were Kennedys.

Beyond question, those things that unite the cousins—genetic, philosophic, economic, religious, and temperamental—are far greater than those that divide them. Yet divisions are there. "They are not a monolithic group," comments John Douglas, who has known them all for years. "They can't be because of their vast numbers alone." Most certainly, there are unique features to the development of each of the six families, and even within the families. These are 29 highly individual young people.

In fact, they resist and reject all that treacle about togetherness, says Harvey Fleetwood, a friend of Bobby Junior: "If you look you'll see a consistent pattern of them trying to put some distance between themselves and the others. They are loyal to each other, but they would just as soon live down the myth that they are one big happy clan that has lots of meetings and does nothing else but congregate and play games. It just doesn't apply to the way they live their own lives."

On the other hand, these 29 extremely attractive, forceful, intelligent, tough-minded, competitive young people look a lot alike and sound a lot alike and think a lot alike and behave a lot alike—a good deal of which can no doubt be attributed to the extraordinarily powerful personalities of both their Kennedy grandparents. Many of the distinctions among the families can easily be traced to the reaction of the non-Kennedy spouse to Joe and Rose. Ethel loved them and their whole manner of life, which at least partly explains why everyone recognizes RFK's children as the most "Kennedy" of all. Jackie and Sargent Shriver were the closest to Joseph Kennedy, yet they each tried to chart a separate course for their offspring. Jackie's remarriage to Aristotle Onassis, when John and Caroline were still impressionable, gave those two cousins an altogether different set of scales with which to weigh things, including other Kennedys. They might be said, for that reason, to be the least "Kennedy" of the Kennedys. Joan, too, erected not entirely unfriendly— and not entirely successful—barriers to what she viewed as the overpowering influence of the older Kennedys. But her Bennett background was not nearly as powerful an influence on her childrens' lives as EMK's Kennedy roots.

The Shrivers and Smiths in looks and attitude are really almost half and half, thanks to the strong father in each instance. The elder Steve Smith happily joined Kennedy ranks, becoming more indispensable to them than blood relatives by his capable management of the family business. Sargent Shriver spent considerable time knocking Shriver certitudes into his children, and it worked. Still, Eunice is probably the most Kennedy of all. The Lawfords are almost pure Kennedy, their contact with their father having been limited because of the divorce.

Age is the measure that loosely defines groups that cross nuclear family lines. At the top stands the oldest, Kathleen, in solitary self-assurance. She has no rivals, no competitors. Next comes a male mélange of Joe, Bobby Junior, David, Chris Lawford, and Bobby Shriver. These five competed fiercely with one another and still do. Right behind them, seven females: Caroline, Courtney, Kerry, Kara, Maria Shriver, Sydney and Victoria Lawford. Paralleling these women are Michael and Steve Smith, Jr. Next, two pair of pals: Teddy Junior and Willie Smith, and John Junior and Tim Shriver. The youngest form the loosest confederation. Christopher and Max seemed joined at the hip. Patrick is close to Dougie and Rory Kennedy and Mark and Anthony Shriver by dint of geography (they all lived near each other). The Smith girls, Amanda and Kym, have so far avoided type-casting and are everyone's favorite moppets.

The almost biblical bond that old Joe Kennedy formed around his family has been weakening with time, and the six newer families have grown somewhat apart under the natural tugs of interests and circumstance.

Even the frightening aftereffects of the two assassinations and of Chappaquiddick are felt less forcefully by the younger cousins. For them, these terrifying and extraordinary events that have so dominated American public life for the last quarter century are history learned rather than reality felt. Finally, those haunting Kennedy voices are growing fainter, or at least changing timbre. The goals and status and the imperative to strive and to succeed, so pronounced for the older children, lay far less insistent claims upon the younger. There are, after all, only so many spots on Olympus, and the older ones get first crack.

Maria Shriver cogently describes the phenomenon. The younger cousins, she says, "did not have the influence of Jack and Bobby and Grandpa that we had while we were growing up. They didn't have White House experiences. They don't remember the Secret Service guards or the helicopters or any of the very special things that were common when the oldest of us were young. It was a much different world. We had the chance to experience the reasons why we were well known. All they have known is the consequences."

Understanding the different Kennedy cousins means understanding their different homes. The 29 of them are as different from one another as any other group of first cousins. They might be loosely compared to the planets in a solar system, each spinning neatly—if sometimes eccentrically—in his or her own personal orbit, yet each held from disappearance into interstellar space by the powerful gravitational tug of that central sun, the family.

The Source—the JFKs

THE UPBRINGING OF CAROLINE AND JOHN IN THE WHITE House and during their early New York days was exhaustively documented despite their mother's resourceful and relentless opposition. The tabloid press was always full of Caroline in uniform entering or leaving the Convent of the Sacred Heart on Fifth Avenue or later the Brearley School, or riding to hounds with Jackie in New Jersey's Somerville Hunt. John's days at St. David's and later the Collegiate School were similarly chronicled.

Maintaining a stable and tranquil home in the face of such persistent intrusion—into her own life as well—was Jackie's mission, which she accomplished. Without question she has been the source of the graciousness in her children and of whatever serenity they have. Few people, even those within the Kennedy cricle, realize what a companionable and solicitous mother she has been.

By all accounts, Jack Kennedy loved the advent of children into his life. He had precious little time for them, but what moments they shared were a balm to him, his associates insist. Of course, he did not live long enough to train them at the dinner table as his brothers and sisters did their children, or quiz them on current events or even teach them how to cope with being Kennedy. But he liked being a parent. According to his aide David Powers, his greatest anticipation was becoming a more available and attentive father after he left the White House.

But it was left to Jackie and a half dozen surrogates—and later Aristotle Onassis—to do the job. They had to do it under unusually difficult circumstances. If the JFKs' life in the White House was an exquisite imprisonment, then life after the White

House was often grotesque. Unable completely to escape the prying, the family hunkered down together.

The first noticeable thing is their closeness. Caroline and Jackie quite literally are chums. They fight and bicker and giggle and play the way old friends would. Irreverence is part of the mixture. Caroline will frequently introduce friends to her mother and then whisk them aside and declare: "Can you believe my mother's voice? Isn't it unreal?"

John, too, is deeply attached to his mother. They speak regularly on the phone, and his friends say John gets great pleasure from what other young men might find an onerous duty.

Jackie's sensitivity to the children and their needs is legend, and truly so. She knew how positively overwhelming their celebrity was and strove tirelessly to soften its effects. When Caroline was not being invited to her classmates' birthday parties, Jackie rightly guessed that other parents did not want it to seem as if they were celebrity-hunting. So Jackie would call the birthday girl's mother—usually startling her—to ask, please, could Caroline come to the party? She understood other people's sensitivity to Caroline's needs, but it was having the opposite impact on Caroline, who felt excluded. Jackie saw to it that such instances were rare. At other times, she swallowed whatever yearning she might have to share experiences with her daughter and encouraged her to go out alone with other adults, such as George Plimpton.

Jackie was a vigilant disciplinarian when it came to Caroline's school work, and Caroline's good grades prove it. John got away with a bit more—he was his father's son, after all, and heaven knows, JFK had been no scholar in his early years. The children were sent to tough schools, not society schools.

Although some of Caroline's life was straight out of Henry James—the travel abroad, the stress on cultural education, all the proper steps to good breeding—there was a distinctly modern thrust to it. In the matter of a society debut, for example, Caroline's wishes prevailed. Jackie had been deb of the year herself, but Caroline wanted no debut, and Jackie accepted her position.

Jackie led a full and entertaining life that included her children at most turns. Her dinner table was populated with some of the most talented and engaging persons of the day—artists, writers, entertainers, and scholars. It was great fun and a great education, and her children and their friends loved it.

Jackie's major message to the children was: Be yourself. Don't let the sycophants spoil you. Don't let the notoriety distract you. The message was successfully transmitted and received.

Caroline and John's links to other Kennedys are much more tenuous than those of the other cousins. Once they had taken the Skorpios tack, JFK's children were more out of the Kennedy orbit than in. They are probably the least likely of all the cousins to call up another to suggest a family party or a night flight to McMurdo Sound. It's not that they don't enjoy the others, it's just that they have been too much away for too long, and have developed interests and friends outside the circle.

As a close observer of John puts it: "After their father was killed, their mother pretty much determined what they did, and she wasn't all that crazy about being locked in with Kennedys. And all that sweaty roughhousing? She hated it! Caroline and John are their mother's children, for all the obvious reasons plus the accidents of history. So it's a bit ironic that interest in the Kennedys should focus so strongly on them."

The Trunk of the Tree — the RFKs

JACKIE ONCE MADE A DRAWING AS A PRESENT FOR ETHEL. IT showed children running in and out of the house, hanging out of upstairs windows, playing on the roof—with the cook carrying her suitcases out the back door and the new cook arriving at the front door.

Better than any thousand words, that summed up Hickory Hill.

By their number, by their staggering energy, by their excesses and by their powerful personalities, the RFKs dominated the rest of the cousins. They are the trunk of the tree, the other cousins the branches. They are the yardstick by which the third wave is measured: How do I stack up to Bobby? Am I better than Michael? As tough as Joe?

The only thing missing from Jackie's picture was Robert Kennedy. He was the center of it all, and the only way to have portrayed him would be sitting above it, perhaps peering down upon it godlike.

His nephew Steve Smith, Jr., speaks about Robert Kennedy the way Robert used to speak about his father: "There was a very powerful presence about him," says Steve. "He was one of those rare persons who defined his environment. When he was around, you wanted to please him and put forward your best effort—not out of a sense of terror, but because if you did well you'd be recognized, and that was the best feeling in the world. He had an empathetic quality that kids can sense. Either you have it or you don't, and kids can spot it.

"I remember him mostly on the river trips around the campfire. He was the general director of affairs. He'd organize the skits and the songs, and we'd all play charades. If you knew a joke, you'd tell it, or recite a poem, and if you did it well, he would be very generous."

Robert and Ethel Kennedy tried hardest of all to duplicate for their children the life he had known with his own parents. At the core of it was his insistence that the children be "like a Kennedy." It was clear what he meant. He wanted them to be tough and to excel.

"Daddy seemed to have the idea that Kennedys should always do better at things than anyone else," recalled young Joe soon after his father's death. "I guess this is why he always worked so hard. He used phrases such as 'Kennedys never cry,' or 'Kennedys never give up,' or 'There's no such word as can't.' We all just sort of grew up with the idea that Daddy never cried or gave up when he was young, so we couldn't. I can remember him showing me scars on the top of his head that he had received when he was young and saying, 'Do you think I cried when I got all those scars?' Of course I didn't think so, therefore, I'd have to stop crying."

He was direct in driving home his message. At the Sunday dinner table, each child had to come prepared to recite a poem or an essay from memory, without notes. "You never screwed up because there was tremendous peer pressure to do well and hold everyone's interest," says Bobby Junior. Then RFK would tell his own story, usually about some great battle and the leading general who plotted it.

"It was his way of telling us that one man or woman could make a difference, could change history, could have an effect on the course of events," young Bobby believes.

The children also had to keep diaries of current events, writing down three a day that seemed to them important. At the end of the week, "Old Moms," as Ethel called herself, would check and criticize them.

Robert Kennedy wanted his children involved in the events of his life—the history that preceded them and the future they were creating. Sometimes he would write them letters about a happening he viewed as especially significant, so that they would have a more nearly permanent record. When Jack as President and he as attorney general ordered the National Guard to remove Alabama's Governor George Wallace from the doorway of the University of Alabama, where Wallace was ostentatiously preventing integration of the institution, RFK wrote about it to

David—even though David had been with him at his office during the day, where they watched on television as the drama was building. Of the same event, he wrote to Michael that he hoped by the time Michael was attorney general such behavior would no longer be possible. Not much later in their lives, RFK began to gather his thoughts and speeches into specially bound books that he gave to the children at high ceremonial occasions. Clearly he wanted to leave a distinct legacy for them.

The children were visibly a part of RFK's public life. They marched in parades with him, sat on stage while he gave speeches, filmed political commercials for him and stayed at his side during campaigns. He also brought his political life before them. "Lyndon Johnson was rather a nemesis to the family while we were growing up," recalls Bobby Junior. "In retrospect, he was one of the best presidents we ever had, but during the heat of battle, the kids all saw him as some kind of ogre." Kennedys, they were taught, live by their loyalties.

It was not all formal and serious, though. Far from it. Much of the special ambience of Hickory Hill derived from sheer weight of numbers and the open terrain. The huge Civil War mansion, which had served as the headquarters for General George McClellan, the first Union commander, sat on almost ten acres when the RFKs bought it from the JFKs. Its four floors were filled with children and servants. The early American furnishings tended to get banged up badly by roistering children.

The house was named after the hickory trees that dominated the property, especially the centuries-old giant that sat in the back, right beyond the patio. A heated swimming pool was the other focal point of the property, and the RFKs built an elaborate bathhouse—the living room of which could be converted into a movie room—for their children and their guests. Farther back sat a stable that accommodated four horses and the family play gear. An obstacle course was erected for the famous Kennedy pet shows and became a permanent fixture on the side of the property.

Above the fireplace in the master bedroom hung two quotations that were important to RFK and important in defining what he wanted to teach his children. One is Edith Hamilton's description of Aeschylus: "Life for him was an adventure, perilous indeed, but men are not made for safe havens." The other was from Ralph Waldo Emerson: "Seek to persuade the sea wave to break—You will persuade me no more easily."

That is how he saw life, and Ethel was in full accord. They ruled the manse sitting side by side at formal meals instead of at opposing ends of the table. Friends say they were a great love match. He was devoted to her, she doted on him. What they wanted, they created—a raffish, indulgent, hyperactive atmosphere.

To them a large family was a commitment to a way of life. Ethel was a natural Kennedy. She believed in the many-hands-make-light-work theory of maternity, which holds that big families encourage unselfishness and self-reliance, and assumes that the older children will pitch in to tend and tutor the young ones as they come along. Time proved Ethel only partly right—a service staff varying in strength from 10 to 17 was always required to fill in the gap between practice and theory.

It is not that Ethel ever relaxed. She had—has—virtually inextinguishable energy. She let practice dictate to theory in the matter of household chores, which were left largely to the staff rather than to the children. But she herself cheerily drove car pools of squalling children (not all of them her own), supervised play and dinner, and saw to many of those time-consuming extras that sap the strength of suburban housewives everywhere.

To some extent, the older RFK children did tend and tutor. Age and gender generally dictated the pairings, which were, older first: Kathleen with Kerry, Joe with Chris, Chris with Dougie, Bobby with Max, Courtney with Rory. Michael from his spot in the vital center seemed happy with everyone, and David was so febrile and sensitive that he did not care much to make special attachments to his siblings.

The pairings were not exclusive, and all the children had other attachments both inside and outside the family. Where there are large families, though, such alliances are natural because emotions must be rationed.

A relaxed mood prevailed at Hickory Hill. "I don't believe a child's world should be entirely full of don'ts," Ethel maintained. She did not slam on the brakes until her children were teenagers. By then, in some cases, it was too late. "They were inside devils and outside angels," said Hyannis Port neighbor Larry Newman. "In essence they could do pretty much anything they wanted when they were home and in the neighborhood. But when they were campaigning or in church, on stage in any way, they had to be—and were—saintlike. I think they believed there were two sets of rules governing the world: the one for the rest of us and the one for them."

That was another part of the RFKs' makeup, unswerving adherence to some basic values. The world really was made up of good and bad, as Ethel captured it in a famous description of RFK: "For him, the world is divided into black and white hats. The white hats are for us and the black hats are against us. Bobby can only distinguish good men and bad, good things and bad. Good things, in his eyes, are virility, courage, movement, and anger. He has no patience with the weak and the hesitant." Actually, he did have patience for some of the weak and hesitant—he just did not like to see it in his kin. Ethel was the same way.

Their oldest son, Joe, noted that there were very powerful distinctions to him between his father and "normal" men. "It seemed that Daddy never wasted any time on elementary talk, such as how much the new car cost or where he was going to get a haircut," he said after his father's death. "He just never seemed to worry about little, unimportant things. Also, he didn't care what other people thought of him. It was just sort of fun to watch him."

Bobby Junior now says it was clear to him that his father and mother tried to teach the children that they did not have to follow the crowd. There were other issues to be pondered. "We really were taught something different from the nineteen-seventies' notion of friendship," Bobby Junior explains. "There are some values that transcend friendship. They are absolutes, and if they are broken, then the person that does it cannot be a true friend."

One example he remembers vividly was ethnic jokes. They were not tolerated, even the mildest. Several persons were thrown out of Hickory Hill for beginning them—some of them dear, or formerly dear, friends.

Towering above all the moral lessons Robert Kennedy tried to teach his children was compassion. He apparently started early. "My earliest memories are of running around my father's office when he was attorney general," says Kerry. "I guess I was three. It was a great place to be—you know, you didn't have to stay off the furniture. I don't know how I figured it out, but it was very vivid to me that this was the place where my father was seeking justice. People expect that we Kennedys will do something good for others. It's not the result of a lot of pressure and indoctrination. It's part of our heart and soul."

RFK taught compassion by doing as well as by exhorting. Bobby Junior was strongly impressed the time his father and a friend, Dean Markham, halted a tennis game after an injured bird fell on the court. It was a grosbeak, the youthful ornithologist noted when he learned the details. The grosbeak has a naturally crooked beak, which helps it to crack seeds. The men did not know this and spent literally hours with tweezers ministering to the injured bird, trying to "correct" its beak. The humor aside, the incident was evidence to Bobby that his father seemed "to care about every living thing. It was unforgettable."

Other things were equally unforgettable. "I think that the most outstanding characteristic of Daddy as a father was his method of encouraging his children," says Bobby Junior. "He never reprimanded us physically except for an occasional slap on the fanny. Yet he could shame us with a mere look of disgust." Like Grandpa Joe, his toughest discipline was "the stare." Once, when he really became fed up with young Bobby, he made the youngster write out "quite a few" pages of Lord Tennyson's "Ulysses."

For Joe, the impression was equally vivid, especially when RFK told the children he was "disappointed" in them. The most humiliating time for Joe was when he and a few siblings and pals got into a food-throwing extravaganza once at Aspen. "Daddy walked into the room and caught us red-handed," Joe remembered. "The only thing he said was that he was very disappointed in all of us. He made us feel like real rats."

On other occasions, RFK could be remarkably forgiving. Again, Joe recalled a time he was sent home for the day from school for shooting rubber bands. When his father found out he simply asked "Why?" That was sufficient. "He would always surprise you with his reactions," said Joe. "If you made a huge mistake he wouldn't hold it against you. The only thing he couldn't take was if someone was just careless or didn't work. As he always said, 'All I ever want you to do is try.' "

Niece Victoria Lawford remembers him much the same way. He made an extraordinarily powerful impact on children. He certainly liked them more than he liked most adults. Victoria remembers the day he broke up another battle in her long war with Kerry—this one over who owned some conch shells. "This is not the way you do it," he said. "You should share and you should be friends and shake hands."

"He was wonderfully good to us," says Victoria.

"He made you feel like you were center stage," adds Kathleen's friend Anne Coffey. "At dinner if you were there, he'd turn to you and ask your opinion about the issue being discussed."

That was especially important to his children. He knew their individual needs and tried to meet them. Because young Bobby was smitten with animals, he had an elaborate terrarium built by experts from the Bronx Zoo in the basement of Hickory Hill. In all, there were 75 different breeds of animals in a perfectly self-sustaining ecosystem. Because Kathleen hated religious school, he encouraged her to go to the ultra-liberal Putney School in Vermont. Robert Kennedy even joked that this put Kathleen in step with the times and gave her a button that said: "Peanut butter is better than pot." For sensitive David, he allowed a liberalizing of the rules. RFK's longtime secretary, Angie Novello, recalls a time when David was visiting his father at a campaign headquarters and began to fidget, asking his father when they could go home. Eventually he started whining and then crying. "Don't cry," Robert Kennedy said firmly. "Kennedys don't cry." It produced the exact opposite effect on David and he howled even more. Kennedy melted instantly and rushed to his son, picked him up and embraced him—physically and with soothing words—until he stopped. For all of them he set aside certain poems, or essays, or stories, that he thought would be especially interesting. "He knew what moved each of us," concludes Bobby Junior.

Strains of both parents ran through each of the children. Courtney, for instance, inherited her mother's yen for family life. She sees motherhood as her mission and looks forward to it eagerly with her husband, Jeff Ruhe, a fast-rising young producer at ABC-TV sports. Kerry, on the other hand, got her mother's kinetic energy and aggressive, affectionate ways. She has a poet's ear and a painter's eye and was a special favorite at the Hyannis Port scene, where a huge blowup poster of her pretty gamine's face dominated one playroom. She also is the socialite of the family, favoring hot New York discos and the company of the likes of artist Andy Warhol. Of Kerry and Courtney, family friend Peter Kaplan remarks: "They are there in the midst of all this action and all this tumult and they are like a warm breath of tenderness and sweetness." Rory, by turn, is the outdoorswoman of the family, and has won an impressive array of riding ribbons.

At times Robert Kennedy's commitment to his children was spectacular. When Kathleen was about 14 she passed up a sailing trip with the rest of the family so she could ride in a horse show. As it turned out, the family began its sail off Newport in a near squall. Soon a Coast Guard cutter barreled down on them at high speed and a voice over the bullhorn alerted them: "Senator Kennedy, your daughter, Kathleen, has been injured by a horse and has head and internal injuries. But the doctors say she is all right. Do not be concerned. Pull your mainsail and we will try to come close enough to reach you."

Ethel went limp. The biggest problem was how to get to shore in the foul weather. The cutter was the only way, but sea conditions were so bad no one wanted to lower the mainsail because they would lose control of the boat. As was his custom, Robert pondered the problem for a minute, then stood up in the 30-mile-an-hour wind, gave the wheel to someone else, and dove into the pounding ocean.

"Over he went," recalled one of the onlookers. "We all held our breath. He bobbed about in the waves, fighting desperately to stay on top. The cutter maneuvered quickly behind us, and he was somehow able to reach its ladder. They pulled him aboard, and we all sighed in unison."

When he reached her bedside, Kennedy found that Kathleen had been seriously hurt, having been thrown beneath her mount. She recovered from a bad concussion and internal injuries, but has been forced to curtail her riding.

Fittingly, Kathleen will have the last word on Hickory Hill. This is the poem she wrote for her mother two weeks after her father's death. Entitled "For Mummy," it, as much as Jackie's picture, says what it is possible to put into words.

Bobby—5 steps and cut to the right
Joe—go along to the left
Kerry—come around in a reverse
   and I'll fake it

Another game of touch football had started.

Tommy—who's faster and who has
   better style?

And then we would race down the mountain
   (trying to keep our knees together)
Or we'd put pennies on the train
tracks waiting for the train
   —at age 6

Riding on Attorney General
trotting off to C.I.A.
then cantering down the highway
and suddenly for a few moments
when no one would admit they
were out of control—we'd gallop.

On New Year's Eve he promised to
   stay up till midnight
but managed till 12:05.

On river trips he'd always be with
   the children
and say that's all right, Ethel
it's good for them to go up
Jack Ass Hill or float down rapids
in just a life preserver.

There was always plenty of
mustard and salt and pepper
whenever we barbecued steer and they
were always very good (?!?)

On the Victura and then the Resolute
we'd drag
or tighten the mainsail
or pull in the jib
or be ballast
and if we were lucky—take the tiller.

Sometimes I could drag him
to dance—but not very often.

There were prayers at the foot
   of the bed

and then a story from the Bible
and sometimes even a
TICKLE-TUMBLE

Tommy is Tom Corcoran, expert skier and family friend. Attorney General was a family horse, and CIA was CIA, which was just a few miles from Hickory Hill. To "drag" is to be towed on a rope fastened aboard a boat, and a tickle-tumble probably needs no explanation. Neither does the mystery of family love. In fact, it cannot be explained, but it is all good things.

Ted — a Good Father

EVERY MONTH WHEN THEY WERE GROWING UP, TED KEN-nedy had his secretaries phone the schools of his children, his nieces, and nephews to find out what activities were scheduled. He did not think the children would remember to tell him about all the plays, field days, expeditions, and the like that filled their lives.

"It would have hurt him to have missed something impor-tant—Senate business or no," says longtime family governess Theresa Fitzpatrick. "There were a lot of times when he'd be the only parent, certainly the only father, at some of these events."

All of the Kennedy children will tell you what a good father he has been. There are doubts about his character in other areas of his life, but it is hard to fault him as a parent.

"The kids in many ways are the center of his life," says an old friend. "There isn't too much happiness in the other parts. His personal relationships are not terribly fulfilling to him and he has few really close friends outside the family. His closeness to adults is usually temporary, both with women and men. His professional life is not all that satisfying either. The Senate is always frustrating, especially nowadays. His kids and his broth-ers' kids are the only thing that makes him happy."

Ted Kennedy was moved about as a child and he apparently determined that it would be different for his own offspring. "He was at so many schools in his life, and lived in so many places, that he has trouble remembering them all," said daughter Kara. "I can remember him saying that he didn't want that for us and that he wanted to make sure our lives were not as com-plicated as his."

He was devoted to the work of parenting. During one semester at St. Alban's School, young Teddy had to memorize three poems a week, and father and son would troop off to the study after dinner and stay there for hours, if necessary, so that Teddy could practice his delivery.

"He had energy for things no other father I know had energy for," said former aide Dick Drayne. "Every little picky thing in his kids' lives was important to him."

Kennedy thought being a father was great sport. A paternal trademark was his elaborate stories and animal voice imitations. He did the usual Donald Duck and Mickey Mouse, but he also could do noises from another galaxy. Breakfast was a favorite time for him to do his rendering of a chicken, as eggs were being gulped. Patrick was always delighted. The older ones were always dismayed. And it did not end at home. Melody Miller, an assistant, says Senate staffers were occasionally confused by barnyard sounds from the senator's inner sanctum. It was only the senator playing hide and seek with the kids.

He seemed not to have inhibitions about it, either. Governess Fitzpatrick remembers once when the senator had invited one of his interns, a reputed tennis whiz, for a game of doubles. Every time the poor guy tried to hit the ball, Ted would squawk "grashaw, grashaw"—his duck sound—to keep Patrick, in the bushes alongside the court, amused. The young man was so perplexed that he dumped most of his balls into the net or drove them beyond the baseline. After that, no one could convince EMK that the young man was any good at all. He refused to believe that his duck sound could have been the cause of such a collapse.

The EMK home, off Chain Bridge Road in McLean, had other amenities besides tennis. An old French country house, it was a great place to grow up. Its five acres front the Potomac River on one of the most appealing vistas in the Washington area. The 15-room house also has the required sauna and in-ground trampoline as well as the tennis court and heated pool. The major differences between it and nearby Hickory Hill were that the EMKs kept a far smaller household staff and the atmosphere was calmer by magnitudes.

It was not sedate, though. No Kennedy home is. As his children got older, EMK kept up the pace. On a recent sailing trip, Kara made the mistake of commenting to a friend about the good-looking guy who was wind-surfing nearby. The next thing she knew, her father had brought the boat about and spent the better part of the afternoon tacking near Kara's mystery man, whistling and calling out to him, much to her embarrassment.

"Superdad" is what Joan called him.

The commitment was the thing that amazed others. "The Dads," as Ted named himself, paralleling Ethel's "Old Moms," was a persistent parent. Often he would fly back to Washington between out-of-town engagements to spend 90 minutes, even an hour, with the children.

"I never had a moment's rest," Miss Fitzpatrick recalls, not unkindly, "because out of the blue the call would come that Daddy is flying in from Seattle for an hour before his trip to Boston and he wants the kids in their suits for a swim."

It became a family joke. Kara would tell friends they would just have to wait for whatever it was they had been planning to do because Ted had suddenly materialized and declared "family time." Now she is a bit more understanding. "He really made an effort to make his time with us good," she says.

When Robert was gone, Ted saw that there was "family time" for Ethel's 11 children, too. They always accompanied him on family outings and many times got first call on his attention. On many nights he would go to Hickory Hill to check on things before he went to his own house. Oftentimes he would end up sprinting out of the house because he had to be home to administer chemotherapy injections to young Teddy or asthma shots to Patrick. Also, despite an aversion to hospitals and blood, he held Ethel's hand when she delivered Rory after Robert's death.

In 1981 Patrick moved to Boston, partly to be nearer his mother and partly because his father was going to be in the region to campaign for reelection. It was a painful moment for his father, though, when he pulled up stakes at McLean, because the big house was now empty, Kara and Teddy having already gone away to school. So the Senator thought of closing or selling the house. "He thought about moving into Washington, where he could find a smaller place more suitable to him," reports Richard Burke, the senator's former administrative assistant. "But he finally decided to stay because he wanted to be near Ethel and Bobby's children. That was clearly his first priority."

It all could have been so good had the marriage worked out. But the questions that never had time to ripen in the John Kennedy home—about privacy, exposure, and pressure from the family and others outside the family—dominated the life of Ted and Joan. Joan was Jackie's natural ally, and felt great affinity for her. "People criticize Jackie for going her own way where the Kennedys are concerned," Joan told reporter Betty Hannah Hoffman, "but this family can be overwhelming. For years I went along with everything they said because I didn't dare do otherwise."

Joan simply had no appetite for political life, and it was her husband's whole working life. She escaped into alcoholism, and he into whatever tolerable pursuits he could find.

At first Ted and Joan had every reason to think they had the world at bay. Joan even thought the whole thing idyllic. "When you are twenty-six and you're the sister-in-law of the President of the United States and your brother-in-law is the attorney general and your husband has just become the senator from Massachusetts—I mean, how glamorous can life be?" she exulted to writer Lester David. But the party was soon over.

"I tried to be like the Kennedys—bouncy and running all over the place," she confided in reporter Gail Jennes, "but I could never be that. That's not me. I'd rather take long walks, sit by the fire, or play the piano."

"Joan was an extremely beautiful Catholic girl, who grew up in a privileged, very quiet, very Catholic world," comments family priest James English. "I don't know if such an uncorrupted world exists anymore. She came out of that world and married Ted Kennedy, and they were dazzled by each other. They never had a chance to just be quiet, young newlyweds aiming to go off and build a house together.

"All of a sudden John was running for the presidency and they were off on the campaign trail. As a Kennedy he loved it. And as his wife, she dug right in. But it was hectic for someone who came from the quiet little Manhattanville world. For a long time she did it, but it was hard on her. She did not like it. Her disillusionment set in more after she lost several babies," a reference to Joan's three miscarriages.

"It was just too fast for them both. He never had a chance to mature slowly through the political process and life's process. He started near the top of his profession and has had to stay there all this time. That's a devastating burden.

"It would have been nice if they had some more time without the intensity of all the travel and all the attention focused on them. They were too young to sustain it. After the assassinations, he was able to carry on and Ethel was able to rise to it. But it was costly, very costly—especially to Joan.

"I think communication was the big problem. I don't think she's a great communicator. And he's not a great communicator at the personal level. So, from the outside it looked glamorous, but from the inside it was a tough, tough, tough time. Ted and Joan Kennedy will always love each other. They just came to a point where they couldn't live together."

Though they could not bring themselves to talk about it together, Joan managed to communicate her pain to outsiders in tortured interviews that laid bare the difficulties in their marriage. Her confessions, perhaps serving some benefit to her emotional growth, were nevertheless hard on her and her husband and devastating to their children. As late as mid-1979, for instance, she told one interviewer that she did not know anymore whether the senator loved her. "I just don't know," she said. "I know that sounds like a cop-out, but I just don't know. I don't think it will end. There is no reason for it to end right now. But we don't talk about it. If I work on myself and stay well, then I'll know much better what I want to do with the rest of my life and it will all come together. I think things will work out naturally for the best, whichever way the chips fall."

Yet all the time their marriage was withering, neither Joan nor Ted ever loaded private griefs onto juvenile shoulders. Serenity in the home was paramount. Whatever it was that was upsetting them, Joan and Ted were always mindful of their children, who stand out as guileless, unaffected, and generous.

In one thing Ted and Joan did agree, and it showed: the children's behavior. Routine household chores and manners were policed far more rigorously in the EMK home than they were at Bobby and Ethel's nearby Anarchy Hall—that is, Hickory Hill. Kara, Teddy, and Patrick knew right from the beginning what behavior was expected of them and that they would be punished if they didn't perform.

Governess Fitzpatrick ran the EMK home with an iron hand—and with the full backing of both parents. She came into a troubled situation, not so much because of the marriage, but because a predecessor had terrorized the children. For months after she arrived, she says, Teddy would wince if she lifted her hand even to mop her brow or emphasize a point. Asked why one day, Teddy said that the former governess—"the last Nazi," he now calls her—would often strike him for no apparent reason and without warning. Kara too was extremely shy around adults.

The regimen was eased considerably under Theresa, but the expectations were still the same and still sanctioned by both parents. The children were punctual and courteous and lived by an exacting code. No one picked up after them, and when they wanted to have friends over they alerted Miss Fitzpatrick with written notes explaining their plans in detail. They did not bring friends into the house until they had permission.

Once the governess was coaxed into taking ten-year-old Patrick, Kara, and a couple of friends to a showing of the R-rated *Serpico*. It took about ten minutes, a wisp of violence and the promise of some juicy sex to convince her to yank the kids out, which she did over their loud protests.

Neither Joan nor Ted tolerated presumption. Theresa remembers that the children "were disciplined for speaking back to the staff. I saw it any number of times. They were told that 'She is not the maid, she is someone who helps Mummy.' They were responsible for their own place settings and they could not watch television unless there was a documentary on." Acting spoiled was a mortal sin.

Life in the EMK home was much less frenzied than at the other McLean branch of the family. Granted there were only three children instead of 11, and two of them were ill, Teddy with cancer and its aftermath and Patrick with severe asthma.

Patrick was so sick one year that he had to repeat third grade because he had missed so much classroom work. He also had to carry a portable inhalator. EMK learned to give Patrick his injections, and was rewarded with a fallibly drawn but trenchant picture of an ogreish nurse who resembled the senator bearing a hypodermic. Patrick called the work "My Night Nurse."

The senator's style was a bit less formal than Robert Kennedy's. His children did not have to perform at Sunday dinner, but they did have to know current events and be able to discuss them. He also was the toastmaster of every occasion, insisting that one and all participate in the festivities, and razzing the ones who failed to measure up. "The Dads" insisted that they have a sense of family continuity. On his Senate office wall was a John Adams quote that he repeated often to his children: "I must study politics and war that my sons may have the liberty to study mathematics and philosophy . . . in order to give their children the right to study painting, poetry, and music."

Kara fondly remembers her father as attentive but not all that exacting: "He's pretty liberal. He heard you out, and he wasn't big on harsh punishments if you did wrong." Kara's friend Abby Kaufman found that "Senator Kennedy is pretty subtle about his criticisms. If you've thrown your stuff all over, he'll leave a piece of it where you'll find it. He can get mad, but he does not make a big commotion." The impact was powerful, however subtle.

As a disciplinarian, Ted was an intriguing mixture of toughness and understanding. Young Teddy's pal Adam Randolph recalls two instances. The first was when he and Teddy swiped two parking meters in Georgetown and were caught in the act by the police. A call by Teddy from the police station and appropriate apologies freed the lads. But then they had to face "The Dads." They expected the worst when he summoned them to his study.

"Puh-leese," he began. "The next time you want to try something like this don't do it in Georgetown and don't do it in broad daylight." That was it. The knowing look on the senator's face and the glint in his eye over those half-glasses signaled an all-clear.

Then, in the summer of 1981, as a protest, both Teddy and Adam were considering not registering for the draft. When the senator found out, he sat them down and talked them through it. There was no mistaking what he wanted them to do. This was not a negotiable matter. "When that became clear, we flew down to the post office and registered literally seconds before the deadline," Adam recalls.

Ted Kennedy's concern about children extended beyond the family. Kara's friend Linda Semans remembers the day at Hyannis Port when she accidentally suffered a head wound from a tow-rope handle flung by Max Kennedy. The senator sped her to shore and to the nearby Cape Cod Hospital, which had come to be thought of as an annex to the Kennedy compound because so many of the family bivouacked there for treatment of broken limbs, sprains, and cuts. Other friends stayed with her, and EMK went back to the water sports.

When he returned a couple of hours later to retrieve Linda and found that she had not even been examined by a doctor, "He just stomped through the place wanting to know why, then he got a pad and pen and went through the waiting room asking people how long they had been waiting and if they were being treated well," Linda recalls. "It was just the way he would have acted if one of his own children had been hurt."

Physical comfort was only part of his concern. His children's friends also recount instances when they found him as affectionate and supportive as their own parents. He has gotten them all jobs at one point or another and, in the case of Cindy O'Brien, checked up on their progress until he made sure they were happy. Sam Medalie, a pal of young Teddy, remembers how the senator helped him when he wanted to drop out of Harvard for a year. First young Teddy wrote him "a very warm and supportive letter that helped me settle my mind." Then Big Teddy, knowing the boy was still troubled, drew him aside one night and listened while he poured his heart out. "It was extraordinarily generous," says Sam.

Adam, too, felt compelled not long ago to write his thanks for the many courtesies the Senator had showed him, especially during some troubled times. "You're a member of the family," Senator Kennedy wrote back. "We're proud of you." To Adam, "no words could have meant as much."

Only one piece of family history needs to be straightened out. The senator claims credit for once having prompted a spirited protest from young Teddy during a battle over school work, but Theresa Fitzpatrick sets the record straight:

It was she who one day upbraided nine-year-old Teddy for poor work on five pages of spelling homework. He could do much better, she scolded, and told him to do so forthwith. Simmering, Teddy left the room.

Theresa went to her quarters to have a cup of coffee while awaiting Teddy's rewrite. Minutes later, however, he slipped a piece of paper under her door: "You are not ascing me questungs abouat the 5 pages. You are not creting my home work. It is a free wrold."

Shrivers Can Cry

BOBBY SHRIVER TELLS HOW HE WAS ONCE SLUGGED—HE DOES not remember exactly how, but perhaps during one of his losing boxing matches with Bobby Kennedy. He was crying, and the others were telling him not to cry, to be tough. His father, Sargent said, "Maybe Kennedys can't cry, but Shrivers can. He can cry if he wants."

"That's the kind of thing my father would say," Bobby recalls. "He didn't want us always to do exactly what the Kennedys did."

The Shrivers certainly had the most stable household in the family and possibly the most intriguing. From their mother the children got a mainline dose of the Kennedy style. From their father they got quite a different pair of spectacles with which to view the world.

Bobby again: "My father is a true intellectual with a classical education in Greek and Latin and literature and history. He reads a tremendous number of books and places an extremely high premium on intellectual values and knowledge. We heard a lot about that when we were growing up." The "we" being sister Maria and brothers Tim, Mark, and Anthony.

"My mother, on the other hand, is more a street fighter," Bobby continues. "She knows how to use intellectuals for her work and how to pick them. But for her, the whole issue is the bottom line—how do you do it and get it done well?"

It is an exceptionally strong marriage, the aggressive philosopher and the pragmatic trench warrior. "My parents are perfect" is Maria's judgment. "Their relationship is very strong, loving, respectful, and allows them both independence. I never heard them screaming or fighting. And we were taught to be very respectful. We always stood up when my mother came in the room."

Some of the difference between the Shrivers stemmed, according to Bobby, from their religious backgrounds. "My father was brought up in tradition of German Catholicism, which is a whole different kettle of fish from Irish Catholicism. The German is much more analytical and theologically oriented. The Irish is more emotional and earthy."

However, there was no dispute about the singular importance of religion in their home. The Shrivers have always been passionately devoted to their faith. There were regular prayer services in the home, often in front of a makeshift altar with candles that Sargent set up. Even after Vatican II, they continued to practice many of the older, more familiar rituals. They frequently knelt to pray the rosary and, as a family, they would follow the stations of the cross.

Once, during Lent, Sargent led the family and some of their friends in the stations. The children became confused and forgot the words. When one of the younger ones got the giggles because of this, Sargent became irritated and ejected the miscreant. This served only to increase the giggling, so one by one the offenders were expelled. Finally, only Eunice and Sargent were left. Then she, too, was seized by the absurdity of it all. And then there was Sargent. "At least I know the words," complained Eunice as she closed the door behind her.

Eunice, of course, is SuperKennedy, living testimony to the family's compulsion to service—especially in helping the retarded. The Shrivers ran a summer camp for the retarded right out of their rural Maryland home—Timberlawn. It was a grand place for such activities, more than 200 acres of grounds. Actually, it was a working farm that the Shrivers rented—they dearly wanted to buy it but the owner never gave in. The rambling Civil War mansion had been built up with additions over the years that left it with two huge dining rooms, nine bedrooms and assorted unused servants' quarters. A 15-horse stable sat at the side of the plot, sheltering some horses and the farm equipment that tenants used. Of course there were the usual Kennedy amenities—heated swimming pool, trampoline, tennis courts, and rolling lawn for football and baseball.

Five weeks each summer for more than a decade Camp Timberlawn was a remarkably affecting place. There was an official camp song ("Camp Shriver," it was called, as Tim remembers) and a flag-raising ceremony to begin the day after the 50 to 60 campers arrived by bus. An earnest trumpeter would sound "The Star Spangled Banner" while all sang.

There was plenty to do—swimming, trampolining, baseball, soccer, the obstacle course, volleyball. The games were under the direction of family athletic director, Sandy Eiler. Every camper had a teenage companion to help him. Most needed assistance to keep from hurting themselves or others. Some wore football helmets to prevent injury. Many of the cousins helped, including Chris and Sydney Lawford.

The Shrivers almost always had retarded persons living with them and helping in the home. Of course the family's commitment to the retarded grew from their devotion to Rosemary Kennedy, Eunice's retarded sister, who has lived for several decades in a convent in Wisconsin. Of all the family, Eunice is the one who has been the most attentive to seeing and occasionally caring for Rosemary.

Eunice is especially honored among the cousins for her great love for the family and her extraordinary capacity to do useful work. There was a time when the Shrivers worried that Anthony, their youngest, was having trouble adjusting to school. He had spent so many of his earliest years in France while his father was ambassador that he was more proficient in French than English. Eunice virtually willed and worked and loved it away. She spent hour upon hour with him, taking him to a special program in Baltimore, reading with him into the night. Sometimes she would sit outside his room at bedtime, singing until she thought he was asleep. It was just to let him know that she was there, and cared. If there once had been reason for concern about Anthony, the problem now is holding down the voluble and strikingly handsome youth. Anthony has dated the likes of Tatum O'Neal and has leavened the sometimes highbrow dinner tables by provoking smiling inquiries about his social life. "We kinda wonder about Anthony," jokes his family alter ego, Patrick Kennedy.

Each of Eunice and Sargent's children had a different and special relationship with the parents. Maria's friends all remark on her closeness to her mother, and when Tim expressed an interest in the circus, his father arranged for him to tour Texas with Ringling Brothers. Mark's interest in baseball was cultivated early. He worked for a summer league on Cape Cod and then whetted his passion for the Baltimore Orioles by landing a front-office job with them in 1982 with the help of family friend (and Oriole's owner) Edward Bennett Williams. Mark is a typically hearty, bluff Irishman who loves his sports. Like the EMK branch of the family they were careful to uproot effrontery in their offspring, though it is likely that these intelligent children figured out eventually that not every kid off the street could express a dream and wind up spending a couple of weeks under the big top or helping in the office of his favorite major league team.

The children are the center of the Shrivers' lives, and they love throwing parties for them. Every year the pre-Thanksgiving party at the house is given in "honor" of them, and they are encouraged to bring their friends and friends of their friends.

After Rose, Eunice is the family's model woman. She has often helped nieces and nephews. Chris Lawford reports, "Eunice was one of the few people in the family who took an interest in me and cared enough to talk to me. She couldn't do enough for me and I think she's the greatest. She was there for me when other people weren't."

"She should have been President," believes nephew Bobby Kennedy. "She is the most impressive figure in the family. She has a carefully constructed set of values, and she will not budge from them. She is highly principled in ways that are more sophisticated than anyone in the family. If you ask, most of my brothers, sisters, and cousins would say they'd like to be like her. One of the reasons Kathleen is so impressive is that she is very much like Eunice."

Eunice was also JFK's closest sibling and held him up to her children as a model. "She thought he was the all-around '*it*,'" says one friend. So much so that her own children used to tease her with: "Well, what about Daddy?"

On the day she married Sargent Shriver, Eunice toasted him, saying: "I searched all my life for someone like my father and Sarge came closest." He also came with old Joe's blessing—he had been running the lucrative Merchandise Mart for several years and was an important financial adviser to Grandpa Joe. The two had deep affection for each other and that is the major reason Sargent never felt oppressed in the sometimes overwhelming family.

Shriver is very much his own man, and the father of his own family, completely capable of handling a little brother worship in his wife. He calmly points out that the name Shriver is a good deal older than Kennedy, and he is serenely self-assured about who he is and what he intends to do. His family lost its fortune in the Depression, which spurred Sargent to combine a will to succeed with his high idealism.

Although he has spent time under Kennedy patronage, he has also made his own way, politically and otherwise. He has run twice for national office—for vice-president on the trounced George McGovern ticket in 1972 and for President in 1976, when several primary drubbings persuaded him to withdraw He also briefly flirted with a run at governor of Maryland in the late 1960s, but found that the water was not quite right. In none of those cases did he have—nor did he seek—the full family blessing.

The Shrivers have never been swallowed up by the Kennedys, nor was there ever the remotest danger that they would be. At times both parents stressed the differences, just to make the point.

Bobby Shriver explains: "They had different styles of dealing with children. My father was discreet. He'll try to help you reach your own conclusions. If you told him something, he'd be likely to ask, 'What do you think? What are the alternatives?' That must have been frustrating at times because you're sure to see your kid knock his head against a few walls before he gets the right answer. It also involves a great deal of trust and faith in your children because you know there is always the risk of pain or failure.

"My mother's approach was 'Do this,' or 'Do that.' She'd tell you what to do at the drop of a hat. I think that was more of the way she was brought up. And you behave the way you were brought up."

Each of Eunice's children will respond assertively, if asked, that "Shrivers are *not* Kennedys." It was a point of honor when they were young, especially with the pesky RFK kids. "You sit in the back seat and I'll sit in the front—because I'm a Kennedy and you're a Shriver," one Hickory Hiller would shout. "No way, Shrivers are better than Kennedys," would come the defiant reply. And to this day lively, friendly competitive comparisons are a feature of family get-togethers.

Yet while the Shrivers carefully maintain their detachment, they are somehow still Kennedy to the core, and deeply concerned with the family past—Bobby's thesis on Grandpa Joe and Maria's on JFK being the most elaborate studies any of the grandchildren have made on their Kennedy roots.

Current affairs was a family pastime. Articles that covered matters of particular interest to different children were clipped or books were set aside with passages marked for study. The child was expected to study the material and be prepared to report on it and answer questions about it at the following dinnertime. Friends, like Theo Hayes, also underwent the same rigors.

Tim's description of the atmosphere in the Shriver home would equally well characterize all Kennedy households: "There was a large achievement mentality that was not really in the form of direct, overt pressure, but was the nurturing environment of our homes."

One family friend says, "Both Shrivers want their children to accomplish things that will change the world," a very Kennedy aspiration. It is also said that "They want to make sure on a daily basis that their children do worthwhile things, so they are constantly throwing ideas out about how they can better themselves. They want their children to be great successes."

Tim notes that his father has 50 million ideas for constructive use of every minute of the day even if one of the children already has his or her own 10 million ideas. This passion for uplift has a distinct Kennedy ring, but it is typically Shriver, too. They are within the charmed circle, but very much on their own terms.

"You work hard, you play hard," Tim sums up. "Above all, you do well."

Peter Who Went Away

CHRIS LAWFORD PONDERS THE QUESTION IN A LAWYERLY WAY, then answers judiciously:

"My mother was terrific." Long pause. "But she had her doubts about bringing us up because she was a female in a male-dominated household. All the examples she held out to us were male. It was, 'Uncle Jack did it this way,' or 'Uncle Bobby did it that way,' or 'Grandpa always used to say . . .' It just brought home to us how important it was that we didn't have a man in our family. Her message was that something was missing."

Chris's father, Peter, got off on the wrong foot with the Kennedys and never got into stride. When he and Pat Kennedy were divorced, in 1965 when Chris was ten, it made their children the first Kennedys to lose a father in that way. It made them different.

Even when Peter was around, it was not too comfortable. When Joe Kennedy heard that Pat had engaged herself to Lawford, he glared and said: "If there's anything I think I'd hate as a son-in-law, it's an actor. And if there's anything I'd hate worse than an actor as a son-in-law, it's an English actor." That left little room for compromise, but Lawford tried, he insists.

"Actually, it took two years of exposure to the Kennedy family esprit before I began to get the message that the secret was participation," Peter wrote. He found the Kennedys "almost overwhelming."

True, his Hollywood contacts did help Jack at certain crucial points in the presidential campaign, and added a little glitter to the White House later. And, true, the Kennedys were not at all foreign to the Hollywood scene. Grandpa Joe, after all, had been one of the first to get into the talking movie business and he was friendly with scores of celebrities—still a family trait.

So the Lawford marriage at first seemed a happy union of two complementary spheres.

Peter did not have the intellectual heft of a Sargent Shriver that would have allowed him detached perspective, nor the savvy of a Steve Smith that would have encouraged assimilation. To him, the Kennedys were "like the Dallas Cowboys"—he could not beat them. Neither, it seemed, could he join them. So he went away.

As he told Anne Taylor Flemming a few years ago: "I always felt that Pat's love for her father took precedence in a funny way over her love for me. The more I saw it in our daily life, the more I understood it. She worshiped him—in the long pull, that was stronger."

After her husband left, one family friend said Pat's reaction was to thrust her children into the rest of the family and hope for the best. "Her instincts were probably right," the friend said. "They needed the connection to a family and she made sure it was a powerful Kennedy connection."

Recognizing perhaps that their own hearty Kennedyism was at least partly to blame for the Lawfords' loss of a father, the rest of the family always has been exceedingly solicitous of the Lawford children. Chris, Sydney, and Robin have been unqualifiedly welcomed into the Kennedy orbit. "Your entrance is timely, as we need a new left end," President JFK wrote to his newest niece at the time of Robin's birth. In later years they went on the raft excursions, the ski trips, and the other family activities. For many years Lawford was an absentee father.

As best she could, Pat insisted that the children keep in touch with Peter and remember him on birthdays, holidays, and Father's Day. "Mummy really made us feel that our father was still a part of the house," says Victoria. "She could have made him an ogre. But she was very good about keeping the kids in touch with him—even if it meant reminding us and staying on our backs."

There was no escaping an acute feeling of loss. The depth of that feeling is illustrated by another anecdote Chris tells: It was Christmas, 1965, and the RFKs had come to Sun Valley to ski, Chris with them. The RFKs all were good skiers, but Chris had never buckled on a ski before, and was afraid. When RFK asked him if he was ready to go, he said no, that he would wait for his mother. Robert must have seen through Chris' excuse, because he immediately sent off his own group and got Chris the equipment he needed and a little tender, loving coaching to get him going. "We got over to the mountain, and by this time I had growing confidence inside me just from hearing him talk," says Chris. "He got us set up and told us not to be afraid and that he'd see us later. I really had a blast that day."

Still, in a fatherless home, growing up was hard. What was missing—the love and attention of a man—was difficult to find, since there were so many cousins seeking it.

The instances of male attention were so rare and so precious that Chris remembers almost all of them. One balmy summer day Robert Kennedy spotted Chris in long pants and urged him to go inside and change to shorts. Chris was overwhelmed by this interest. "It meant that there was a grownup who took an active interest in what I did on a particular day. There always seemed to be people interested in how I spent blocks of time— like where I was at school, and how I was doing and what my vacation plans were. I was pretty well taken care of when it came to groups of days. There were adults who seemed to take an interest in that. But a lot of the time there wasn't interest on particular days."

Victoria describes a similar kind of pleasure at the attention her Uncle Ted gave her when she was at college near him in Virginia. "He was very kind and always interested in what I was doing," she says. "He was great for having long talks and he helped settle a lot of issues in my life."

One of the toughest for her was the search for a job. She wanted to get into broadcasting, but it was not easy. For more than a year and a half, she went to scores of fruitless interviews. Many prospective employers really did not believe that she was applying for an entry-level job. They thought that she, as a Kennedy, would quit in a moment when a glamorous job offer came along. Several interviewers just wasted time asking her about the family.

There was no glamorous job waiting for her, but Victoria's persistence eventually paid off. She now works in a cable television outlet covering political and public affairs and is angling for an on-camera slot.

Perhaps to compensate for their loss, the Lawford children became strongly attached to one another. "I have the three greatest sisters in the world," Chris now says, remembering the times they doted on him. No matter where any of the Lawfords are, for instance, they will rush back to New York to see one of Robin's off-off Broadway theatrical productions. Victoria adds that the worst thing about a two-year stay in Paris with her mother and Robin was that Chris and Sydney were not there.

Inside the Lawford home the Kennedy rigors were maintained. There were mandatory poetry recitals every Saturday night. Pat also required that they write formal book reports about their current reading and present them to her. In addition, she asked each of the children to spend part of an evening every so often reading to her from their school books. "If you ever messed up, she'd make you read it again," reports Victoria.

When the family's favorite non-Kennedy, Lem Billings, was a guest, which he frequently was, the Lawfords would bring a map of the United States to the dinner table and then be grilled on the states—or perhaps prompted to name the Presidents of the United States, sometimes backward, sometimes forward.

It was a house that in many ways was as fully exacting as the others. "Mummy was always doing things with us—taking us to museums and concerts and art shows and stuff," says Victoria. "I'd want my children to have the same kind of life I had. I never thought about it until recently, but it has become clear to me that my mother was there for us all the time. We were her life's work." Chris agrees: "No matter how hard it got, no matter what kind of trouble we gave her, my mother never failed to let us know how much she cared about us. She was the source of the happiness we had in our lives and it was very tough work for her. We weren't very easy sometimes."

Among the Lawford children, the deepest sense of family mission runs in Sydney, the oldest daughter. Like her mother, she has a passion for family details such as birthdays and important other milestones and will throw a party in honor of something or other without any prodding. She is also especially close to Grandma Rose, due in part to their living near each other for a while during a time when Sydney went to school in Florida. She has a model's good looks and a clown's temperament and is now engaged to Boston television producer Peter McKelvey.

Always, there was the Kennedy exhortation to do well. "My mother always used to say to me that she didn't care what I was, she didn't care if I didn't want to be President, as long as I tried to do the best that I possibly could," says Chris. "I'm not so sure she was telling the truth. I'm sure she'd like to see me do as much as I possibly can with the maximum effect. In our family, great things are expected."

Not Just Another Guy Named Smith

IT IS NOT RECORDED DIRECTLY WHAT JOE KENNEDY THOUGHT of his son-in-law Steve Smith, but most likely it was the measured approval one accomplished person gives to another, especially when the resemblance between them is close. With Smith as with Joe, most people rarely see more than the tip of the iceberg. When he is asked the wrong question, his response is the famous Smith stare, as cold and cutting as a Damascene blade.

One friend recounts how he once innocently asked Smith about a forbidden subject. "The dialogue was so brief that it was easy to write it down when I went home." Here it is, reprinted in its entirety:

"What exactly is it that you do for the Kennedys?"

"I run the business."

"What does that entail?"

"Keeping track of things."

"What exactly does that mean you do? Whom do you talk to? How do you do it?"

"I do lots of things."

"Well, could you tell me the first thing you did this morning after you took off your coat?"

"I can't."

Discretion is the linchpin of Steve's character. "I sometimes think he could walk with his back to the sun and never cast a shadow," says the friend who tells the anecdote. His decisions affect the well-being of the entire Kennedy family, and in most cases Kennedys and others do what he asks.

To the public he is an invisible man, the unknown Kennedy. Yet Steve is not just another guy named Smith. There are two great lines of authority in the Kennedy family. One stretches to Ted Kennedy because he is now the head of the family—with his three sisters having veto power over him if they act in concert. The other line runs to Steve Smith, who is the minister of finance and attorney general wrapped into one. He controls the purse strings and lays down the law, zealously guarding family interests. He is also the crisis manager, having handled Chappaquiddick, David's drug problems, and countless everyday difficulties.

He has been offered chances to run for office in New York State, but long ago decided that he was not an open-field politician. "He prefers the back room, where the real decisions are made," says an intimate.

Being the "no" man is a difficult role, and most of the cousins have sometimes resented him and his barbed humor and iron will. Only recently have they begun to understand that he has always acted out of unwavering concern for them. "Steve and I have had our problems," observes Chris Lawford. "But he cared about me, and that was hard to see at times."

"Steve bleeds for them in his way," said another friend—again asking for anonymity because no one wants to be named when talking about the Smiths. It is a measure of respect, if not quite fear, that Smith commands. "I think it bothered him more than anyone that he had to crack down so hard so often," adds another family intimate. "Steve is tremendously loyal—that's the overriding thing about him—and very intelligent."

If Steve is hard as a walnut, then Jean Smith is soft as a willow. She, too, has a special place in the family—a kind of female version of Uncle Ted, tender and tolerant. Teddy Junior puzzled for years over choosing a new godmother after his original one, Mrs. Edward Moore, from whom both he and his father got their forename, died. "Finally I decided to ask my Aunt Jean," he says. "She's been so nice to me and my father. She'd do anything for us. She gives great advice and she is very understanding—and she's got a great shoulder to cry on."

The Smiths, Jean as well as Steve, move with easy assurance through the many power centers of New York City, where they live. During the past few years they have begun taking their sons, Steve Junior and William, along to introduce them early into the nation's financial, journalistic, literary, artistic, and musical centers, and the boys have learned how to use such access advantageously.

Like the Shrivers, the Smiths have always supported the handicapped. Jean has developed an arts program for the retarded, and last year began working with choreographer Alvin Ailey on dance training for the blind.

Also like the Shrivers, the Smiths turned their getaway home in Pawling, New York, in the Hudson Valley, into a summer camp for the mentally handicapped, after first having fended off an effort by some local politicians to deny them the required zoning variance.

Michael Kennedy was one of those who joined his Smith cousins in working with the handicapped—swimming, baseball, exercising, trampoline, and crafts. Steve Junior proudly remembers one of his charges, an extremely bright autistic child who refused to speak. "He'd been to all kinds of programs and still had never spoken a word," Steve says. "Then all of a sudden, during some of the games he began saying 'yes' and 'no'—it was a great feeling for me."

The Smiths have nurtured in their children a typical Kennedy seriousness of purpose and social commitment. Steve Junior has his father's keen mind and eye, and possibly a promotable political personality. William is more retiring, like his mother, and instead of following his older brother to Harvard, went to Duke University, from which he graduated in January 1983. He agreed with his parents that it was best for him not to get caught up in the Kennedy whirlpool in Cambridge. William is very guarded about the family's doings and is likely to be the first to express reservations about the motives of outsiders who want to get close to the cousins. He once urged Kara to stop dating a journalist because he was sure that the man was using her for a story.

Steve and William are good friends as well as brothers, though they are very different persons. Where Steve is rugged and unrelenting, William is tender and sensitive. When Steve was likely knocking heads on the playing fields, William took up art and now is quite good at it. Yet the Smith brothers share many things, most recent of which was their study of Spanish before a trip to Costa Rica for work with a social service and political agency. Now, when family teasing gets tough on them, they switch into Spanish. "They obviously enjoyed going through it together as brothers," says their friend Peter Emerson.

The Smiths refuse to discuss their adopted daughters, Amanda and Kym, out of concern that it might hurt them. "I don't want to talk about my daughters," says Jean. "I don't want them to feel different." It is known that Kym was one of the last Vietnamese children flown dramatically to the U.S. as the war in her country was drawing to its calamitous close. But one does not learn this from Jean Smith, nor anything whatever about Amanda, who seems to be quite shy.

It is clear to friends, though, that whatever the Smiths did to prepare their home for the girls and open their hearts to them was right. "They are both really spectacular kids," says Andy Karsch. "They are the center of life in that house. They have great wit—true Smiths." Their father privately delights in their accomplishments and boasts to his friends what "life enhancers" they are.

Amanda has followed the footsteps of her brother, William, when it comes to art. Their drawing and paintings, much coveted, are given to the family as gifts. She has also done very well at school, and been rewarded with a year's study in France. She hopes to go on to Oxford, which would be a Kennedy first.

Kym has all the unabashed Kennedy gregariousness. A delightful chatterbox, she will strike up a conversation with anyone she meets. Curious about everything, she is completely unselfconscious. She has wrapped the most hardened of her male cousins around her pinky and she tirelessly enforces the privilege of her rank—the youngest.

"It's a real challenge to explain your career and your life to a nine-year-old, but Kym insists on it and she is infectiously engaging," says Emerson.

Like Grandpa Joe, whose role in the family he inherited, Steve Smith watches over the whole stormy brood of cousins with a dedication that is guardedly affectionate. When great issues and large sums are at stake, one must act prudently. It is not wise to leave too many chinks for clever youths inventively to exploit. Smith has taken on the toughest role in the family— that of the enforcer and protector—and those who have watched the family assert that no one else could have assumed that part.

Someone who was also there remembers the time Steve took his sons to see *The Godfather*. "He watched the movie very intently," reports the observer, "and when it was over, he sat in his seat a bit longer than necessary, smiling and nodding his head." He later told his sons that he knew exactly what it was like protecting a family's enterprise, making deals, and moving in the back corridors of power.

Homeland of the Heart

"EXTRA! EXTRA!" DAVID'S MAKESHIFT HEADLINE SCREAMED! "Despite the belief in some quarters that Chris Lawford is the favorite grandchild, David Kennedy is in fact Grandma's favorite grandchild," the appended story explained.

The reasons were ample, according to David, but Chris saw it differently. His own story argued that he was No. 1 because he knew while still a child where the Pilgrims landed. And he knew the church holidays backward and forward. In addition—and this was important to Grandma—he was the best golfer.

The pitching and heaving for favor came in a book of tributes to Rose Kennedy that Bobby Shriver, then an editor at the *Yale Daily News*, had his cousins put together for their grandmother's 85th birthday in 1975. The book of pictures, puzzles, poems, and commentary said, in Chris's estimation, what all the cousins believed: "My grandmother is very, very special."

Towering over each of the six separate families of this generation of Kennedys are a dead grandfather's still vital memory, and one grandmother's living exceptional presence. In very different ways the influence of these two unusual people, Grandpa Joe and Grandma Rose, is the reason their 29 grandchildren see themselves as especially privileged beings. It is not because any one of them is individually that extraordinary, but because corporately they constitute an entire spiritual ecosystem—self-sustaining, self-regulating, self-regenerating, self-informing, self-enhancing. They need one another as they need air to breathe, and they do not really need anyone else at all. It is an amazingly buoyant and comforting circumstance.

"Our whole family is pretty hard to get to know," notes young Teddy Kennedy. "It's not just my generation, but my father's too. We've really had to stand by ourselves because you have to be wary. I've spent probably more time with my immediate family and my cousins than probably any other person or group of persons. I enjoy them. It's partially out of knowing that we've shared so many of the same things. And it's partially that this is the way we were raised."

They reinforce each other, as well, though it tends to be strong support rather than introspection that they seek. "The hardest question you could ask a Kennedy is, 'How are you?' " says Father James English. "They really can't cope with the ramifications of that question. To them it is an extremely private matter and the presupposition is that they are all fine, all the time, under all circumstances. If you ask the question they will just go into confusion and muttering. They deal entirely with each other and even there they see their main job as telling each other that each is doing all right and that the others in the family should do the same. It is an immensely strengthening activity that comes from their grandparents. It's also very Irish."

Adds Chris Lawford: "I do not want to let people get too close. It was important that the family stick together because we could trust each other the most. You could never be sure what outsiders were really after, but you could always be sure of the family."

"They're their own best friends and their own best fans," says Theresa Fitzpatrick, who was governess to Ted and Joan's children.

They love to salute and entertain themselves, and do not require prompting. During summers at Hyannis Port there was much more than sailing, tennis, swimming, and getting into mischief together. They would also write and produce all manner of well rehearsed plays such as *The Wizard of Oz* and *Cinderella* for themselves and their parents and grandparents. Maria Shriver is remembered as the most prodigious playwright, but they all participated in the dinner-table debates on nuclear arms or protectionist tariffs.

Sometimes the self-congratulation could become cloying. Karen Kelley remembers how Ethel used to prep all the neighborhood children at Hyannis Port to sing and dance to popular songs about the Kennedys in order to perform when the President visited—songs like "PT-109" and "Caroline's Pony, Macaroni" and "My Daddy Is President."

Their childhood was "like a camp organized around ourselves," Maria Shriver remembers. "There was always the sense, the very strong sense, that the family was the most important thing in the world. I didn't go over to my friends' houses for the night. They came to mine. My parents would accept any number of my friends around as long as I was there so it kept the family close."

They assigned privileges to each other that suggested that the act of doing things for the family was—and is—of vital importance. Chris Lawford still proudly recalls that he was the one honored to raise the presidential flag at his Santa Monica home when Uncle Jack came to visit.

The commitment to each other came from deeply programmed responses that were taught to their parents. As Rose once remarked: "Years ago we decided that our children were going to be our best friends and that we never could see too much of them. If any of us wants to sail or play golf or go walking or just talk, there's always a Kennedy eager to join in."

That message to her children obviously has come through with undiminished force to the third wave. They love to travel together—shooting the rapids on the Snake River or the expert trails at Aspen, climbing mountains, flying over the top of the world, making the Grand Tour of Europe. John Kennedy, the Lawford girls, the Smith boys, Bobby, Michael, and Max, young Ted and Kara, and Tim Shriver all still talk about the traveling they did together; it is among their fondest childhood memories.

Chris Lawford: "The fact that we all feel so strongly about one another and the fact that we all really have the same core of values and beliefs means that it had to come from somewhere—and that place is our parents and our grandparents."

Everyone knows, or at least has heard, of big families that grew upon the nourishment their members drew from one another. At the risk of sounding excessive, it is probably fair to say that America has never had anything quite like the Kennedys—nor has anyplace else, for that matter, in modern times witnessed a family that has had an effective span of three generations and was as daring, ornamental, resolute, and downright tragic as the Kennedys. Most Americans, and millions of people around the world, no matter how they feel about the Kennedys politically, are still fascinated by them for that reason.

It cannot last. The logistics will not allow it. This is the last generation that can be described collectively as "the Kennedys" without having to specify which branch. And the only reasons the effect has lasted this long are the remarkable strengths they

*Unto the fourth
generation...*

At Hyannis Port in the
summer of 1981, ages as of
Oct. 1983: Grandma Rose,
93, with her son, Senator
Ted, 51, granddaughter
Caroline, 25, and great-
granddaughter Meaghan
Townsend, 5. Meaghan's
mother, Kathleen Kennedy
Townsend, daughter of
RFK, is Rose's oldest
grandchild at 31 and has a
second daughter, Maeve, 3.
Kathleen's brother Michael,
, at right, with wife, Vicki
Gifford, already has entered
Michael, Jr., 1, in the fourth
wave, and brother Joe, 30,
has added twin boys, Joseph
Patrick III and Michael
Rauch, 2.

The Kennedy's have the
ability of natural politicia
to look like winners even
while losing. Here a grou
of the cousins watches as
Uncle Ted falls short at th
1980 Democratic Con-
vention in New York City
Above, in front: Chris an
Joe Kennedy with sister
Courtney, 23. In back,
Mark and Maria Shriver.
Left: Earlier in the cam-
paign, Chris, then 17, and
Mark canvass for votes in
New Hampshire. At right
John Kennedy, Jr., leavin
the St. Regis Hotel in
New York after wedding
reception for cousin Mich
in March 1981. Although
he worked hard in the
'80 campaign and certainl
has the Kennedy presence
John, 23, who graduated
from Brown University ir
1983, has not yet settled o
a career. He enjoys acting,
but has turned down sever
show business offers.

The joys of summer

For the Kennedys, summer still centers on Hyannis Port's sun and sea, but they celebrate the outdoors wherever they are—usually with a roster of well-known guests on hand to assist in the fun. Opposite page, top: Tennis star Ilie Nastase and model Cheryl Tiegs flank Dougie Kennedy, then 14, at the 1981 RFK memorial tennis benefit. Below left: Lawford sisters Victoria, now 20, and Robin, 21, at the 1979 RFK tourney. Center: Rory Kennedy, 14, with one of the big dogs favored by the RFKs. Right: Kerry Kennedy, 22, carries a camera on such occasions to snap other celebrities. On this page: Ted Kennedy, Jr., 21, gets ready for a sail; sister Kara, 23, poses fetchingly on the dunes; and kid brother Patrick, 15, heads for the waterfront.

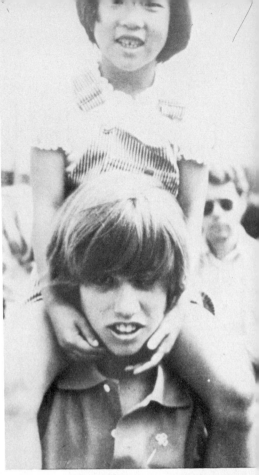

The company they keep

The Kennedys, a self-sustaining ecosystem, thrive on one another's company. "It's as though I had 28 brothers and sisters," is how Chris Lawford, 28, below right, with his fiancée, Jeannie Olsson, puts it. Right: Max Kennedy, at 14 in 1979, happily hoists the littlest Kennedy, Kym Smith, then 7. Below left: Sydney Lawford, then 23, heads for the 1980 convention with mother, Pat. Opposite page, top: John Kennedy and Tim Shriver, 23, are best friends as well as cousins. Below: John, left, with Ted, Jr., and Uncle Ted.

Thinkers and testers

Oldest of the cousins, Kathleen Kennedy Townsend, pictured here at 30 in 1981 with lawyer-husband, David, and daughter Maeve, then 8 months, is very much RFK's daughter, testing accepted family views, yearning for a just society and still struggling with the dilemma of career versus family. She writes long, thoughtful essays on politics and has a yen for public life. She gave birth to both Maeve and her other daughter, Meaghan, with the help of only David and a midwife in Meaghan's case and David alone in Maeve's. Kathleen's brother David, 27, left, shattered by his father's murder, went into a desperate emotional tailspin from which he is only now emerging. He has a penetrating wit and is a facile writer.

Attractive, determined women

Caroline: At 25, she speaks softly, is feminine and funny, but has an iron resolve to shun publicity, in which she is generally successful. She works in art history at New York's Metropolitan Museum. Although there's no talk of marriage yet, she has an active social life and is great pals with her mother and brother.

To RFK, she was his "beautiful Courtney." To Jeff Ruhe, a rising young sports producer at ABC-TV, Courtney, 26, is a loving and dedicated wife. Amanda Smith, 16, below with cousin Rory, is a standout student who hopes to matriculate at Oxford, which would be a Kennedy first. Maria Shriver, 27, opposite page, wrote her undergraduate thesis on the Catholic issue in her Uncle Jack's presidential campaign. Now she is a television personality in her own right. Maria, who regularly dates body-builder/entrepreneur Arnold Schwarzenegger, hopes soon to have a family of her own.

"I knew the moment I saw those eyes that here was a girl who liked to have fun." That's how Linda Semans, Kara Kennedy's best friend, characterized Kara more than a decade ago. The evidence in this spring 1983 picture of Kara and her mother, Joan, reaffirms Linda's finding. One reason Kara is happy now— as are brothers Ted and Patrick—is that Joan has conquered her drinking problem and is happy herself. After her graduation from Tufts in '83, Kara was thinking about a career in international relations.

Strong, confident men

The face is familiar. From certain angles, young Bobby Kennedy looks
hauntingly like RFK. Voluble and talented, Bobby, 29, was deeply shaken by
his father's death and behaved erratically for several years. Now married and
with a law degree, he is determined to take up the business that his father left
unfinished. He has prepped for a political career in the New York County
district attorney's office.

If the first "Kennedy" of the third wave to enter politics were to bear a name other than Kennedy, it could very likely be Smith. Steve Smith, Jr., far left, 25, has the quiet competence of his father, who manages all Kennedy financial affairs and is the family's principal political strategist. In addition, young Steve is very personable and very articulate. His brother William, 22, left above, although equally determined, seems to have inherited his father's preference for the back room. Anthony, youngest of the Shrivers at 17, below, has striking good looks that have attracted the likes of Tatum O'Neal. The oldest Shriver brother, Bobby, 29, right, after a brief but noteworthy career as a reporter, is now a lawyer in California. He wrote his Yale undergraduate thesis on his Grandfather Joe Kennedy, and intends, at least for a time, to emulate Grandpa and make a lot of money. He was a teenage rival of Bobby Kennedy, and has a large installment of the family's forensic and magnetic gifts. So there would seem to be politics in his future, too.

If courage and grace were the principal criteria, Ted Kennedy, ~ left, might be everyone's favorite candidate Kennedy. Young Ted's personal triumph over cancer and his selfless work for the handicapped have given him a maturity beyond his 21 years. His cousin Joe, below, with wife, Sheila, in 1980, has also overcome great handicaps, including severe school difficulties and a car crash, in which he was the driver, that left several people injured, one permanently. But with Sheila's inestimable help, Joe took hold of his life. He now heads what is certainly the most unusual, if not the most profitable, oil business in the United States.

All photographs by Brian Quig

drew from Grandfather Joe and Grandmother Rose—that plus the imperative pull of the murders of Jack and Bobby and Ted's long night at Chappaquiddick. The glue that makes the Kennedys stick—to one another and, persistently, to all Americans—is one of shared ordeals.

In a sense, the publicity that came with the tragedies has served to increase the cousins' instinctive tribalism. They seem to be most at ease among themselves. Still, they do allow intimacy to certain well screened people: "I felt as if I was on probation for a while, then all of a sudden things opened up to me," one friend of several RFK children remembers. "They are looking for the right stuff in people. I think that's a mix of athletics, energy to keep up with all their games and the ability to hold one's tongue at critical moments. They tolerate some sycophants because I think they realize they are inevitable and because we all like to be told how great we are. But they weed out the extremes—those who are too smitten with the Kennedys and those who are on the make."

Those admitted to the Kennedy Auxiliary find the excitement quite heady: "The Kennedys want to sweep you along with their lives," remarks sweepee Peter Kaplan. "It is a great picaresque novel—incredibly adventurous, glamorous and fun. They leap over all obstacles and pull you with them."

Yet all that leaping and glamour can intimidate outsiders. Victoria Lawford remembers that some of the beaus she brought home—handsome and well spoken as they may have been—could barely open their mouths in the presence of her cousins. "We don't think of ourselves as intimidating, but that has happened any number of times," says Victoria.

Perhaps the reason is that the Kennedy cousins were so magnetic and had such a sure sense of themselves and their past. Nothing in the Kennedy legend rings hollowly to them. The pictures on every wall, the cadences of conversations and the repeated references to the family first formed their view of the world. They believed their fathers and uncles ignited a new spirit in America and that a return to it is something fervently to be wished.

"This was a special enterprise—this being a Kennedy. The kids learned it pretty quickly," comments Adam Walinsky, a former associate of RFK.

Collectively, their past and their politics affect hundreds of decisions in their lives right down to the planes they use (never

Concordes because they are non-American) to the places they visit (Costa Rica is in) and whom they meet (Was he a friend or foe of Daddy's? Is he a friend or foe of Uncle Teddy's?).

Rose would always try to instill the Kennedy discipline by pertinent reference to family glory. For intance, if some cousins favored foods such as popcorn and candy, she would tell them that they would not be able to play football or swim as well as their fathers and uncles had. Then she would drive the nail home by perhaps producing a drawing of Uncle Jack's heroic rescue of a shipmate after *PT-109* was sunk in the Solomon Islands during World War II—Jack had swum for hours holding the unconscious man afloat by clamping his lifejacket belt in his own teeth. Grandma Rose says she always got immediate results. "In a few minutes," she once told a reporter, "all the youngsters are drinking their milk or their orange juice."

Despite the infirmity brought on by his stroke in late 1961, most of the cousins remember their grandfather as "the predominant pervasive force" of their childhoods, as Steve Smith, Jr., tells it. Grandpa had described his children as his "hostages to fortune," and that attitude was perpetuated with his grandchildren. "Every activity at the Cape seemed to be geared to him," young Steve goes on. "We made elaborate presentations for him that we wrote and rehearsed and acted out just like a drama—skits, memorized quotes, debates on things like the Test Ban treaty and civil rights. He was an incredibly powerful force. You felt his presence, and you knew whether he was pleased or displeased. It was important for all of us to please him. When you did, you felt terrific."

His grandchildren were carefully encouraged to pay homage to him, as well. The RFKs had carefully mounted an old picture of him in their home with the inscription: "Dear Bobby [RFK]: This is how I looked at your age [about four or five]. Note the clenched fist, showing determination. Note the keen eye." And that is how they treated him even after he was bound to a wheelchair. "Everything we have, we owe to Grandpa. Everything. So when you go in to see him, remember that everything you have, every toy, every pet, the house we live in, everything we owe to Grandpa," Ethel would tell her children as they lined up before going in to greet the infirm man, according to nurse Rita Dallas.

On his birthday they would stage an especially extravagant production, line up to give him a kiss, and then stand back in choir with their parents to sing "Happy Birthday." Said nurse Dallas, "Physically, he held the reins on the place. His piercing blue eyes told you everything you needed to know—was he happy, sad, angry. Their parents would tell the grandchild, 'Grandpa says win. . . . Grandpa says do this. . . . Grandpa says do that.' In a way, he really wasn't debilitated. He was strong and determined and he got his way, even though he was in a wheelchair and could only say, 'Nooooo.' "

Rose too got grand treatment. There are regular productions in her honor—the last of which featured young Rory Kennedy in the title role of "The Story of Rose," a bravura drama that portrayed Grandma during the JFK presidential campaign. They even staged a parade for her in Hyannis Port in 1981 when she turned 90.

Rose's relations with her grandchildren tend to be somewhat formal, in part because there are just so many of them. At Hyannis Port, she would invite a few over at a time, grouped by age, so that they could have a talk about things "suitable to their age and experiences—as I did with their parents." She would also tell them about the family, because, as she wrote once: "Naturally, as I see them sitting there, often in the same chairs where long ago their parents sat, I want them to get a little sense of family history, our family life—where they are, where they came from, what it was like, what good times there were."

She would also quiz them closely on their religious practices—what the priest said at mass, what holy days were coming up, what the Bible said about this or that. And grammar. She was a stickler, often pouncing on solecisms with written chastisements.

The devoted relationship the grandchildren had with their grandparents sometimes surprised cynics or peers who did not believe such family loyalties were common. "I know people who thought of their grandparents as doddering fools who had to be tolerated, but were more pathetic than not," states young Teddy Junior. "It was hard to believe anyone could think that way of a grandparent. It just would never have occurred to us."

Whatever Rose told them on those lingering summer afternoons over the easeful clinking of Georgian silver on fine porcelain tea services made an impression. She stands out as a figure of awe and respect for her grandchildren. "You can tell when my father is around her how important it is to him that she be happy and that she be in touch with us all," notes Teddy. "It's a major reference point for him. 'Where's Grandma? Let's take Grandma.' She's a fantastic woman and fun to be around when you get her talking about the old days. She has an incredible memory for dates, times, places, and even the most minute details of her surroundings."

First granddaughter Kathleen did not always hold Rose to be as special as cousin Teddy does. "Seven years ago I wouldn't have thought so, but I think she's terrific now," Kathleen acknowledges, with maybe a touch of surprise that time, reflection, and conviction have softened her views. She has become the grandchild who, in a way appropriate to her own age, perhaps best exemplifies Grandma's piety, personal, familial, and religious. Today she says of Rose: "She's had an impressively full life, and is to be admired for it. We've had major differences—still do. But I'd say now she is wonderful and fantastic."

At the center of it all was the family's supreme collective enterprise—politics. Or, as Ethel put it, their "great exhilarating adventure." The children were as much a part as the adults and deliberately so. Their parents conducted their lives with their children at the center. They were always included in everything. One of the essential benefits of this was that they helped create the right impression of vigor, youthfulness, virility, and emotional warmth that leavened the business of politics.

"Politics is bred into you," says Maria Shriver. "The children of doctors and lawyers tend to do what their parents do. If you grow up hearing that public service and politics is the best, most exciting, most worthy part of life, then it is inevitable that some of that will wear off and some of you will get into politics."

They sat on the knees of world leaders and celebrities, and it had its effect. "We were taught that it was inexcusable not to be interested in the world and the great issues of our time," says young Steve Smith. "When you have the opportunity to meet the people we have and see the things we have, it rubs off. You couldn't be a member of our family and not be interested in politics."

Politics and the family were one. All the adult cousins have a more than passing interest in public life. "It's the most exciting thing you can do, unless you're a gifted musician or athlete—which I am not," says Bobby Shriver.

"We're all very committed to public service," adds Steve Smith, Jr.

"I'll probably do something in public life," muses Teddy Kennedy, Jr.

"Maybe I'll try it, later on," thinks Chris Lawford.

"It does have its appeal," agrees Bobby Kennedy, Jr.

Politics and family, or, better, family and politics, dominated one important weekend in their lives—the Thanksgiving weekend of 1982. There was an exceptionally full family complement at Hyannis Port, because for Senator Ted it was a weekend of decision, during which he had resolved to determine whether or not he would try yet again for the presidency. Except for Ethel and the Shrivers, all the family powers were there to help him, and the arguments for and against were put on the line and beaten for hours, like rugs, until everyone, even the third wave, was exhausted, and there was no dust left to settle. Then they would rest, or take a walk or have a drink. Then they would go at it again. The Kennedys are very thorough about politics.

Given her age and growing infirmity, Rose was not involved in the sessions, although everyone was aware of her as an affectionate presence and mindful of her needs and comfort. With the issue still unresolved, the family—more than 20 strong—sat down to Thanksgiving dinner, the senator, as senior male, in his father's place and Grandma in the chair she has occupied for more than 60 years.

Suddenly Rose was on her feet and had something to tell them all, especially the grandchildren. There was total silence in that huge dining room during the ten or twelve minutes she spoke.

She began by recollecting her own childhood—joking that she had always been afraid that her sister Agnes had been prettier than she—about the houses she had known and the laughter with friends, about the joy of picking berries with her family and the rollicking times with her uproarious father, "Honey Fitz."

Then she told them about meeting Joe Kennedy and falling in love, pointing out carefully that she loved him before he had any money. "The love came first," she said. The story then turned to the beginning of their family, and of how the house in which they were sitting to enjoy the bounty of the earth had become the central hearth for that new family, the place they always came home to, the place where they learned of one son's triumph and the murders of two. "We have gained strength from our misfortunes," she reminded them, and faith in God had been the undoubted source of that strength.

Turning to the third wave, she wanted them never to forget that now it was their home. She was so happy that they all continued to return year after year. "You are always welcome," she said, as if they didn't know. "So many people in these turbulent times forsake their families. They make lives of their own and never come back."

But Rose sensed that her family really enjoyed being together, young and old alike, and that comforted her. It was wonderful that they could continue to come together like this, "because that has made the difference in our lives."

It took quite a while for everyone to get emotions under control. Later in the evening a subdued Edward Kennedy called everyone together for a family recitation of the rosary, which was an unusual and touching gesture for him. Grandma had pulled them back from the commotion of the immediate political issue to remind them of the great lesson she had tried to teach them all their lives—that the family comes first, even before the nation, because it leads on to eternity. The next day would be time enough to think about the presidency again.

Tested by Tragedy

FORTUNATELY FOR THE KENNEDYS, WHEN JACK'S ELECTION to the presidency thrust them into the center of international attention, there was already in place a supple and unusually supportive interfamily network, enhanced by a strong religious faith, to help them cope with crises like television and impending adolescence. Periodic reinforcement—such as old Joe's rebuke to the President that 1961 evening in Hyannis Port— kept it fresh. It was there when they needed it, and it had worked. To that point.

The resilience and strength of the network was not fully known, however, until it had been tested by three tragedies that would have overwhelmed lesser defenses: the killings of Jack and Bobby, and Ted's debacle at Chappaquiddick.

Within six years the cousins lost two men who had been at the center of their lives, and the character of a third had been darkly questioned. Naturally, the shock of each incident was greatest for the single family personally affected, but the network's resonance involved them all in what seemed to be an endless chain of tragedy.

If Jack's death was a tragedy, Robert's made the family feel that there was a curse threatening their very existence. Then, with stunning suddenness, came Chappaquiddick, a travesty threatening to trivialize the family and its achievements. The stricken family rallied around the survivors, but it would be hard to overstate the extent of the hurt, and the wounds that remain.

The world, of course, was witness to it all and that made recovery even more difficult. The Kennedy tragedies were intimate affairs in every household in the nation. There was a period during which the Kennedys were in their prime when most Americans saw the Kennedys on television more than they saw their own families in person. JFK's funeral, with three-year-old John saluting the coffin and Caroline, six, kissing the flag atop it, are part of the memory trove of virtually every American old enough to have been aware of what was happening, and millions of others around the world. In the immediate aftermath of JFK's death the children must have thought that the entire nation, if not the world, had turned into a giant memorial. Schools, roads, public buildings, airports, even the nation's space center were renamed after John Kennedy. There were reminders of him everywhere. It was upsetting—and distorting—because they could not escape.

Interest in the family, often obsessive if not perverse, intensified with Robert's audacious career and culminated in his own murder and funeral, again made memorable by the exceptional behavior of children. This time, since the older ones were able fully to grasp the significance of the event in a way that the President's children could not, their deportment was even more remarkable.

The image of the Kennedy cousins is frozen in a tableau of tragic pictures. "There is no question that they have been seriously scarred," Ted Kennedy said later. "But they have shown important qualities of resiliency and strength. It has obviously had different impacts on each of them. I think the main force for good was a large family." Referring to the family's ability to suppress grief in the face of apparently pointless tragedy, Father English suggests that "internally it takes a terrible toll, because they don't like to admit that part of themselves and they certainly don't show that part of themselves."

Most of the third wave of Kennedys were too young to understand Jack's death. Chris Lawford, then nine, offers a simple and anguished explanation of his behavior that day the President was killed: "I became aware that everyone was paying attention to me and I got a little mad. They asked me if I wanted to go home, but I said no. And that afternoon we played kickball and I was so mad I kicked three or four home runs. I just wanted to show them all I was not a freak.

"I was asked if I wanted to go to the funeral and I said no. I had invited a friend over for the weekend and I didn't want to disappoint him. It was unbelievable that I thought that way as a child, but I did. My mother tried to explain it to me, but I didn't understand."

Steve Smith, Jr., then six, remembered he was aware something was wrong the day his uncle died, but he could not figure it out. He left school early and started badgering his mother with "whys." "At first I didn't comprehend how terrible it was," he said. "I knew it was an awesome, terrible, special development, but its importance to me did not come until later. Actually that was the first time I realized I was different from my friends, because people treated me as special after Jack's death—I was unique because the tragedy had a terrible, direct impact on me and my family."

Caroline was a "changed child," according to Rita Dallas, who nursed ailing Joseph Kennedy. "She seemed to age before our eyes. She stayed to herself, lost in thought, and her eyes, once so pert and dancing, were listless. Children seldom clench their fists, but her tiny hands were always knotted."

Although John did not comprehend the full implications of the death of his father, he clearly sensed at a point soon after his death that Daddy was not coming home. His cousin Jamie Auchincloss remembers John trying in several ways to conjure the memory of his father in the first months after his death. John remembered that his father liked the sea, and apparently would ask many more questions about Daddy when he was taken to the beach. What was unbearably hard to observe was John's recollection that his father loved to see him dance, so he would often bound into a room and begin dancing for no apparent reason, as if trying to summon Jack. "Are you a Daddy?" he once asked a startled Bill Haddad, longtime Kennedy associate. When Haddad said he was, John asked, "Then will you throw me up in the air?"

Both Jackie and Robert Kennedy were determined that memories of John Kennedy would not fade. Robert was intent on having his children remember every aspect of their uncle's funeral, including them in every ceremony and event. In addition, he wrote them letters urging them to emulate Jack in being kind to others and in working for the country.

Either by prompting or through training, some of the children responded by offering to sacrifice favorite pleasures such as candy in remembrance of their uncle. They knew it was important to their father and it was, in their way, the most significant thing they could do to show proper respect and share the pain RFK was going through.

Secret Serviceman Bob Foster became a strong father factor

in John and Caroline's lives. "There is no overstating the case of how close Bob was to those kids," says Larry Newman, a Hyannis Port neighbor. "The sad thing was that they became too close. The children started calling him 'Daddy' after a while. He tried to discourage it, and you could see the children were more confused than anything else. They knew there was another man in their life who had been called 'Daddy.' But they also knew other children had daddies, so they kind of naturally would use that word for the man who was with them the most. It was very hard for Jackie, and eventually she had to ask for Foster's reassignment."

"I sometimes used to say to myself, 'He'll never remember his father," Jackie said of young John at the time. " 'He's too young.' But now I think he will. He'll remember his father through associations with people who knew Jack well and the things Jack liked to do. I tell him little things like, 'Oh, don't worry about your spelling, your father couldn't spell very well, either.' That pleases him, you can bet."

Hyannis Port lawyer Richard Rougeau, who worked as a summer police officer outside the Kennedy compound in addition to serving as an occasional chauffeur for the Kennedys, recalls the day a couple of years after the murder when he and another man took ten of the Kennedy cousins to an amusement park. On the way over, he looked in the rear view mirror and saw Caroline reading quietly and then silently bursting into tears. As he reached back to comfort her he noticed that the comic book she read was about the death of her father. She gave it to him when he asked for it, saying: "I don't want to read it anymore."

Robert Kennedy's murder was almost as excruciating for John and Caroline as it was for his own children, for he had been the central masculine force in their lives once Jack was gone, and he had welcomed them into his own swarm of children, where they had found protective warmth and shelter.

When, a few months later, Jackie married Greek ship owner Aristotle Onassis, it was taken by the public as a personal affront, and seen by a cynical world as the ultimate marriage of convenience. Overnight, Jackie changed in the public eye from noble widow into just another gold-digging jet-setter.

"You know, nobody could understand why I married Ari," Jackie once told a friend of her children. "I just couldn't live anymore as the 'Kennedy widow.' It was a release, freedom from the oppressive obsession with me and the children."

Once again, the children were dramatically thrust into the public eye. This time they also had to cope with their own family crisis, as well. Adjusting to a stepfather was not easy, although Onassis apparently tried hard to be a father to them.

Whatever faults the multitudes could find with Jackie, everyone who knows her says that she has been a good and attentive mother. "She was always available to her children and took particular pains to make their lives complete, normal, and happy," says JFK's secretary of defense, Robert McNamara, one of the many men Jackie brought into their lives after their father died. "She was constantly in touch with them and had a great sense of what made them tick."

Tragedy was a way of bracing people or of breaking them. The killing of Robert Kennedy brought about some of both within his own family.

Many otherwise sane people saw the second Kennedy murder as part of a plot to wipe out the family, so it is hardly surprising that some of Robert's children saw it that way, too. Even before his own death, Robert's profound melancholia over Jack's death infected some of them. "Maybe we are all doomed," he said on more than one occasion. David started to have prophetic nightmares from which he would wake up screaming from "seeing" his own father's death.

Early on June 5, 1968, Robert had pulled David, nearly 13, from a dangerous undertow in the Pacific near Los Angeles. Later that night, while his brother Michael, slept peacefully in the other bed in the room, David watched his nightmares unfold on television. Theodore White, the writer, raced into the room to find "the brave youngster still awake, fighting back his tears at the horror he had seen"—a horror that David has not yet fully overcome.

On the opposite coast, the older children had other agonies. Dick Clasby, a friend of Robert Kennedy, went to Milton Academy in Massachusetts to tell young Joe Kennedy, 16, that his father had just been shot and to take the boy to Hyannis Port. "You almost could see in the hour drive to the Cape that he was changing," says Clasby. "He realized that he was the oldest son. He mentioned things like his concern for his mother and he wanted to know where each of his brothers and sisters were. It was a situation where one minute he was a young prep school kid and the next minute he really was a young man—the oldest son—of a very large family. He just sort of took on the weight of being the man of the house—maturing in front of my eyes." Joe flew out to Los Angeles to join the others and was able to be with his father when he died. He then told the news to some of the other children.

Kathleen was awakened by a school official at Putney and tenderly brought to his residence with her friend, Sophie Spurr. There they sat through a horrible night of doubt and questions about Robert Kennedy's true condition before she could leave the next morning for her own trip to his bedside.

At Hickory Hill, young Bobby had gone to bed euphoric at the good news coming from California. He awoke at 4 A.M. still tingling with excitement and went immediately to the front door to get the morning paper to read about the final results. The headline on the front page of the *Washington Post* devastated him with the news of the shooting. In a numb trance he read the story, then took the paper to the fireplace and fed it page by crumpled page into the flames for more than a half hour.

After the funeral, Michael told his friend Juan Cameron that he could not rid his mind of the image of himself racing through his schoolyard just days before the killing throwing out "Sock It To 'Em Bobby!" buttons to pursuing—and laughing—classmates.

When RFK was shot, the family immediately closed its emotional fist. "I can't let go now," the anguished Senator Ted told his aide Dun Gifford moments after he'd heard the news. "If I let go, Ethel will let go, and my mother will let go, and all my sisters." He did not let go.

Neither did Robert's children or their cousins. There were no tears, at least in public. They were all part of the living memorial, standing watch over their father's coffin and greeting mourners on the funeral train. It was not until a month later, on July 4, that Karen Kelley saw young Joe go to a secluded place on the beach at Hyannis Port to release his sorrow. "He said it felt good to be in a familiar private place and let it all out," Karen recalls. "He didn't feel safe or appropriate doing it anywhere else."

Similarly, Bobby Junior remembers, "It was not easy to have

public attention so riveted on you in the worst moments of your life. Just having the spotlight on you makes it difficult to show emotions in difficult circumstances."

The older children wrote touching remembrances to their father that Aunt Pat Lawford published in her privately printed memorial, "That Shining Hour." Ten-year-old Michael wrote: "In the last part of his life Daddy did everything he could for this country. He helped the Indians; he helped the Negro. He loved his country very much. He took us to see the wilderness of this country. He loved sports. We played football all the time when he was home. He did almost as much for his family as for his country. He had many different friends; some black, some white. He had a lot of professional athletes for friends. His country, his family and his friends all miss him very much."

If there was a touch of learned response in Michael's tribute, it should be remembered that he was barely ten. Still, by any standard, 13-year-old David's farewell was exceptional: "Daddy was very funny in church. He would embarrass all of us by singing very loud. Daddy did not have a very good voice. There will be no more football with Daddy, no more swimming with him, no more riding and no more camping. But he was the best father there ever was and I would rather have him for a father for the length of time I did than any other father for a million years."

Courtney, then 11, was bereft. Bravely, she too tried to summon happier memories. "Daddy loved us all. He did everything he could to be with us. . . . Every year for the past three years we've been going to Sun Valley. On the last day of skiing we had partnership races. Last year Daddy was my partner. We both tried really hard. Unfortunately, I fell the first time . . . then Daddy fell. We were both failures. We had lost the race. Even though we had lost the race our spirits were high. This shows that the Kennedys are born fighters and we are all proud of it."

On the funeral train, young John Kennedy, then only eight himself, asked his cousin Chris Kennedy, not yet five, whether his father still went to the office. "Oh, yes," replied Chris, "he is in heaven in the morning and he goes to the office in the afternoon."

For his older children, Robert Kennedy's reaction to Jack Kennedy's death gave them the model for their behavior concerning his. "They wanted to follow that lead," says Kathleen's friend Anne Coffey. "It was extremely important to Kathleen to show that it did not get her down. She thought that would help the younger children get through the worst of it."

Kathleen's own explanation was that it was crucial for her and the others to forge ahead. "How could I do otherwise?" Kathleen asked. "That's just saying 'forget it' to everything that Daddy ever worked for. He had a ten times worse loss when his brother was assassinated, yet he went on and tried. If I didn't keep trying that would be forgetting everything I've lived for."

Most of all, Robert's children memorialized him through emulation, by doing things that they saw as pure "Kennedy"— things that were daring or helpful—often spurred by their mother. Ethel immediately decided to keep Hickory Hill just as Robert Kennedy had left it. Pictures of him, his favorite trinkets, and memorabilia were left all over the house. "Robert Kennedy is alive to this day at Hickory Hill," notes family friend Tom Koutsoumpas. "I gather that very little has changed. His face is everywhere. Reminders of him and his thoughts are all over the house. They are very comfortable with it that way. His presence is just there."

"I expected things to be gloomy," adds Anne Coffey of her first visit to Hickory Hill after the funeral, "but nothing had changed."

Yet, in her grief, Ethel drove herself mercilessly even though she was pregnant with her eleventh child, Rory. Doggedly bright with friends, she cracked down hard on the children, perhaps fearful that they might get out of control without paternal discipline.

Robert's death "had to have a meaning for her," suggests her husband's friend and assistant John Seigenthaler, and the children doing good deeds "was the most important way she could conceive to follow the unfinished path Bobby had walked."

Such service was important to Uncle Ted, too. He had written to the children that their father "would have been distressed, if you did not involve yourself in some way in the problems of mankind. He would expect you to devote your lives to continuing his search for a newer world."

Eventually they rebelled at participating in elaborate public memorials to their father. For the first three anniversaries, Ethel arranged large memorial masses at the grave at which each of the older children would have to do something special, such as give a reading for those attending. After the third year, led by Joe and Kathleen, they sat down with their mother and told her they could not do it anymore.

They did not want public displays of their grief. Now there is private mass at Hickory Hill each year. Several of the older children made the same point about the publicized events of the Robert F. Kennedy Memorial Foundation. Again, they preferred to honor their father's memory privately.

Sometimes the children's natural inclination to emulate their father stumbled over their mother's insistence that they do so. Execution at times fell short of expectation when they were doing their service projects. For example, it had been arranged for Michael to teach swimming at a Navaho reservation, but he arrived there to find that, at 15, he was too young to be allowed to do the job. Similarly, Kerry and Courtney set out several years later to work on a Mormon ranch, then found that women are not permitted to do heavy farm work in that society. And David's sojourn once at a dude ranch in Wyoming ended with his loafing in the bunkhouse or seeing a girl friend in the nearest town.

Most of the time, though, these summer work trips and year-round projects were successful. Joe worked with Chicanos in the West. Bobby went to Africa and later toured the continent for a television show. David helped Cesar Chavez organize migrant farm workers in Southern California. Michael joined Steve Smith for a second, more productive, session with the Navahos. Kerry worked in an Amnesty International program involving refugees from El Salvador. In her case studies she found horrible examples of refugees who had been denied entrance into the United States because they did not meet the law's requirement that they be fleeing violence or repression, and who were therefore sent home, where at least some were reported to have been killed.

Ethel had other plans for the children, too, especially the older boys. She determined to supply the lack of a father as best she could by nominating certain male friends to fill the role. Ted Kennedy, of course, became a second father to all of them, spending almost as much time at Hickory Hill as at his own home nearby, attending all the important school and religious functions, and taking over as leader of the family raft, sailing, and camping excursions. With eleven RFKs to account for plus three of his own, and occasionally John or Caroline, Ted was a busy man.

There is no question that his great efforts over many years for Robert's children have earned him an ineradicable position in their hearts. Just trying to speak of how she felt about Uncle Ted caused one of his nieces to collapse in tears. It was some moments before she could continue, but it sums up what all RFK's children feel: "When you think of what happened to his brothers, to his son and his problems with his wife and then you see what he has tried to do for all of us, it is hard not to cry out of gratitude for his strength and his presence. It would have been easy for him to decide that there were other more urgent priorities. No one would have blamed him. But he made it clear we were his priority. There wasn't a thing you couldn't ask for from him. He was always very understanding and tender."

Fortunately, Ted Kennedy did not have to bear all the burdens alone. Ethel's recruitment enlisted David Hackett, John Seigenthaler, columnist Art Buchwald, lawyer John Douglas, Tom Koutsoumpas. All made great efforts to recreate the full measure of Robert's presence among his children. They could not do it fully, but they tried, and it helped.

A singularly important figure to the oldest children after Robert Kennedy's death was LeMoyne Billings, who had been John Kennedy's prep school roommate. He had once been in love with JFK's sister Kathleen, and eventually became the most important friend of many in the second and third generations of the family. Of the third wave, he was closest to young Bobby, whom he viewed and promoted as the heir apparent. But he was also a key figure for many of the others, including Michael, Kerry, Chris Lawford, and Tim Shriver.

Billings was the greatest Kennedy admirer. He was a walking history of the family and was devoted to its well-being. Once, for example, when one of young Bobby's friends said he did not want to go to a party with Bobby, Billings upbraided him. "It's your duty to be with Bobby," he stormed. "I did it for Jack and you should do it for Bobby."

As the central adult figure in many of their lives, Billings was extraordinarily tolerant and generous. "He opened parts of Bobby's heart that could have been permanently frozen over," says Peter Kaplan. None of Bobby's gambols seemed to faze Billings. In fact, he went right along for the ride on some of them. Sometimes that was not what Ethel wanted for her son.

Robert's death almost immediately split his children into two groups—those old enough to have known him and been influenced by him, and those who were not. The differences are quite striking. When so powerful a personality as Robert's is extinguished, those who had not learned to see by that light have to seek a different source of illumination. In the normal course of things, Ethel was the light for the younger children, and it was not the same. Kathleen explains:

"There was great pressure from Daddy on us to do well. Mummy just couldn't do that. She had her hands full just bringing them up. He was someone you could turn to, play with and talk to. He was far more interested in public policy and government than Mummy. After he was gone the atmosphere changed. Basically, there are two aspects to being a Kennedy. The first is that the family has been given a lot and should give a lot in return. The second is that Kennedys are famous. Without Daddy the focus tended more to the second."

As Kathleen's friend Sophie Spurr puts it, "Those ideas about change and making a difference didn't come from" Ethel but from Robert. "After his death she adapted them to her way of life, but it wasn't the same."

Because it was not the same, the older children and their cousins tried somehow to recapture what it had been like. They plagued any adult who knew anything about their father for details of his life. "You never got a very good sense of what the kids were thinking," said Seigenthaler. "They were sphinx-like, but at the same time they were thirsty for knowledge. It was as if they wanted to see behind a curtain they never got to pull back themselves. They wanted others to explain it to them. There was a great sadness about experiencing this from the kids.

"They were completely dependent on those of us who were around. And there were times when I felt they had prepared an alphabetical list of questions they wanted answered. It was very methodical. They would go down the rollcall, almost. 'Now, what did so-and-so really do for Daddy?' or 'Was he really that close to so-and-so?' They would literally drink in the anecdotes.

"What they wouldn't do, though, was take your word entirely. They wanted to make their own evaluations. Almost all of us who were around have been asked the same questions."

Another associate of Robert Kennedy sensed an even keener despair on the part of the children: "It was like exploring Camelot a century after everything went wrong. It was a universal phenomenon. The Smith kids did it, and the Shrivers and the Lawfords and Caroline and John—all of them. They were incredibly frustrated at getting all their information second hand, but they really craved it. They wanted to know their father's or uncle's mistakes and why they were mistakes and they really hit you hard if they thought you were dodging the question or just giving an answer full of platitudes.

"The most unnerving point for me came when one of them asked me what Robert Kennedy thought about death. It totally unhinged me. I don't even remember my answer, it was such a horrible moment. I sensed that his question really meant, 'Would my father have tried to become President if he had known the true dangers and known that it would have devastated his family if we ever lost him?' How can you answer something like that?"

"When you lose a parent that way you are impelled to wondering what it would have been like had he lived," says Lorenzo di Bonaventura, Michael's friend. "You wonder what your father was really like. Some of them have spent a lot of time trying to answer that kind of question. It has become important work for them and it guides a great deal of what they do."

Although the vacuum could never be filled, the children were grateful for what they got. "I was luckier than most people who have lost their fathers so young," said Bobby Junior, who was 14 when RFK was killed. "I had the advantage of being able to read about what he thought and to talk to his friends. At least I had a chance to do it. Not many others get that chance."

Chris Lawford developed a consuming appetite for knowledge about his Uncle Robert, because he was the model for all the cousins. "My mother was very close to Bobby and his death was especially hard on her. The things Bobby believed in— challenges that had to be met and doing things outdoors—the competitive spirit which he embodied became much more a family credo after he was gone.

"It was a point in my life, too, when a lot of people tried to make it clear to me that I would have a lot of responsibility because I was the man in our house. I was really terrified because I didn't know what to expect and what to do. His was the life that was the ultimate representation of what we as a family were supposed to be about." Chris was deeply depressed by Robert's death. He broke with the church, did poorly in school, stopped playing sports.

Steve Smith, Jr., too was inspired to learn as much as he could about Uncle Robert, and to this day he will quote great chunks of Robert's speech to South African students made a year before he died—the same speech that Joe used so effectively at the Kennedy Library dedication. Like many of his cousins, Steve recalls with pellucid clarity the funeral mass for Uncle Bobby. He remembers Uncle Teddy's tearful eulogy, and how moving it was that his young cousins served as altar boys. He still can summon visions of the amazing eight-hour train ride from New York to Washington for the burial, where tens of thousands of citizens lined the tracks, waving and crying and holding signs praising Uncle Bobby—crowds so fervent that some were injured when they got in the train's way as it ambled through the most jammed sections. Finally, he still can see himself standing with the family and looking out at the throng spread over the hillside at Arlington Memorial Cemetery during his uncle's burial.

Eunice Shriver remembers that her younger sons, Mark and Anthony, became very sensitive and spoke often of death in the months after Bobby's killing. It was especially devastating to them because they had just moved to France for Sargent to become Ambassador there. Still, the family's commitment to carry on was no more ardent than in the Shriver home. Neal Nordlinger, a friend of Bobby Shriver's, was with him when they woke up to hear the terrible news of RFK's shooting. "Bobby just got on the phone and started arranging how things would go for him and his family," says Nordlinger. "At one point I heard him say, 'There will be time for that later,' and I think he was talking about grieving. His most important duty was to make sure others in the family were all right."

Maria Shriver captures the ever-onward attitude: "Our response to the things that have happened to the family is to fight back. Your feeling is, 'My God, someone got killed.' It is impossible to believe that somebody could kill someone so precious to you—could just rip them out of your lives and hurt your cousins so badly. It made you even angrier. Your reaction is 'I'm going to carry on the values they had and the work they did so their loss was not in vain. I'm going to make sure that I make a difference in this world.' "

Fear overtook the Edward Kennedy home after Robert Kennedy's death. Teddy Kennedy, Jr., was paralyzed with fright for several years every time his father left the house, especially when he was out of town for the night.

Without Robert's restraining influence, some of his older children, most particularly Bobby Junior and David, went through a very dangerous patch. It was a merciless era for all parents and all children—the generation gap was really a generation war—and the startling thing about it was that it came on so suddenly. Some of the Kennedy children were crack combatants.

Bobby and David both teetered on the brink of delinquency. "I used to be in a state of rebellion," Bobby acknowledges. "Rebellion" is putting it mildly. He was out of control, ran away for months, wandered all over the country, broke with his mother, and came back only when he was tired and destitute.

Along with a dozen or so other teenagers in Hyannis Port, including Chris Lawford and Bobby Shriver, he formed a gang called, not especially inventively, the "Hyannis Port Terrors." Purpose? The creation of mischief. Wearing black capes emblazoned with a skull and crossbones, and with cigarettes pasted in their faces, the "Terrors" would meet with their girls in a dry well in the woods near the compound and plot the day's activities.

First, of course, any Kennedys involved in night games would have to sneak past a parent or other overseer, but that was child's play for Bobby, usually via rope ladder from the second story. "They would walk in the front door, say 'Goodnight, Mom,' walk upstairs and hop out the window and meet us outside," reports Karen Kelley. "It was a snap." Other times they could gull Ethel into letting them stay in the backyard playhouse that was big enough to sleep several persons, but it was never used for that purpose. One time a Secret Service agent "ratted" on them, forever earning their disdain.

Once outside, there might be skinny-dipping at the pool or a trip to the village. Or some liquor swiped from a parent's cabinet would fuel the fun. Or they might "borrow" a family car to coast around town, sometimes blasting away at inanimate objects with beebee guns. If cars could not be had, then the harbor was the place to get behind the helm of a commandeered boat—usually a Boston Whaler. The real thrill was when the harbor police spotted them and gave chase.

None of the Terrors was ever hauled in for boat-borrowing, although they were cautioned more than once. The thought that Kennedys might be getting special treatment infuriated the townspeople, and produced stinging letters from the yacht club and country club about the children's behavior.

Marijuana and amphetamines were the big problem. Drugs eventually led to the downfall of the Terrors, although there is no evidence that the Kennedys were anything more than experimentally involved with pot, hashish, or "black beauties," as the favored amphetamines were called. Yet drugs led to real trouble, for both Bobbys—Kennedy and Shriver.

Early one day in the summer of 1970, Bobby Kennedy lost a prized hawk. It was reported in a tree in a nearby community, but no car was handy to borrow to go to retrieve the bird. Andy the cab driver offered free service. The boys accepted, and Andy became an instant pal. It never occurred to them that he might have had a motive.

As Bobby describes it, he and Bobby Shriver and some others were driving to pick up the hawk when Andy offered them some marijuana. They all smoked a bit of it. "I really didn't like it, but I guess I thought it was a thing that a teenager should do," Bobby Kennedy said later. Other youths recall that some Terrors had Andy make liquor buys for them and even openly discussed their drug deals with him. Virtually everyone who befriended him was later rounded up in a bust that soon shocked the town. Andy was a nark.

A month later, the chastened Bobbys pleaded not guilty in Barnstable County Court, and Judge Henry L. Murphy continued the cases "without finding"—a standard procedure in juvenile cases that essentially put defendants on probation for about a year.

At home there were periods when things fell apart as well. Several adults remember times when they would go to Hickory Hill and find youngsters—some of them Kennedys and some of them friends—in various states of drug-induced euphoria or lassitude. Yet another side of their life was equally apparent. Ethel was exceptionally tenderhearted, for instance, to Mary Alice Cook during a period of turmoil in her family. "She was grand to me," says Mary Alice. "She would call me and pay special attention to me when I was with her. I remember once walking down the stairs at Hyannis Port in tears because I couldn't set my hair right—it was a dumb girl thing, but she knew I was upset about things other than my hair. 'Come on,' she said, 'let's fix you up.' And we spent the better part of the afternoon talking. She was my savior."

The RFK children who did not know their father deeply suffered less from his loss and rebelled less, if at all. They accepted Ethel's values and have been relatively happy with them. Christopher Kennedy is a perfect example of this adaptation: "Our lives have not been as extreme," he says with surprising sagacity for an eighteen-year-old. "We have not had the adventures or the excitement or some of the problems the older ones have had." He is perhaps the best judge, too. Those outside the family describe him as the leader of the youngest children—the most protective, the most responsible, and the most serious.

"He was the one who was always in charge," remembers Theresa Fitzpatrick, the EMK governess. "He saw that the garbage was taken out and the lawn mowed. He had a tremendous paternal streak." She cites the time when Chris single-handedly coaxed a score of adults to stop a party and start picking up on the Hyannis Port grounds because "I'm not gonna lug all this furniture back in the house tomorrow." He had them scrubbing the kitchen floors until 4 A.M.

Chris and Max and Dougie have latterly begun their own private search for their father, with the help of their Uncle Teddy. As Chris tells it, their uncle "sometimes spent a great deal of time talking about Daddy with us. It was important to him and to us. He liked to tell the funny stories about them as teenagers and young men. They were good, he would say, because they knew how to have fun."

In addition, Ethel picked up Jackie's habit of giving presents that recalled events in Bobby's life, and there were the many anecdotes in "That Shining Hour."

Still, men who were connected with Robert Kennedy and men who later entered his children's lives after his death found some of them painfully aware that something big was missing from their lives. When they got even a hint of it, they hated to share it. Tom Koutsoumpas, who began his association with the Kennedy family by helping arrange the pet shows for which Hickory Hill became famous, remembers the time he brought a girl friend to dinner at Hickory Hill. The youngest RFK children tested her in conversation and with bad manners to see if she were up to the important job of being a friend to their friend. Later they bombarded him with questions. Did he plan to marry her? If so, would he still come to see them? What was her background? Was she really good enough for him? He sensed a fear in them that he might leave and they already knew the pain such losses could bring. It was raw and unyielding.

Another man said the youngest children would occasionally take him aside and ask which child he liked best. He believed it was their way of seeking reassurance and affection, not in the sense of being vicious or trying to lord it over the others. They simply craved adult affection.

Edward Kennedy saw it as his duty to get life moving again. Speaking to, as well as for, the cousins and his sisters and brothers-in-law, he told a gathering in Worcester, Massachusetts, months after the killing of Robert: "Like my three brothers before me, I pick up a fallen standard. Sustained by their memory of our priceless years together, I shall try to carry forward that special commitment to justice, to excellence, to courage, that distinguished their lives."

So Ted Kennedy picked up the family standard, but within a year he had carried it to a point of emotional exhaustion. All the cousins made claims upon his attention, and his own children were frightened half to death about his safety. On top of that were piled the worrisome effects of Joan's drinking, whatever the causes of it might have been. The illness began before Chappaquiddick and progressed insidiously.

Joan told friends about a year after Robert's death of an incident that had occurred on a plane trip she took with Ted. "A child exploded a balloon right behind us," she said. "It sounded just like a gunshot. Ted jumped so. What a terrible thing! A balloon pops and my husband thinks he's being shot."

Joan also spoke about the effects of Robert's killing on young Teddy, then seven: "He wants to know why all these things happened to Uncle Jack and Uncle Bobby, and will they happen to Daddy, too," she told an interviewer, and family friends still quote young Teddy's haunting question: "If Uncle Jack was shot and Uncle Bobby was shot, will Daddy be shot?"

Ted Kennedy coped with all this as best he could, but the strain began to show in little things. "Do you know what it's like," he demanded of a reporter once for no particular reason, "to have your wife frightened all the time?"

His deterioration in the months after Robert's murder was widely observed but not publicly chronicled. It became troublesome to those around him as the first anniversary of Robert Kennedy's death arrived. His long and lonely sailing trips came more frequently, and he began to drink heavily and to behave more erratically. Then on July 18, 1969, just slightly over a year following Robert's death, Kennedy drove his two-year-old Oldsmobile 88 off the Dike Bridge into a tidal pool at the east shore of Chappaquiddick Island, carrying Mary Jo Kopechne, 28, to her death. Along with the senator and five other men and five other women, she had been to a reunion party on the island for the "boiler room" girls who had worked in Robert's presidential campaign.

Mary Jo's death, Kennedy's 12-hour delay in reporting the accident, and the suggestion of sexual scandal catapulted the event to a prominence that almost eclipsed the first steps of man on the moon. It brought an unprecedented storm of censure down upon Kennedy and the Kennedys.

The senator later characterized his behavior as "indefensible," "inexplicable," "inconsistent" and "inconclusive." It left an indelible stain on his career and grievously wounded his children. If he has ever talked about Chappaquiddick with them (or with Joan), no one else knows it. "I don't think he has said any more to them than he did at the inquest and in his speech," guesses an old friend. "That's the whole story." More than ever, the EMKs felt themselves under siege.

Every so often other kids would shout at Kara on the playground, "Your father killed a woman. Your father killed a woman." Kara became totally withdrawn. "The expression on her face was always blank when I first knew her," said a former staffer in the senator's office. "You never could tell what she was thinking or feeling. She was very passive and emotionless and she never, ever smiled."

Patrick recalls being tormented with the word "Chappaquiddick" before he even knew its meaning. It was only after long talks with his father that he was fit to face them down. "There were always little incidents at school aimed at me," he said. "My father could always sense when things were wrong and he'd try to explain it to me. He said some people were always going to hang around me because I came from a special family, and others were going to heckle me because they are jealous and they think they are missing something from their lives. It bothered me a lot at first, but I got used to it after a while. My father was very patient."

Patrick was a bundle of raw emotion, however. He would frequently and inexplicably burst into tears. He loved the company of his family most of all and he clung to them desperately.

"There were days when he must have thought the whole world was crashing in around him," says a cousin.

Young Teddy, on the other hand, became aggressively gregarious, always looking for fun and turning serious probes aside. "It was a wheels-within-wheels situation," says a friend of Teddy and Kara. "I would look at them and wonder what they were thinking about what others were thinking about them. I think they were hyperconscious of people's mannerisms, their looks, and the way they approached. They had to be on guard all the time. They both became very good at keeping the world at a distance—Kara by holding everybody off and Teddy by clinching everybody in a bear hug."

One acquaintance remembers a friendly get-together with Teddy and others where the conversation turned to families and their foibles. Teddy became very quiet during the session and when one of the others tried to draw him out with a "What's it like for you?" he said, firmly: "I think you're thinking too much about this."

It was left to Joan to stand by her man. Swallowing whatever pain and doubt she might have had, she did. She has continued to, divorce or no divorce. "I believe everything Ted said," she said at the time. Ten years later, however, she admitted that the toll on her had been tremendous and that she compensated by drinking more and more heavily.

"Of course" she had been hurt by all the stories linking Ted to other women—true or false—she told an interviewer. "They went to the core of my self-esteem. And I began thinking, well, maybe I'm just not attractive enough or attractive any more, and it was awfully easy to then say, 'I might as well have a drink.' And, unfortunately, I found out that alcohol could sedate me. So I didn't care as much. And things didn't hurt so much."

There were other troubles as well. Joan had three miscarriages, two at six months and the other at three months, plus several false pregnancies. "I supppose subconsciously I'd like to have been like Ethel and had one baby after another," Joan said.

Like Joan, each cousin is obsessed with measuring up. How can I fulfill in my life the example of Grandpa, Jack, and Bobby? they always ask themselves. It is their desperate reckoning. They are under constant scrutiny, both within the family and without. Sometimes it becomes unbearable. Then, like Joan, all the cousins yearn for some separate identity of their own, something to keep them from disappearing in the family orbit. For most, it will not happen. They are anchored to their past and cannot—dare not—stray too far. Perhaps their own children will be able to chuck the whole thing, beginning with Meaghan and Maeve Townsend, Joseph III, and Matthew Rauch (Joe and Sheila's children) and Michael's Michael Junior. But this generation has to play the hand that has been dealt. All the cousins have felt the way young Doug Kennedy responded to a prep school application question: "I am often asked if I want to follow my father [RFK]. I want to follow him, but I want to make my own tracks."

For the most part, the Kennedy voices have prevailed. Those who have spun off for a time—Joe, Bobby, and Chris Lawford most notably—have now made their accommodations and have taken reasonably well to bit and bridle. They are serious, if not solemn, young men. Young Kennedys. David Kennedy is the tragic exception, though there is hopeful evidence that he too might have ended his dark days.

"There was an awfully loud banging around them that for a while overwhelmed the family's notions," Bobby's friend Peter Kaplan believes. "Finally, it was the persistent voices of Ethel and Senator Kennedy that got through. There is a strong consistent set of values in that family that, in the end, is pretty hard to turn away. They got these potent doses of idealism throughout their lives and that is what stuck. They were always being urged back and finally they came."

Chris Lawford describes how his Uncle Ted got through to him: "He taught me there was a possibility to live a normal existence with all of what that is," says Chris. "The thing that can be most disruptive about being in this family is that Kennedys live under extremely abnormal circumstances. Our highs and lows are different. The important thing to Teddy's message, though, is that we can get satisfaction from life in our own way."

Despite the dilution of legend they still hold tremendous sway over the public imagination. "The problem in many respects for them now is the tragedy of enormous expectation," notes Andy Karsch, a film producer who met Caroline in prep school and has become a friend to many of the older cousins. "How can you be any less than a god and meet that expectation? And they are locked, too, in a Freudian battle with their fathers. The questions are: Do I want to take his place? Can I get there?"

Their mission was clearly laid out before them and the standards set were high. Moreover, they had to perform before the whole world. There were scarcely any secrets between them and their parents, so fully had Kennedy training been articulated. Yet even if the family insistence on competition and success had not been so widely known, they would have faced exacting standards simply because of who they are. "High expectations are on the shoulders of everyone in my generation," says young Teddy Kennedy.

What galled, though, was that their family lives were so open. Even among the children of the famous who surrounded them at school, the Kennedys stood out. They became accustomed to the claim when they were introduced to someone that the stranger inevitably had a "contact" with "your uncle" or "your father"—or simply had read or heard many family stories.

There were disarming instances where the persons they met knew more about the family and its history than they did. "People hear so much and read so much they think they have an idea of what you do and who you are even before they've met you," says Teddy Junior. "They have a picture of you—mostly it's a media phenomenon—that is hard to shake. They see you the way they want to, not the way you are. I have often asked myself why this is so important to them, and I just don't know the answer."

Though it often did not change the way they were, the cousins also got the sense they were being judged with highly critical eyes, looking perhaps for telltale evidence that they were spoiled or selfish or not up to standard. "People are always judging me as my father's son," notes young Bobby Kennedy. "Someone always seems to notice me. Someone is always scrutinizing me."

Bobby's cousin Kara turns the idea around, saying that her sense is not so much that people were watching when she was there, but that they would be buzzing with curiosity if she did not show up, even for a class: "I always wonder about whether people will notice if I'm missing, will notice that I'm gone. I always felt someone was looking extra carefully for me and it was important to me what they would think if I wasn't there."

The scrutiny produced its own inhibitions and distortions. Some of the cousins developed artful contrivances for avoiding attention. Caroline, John, Kathleen, Joe, and Kara all have gone through periods when they would not disclose their last name when encountering strangers. On the other hand, Bobby, Chris Kennedy, and Max were never shy about using it.

Young Teddy, according to his friend Akiva Goldsman, is "completely unaware that people are watching him because he is Ted Kennedy, Jr.," said Goldsman. "We went to a farm stand once, and the salesgirl was absolutely enthralled. Whenever she could break away, she'd go to others and whisper, 'That's Teddy Kennedy.' I told him later on that they were looking at him because he is a celebrity, but he didn't believe me."

The cousins recoil from being cast as a type. Kerry Kennedy has a simple strategy for exploding preconceptions: Be yourself. "If the person is half serious," says Kerry, "once you open your mouth, the preconceptions will vanish."

Some of the ramifications of being a Kennedy are not so lightly dismissed. Kidnap threats and the threat of real violence have followed the cousins for years. The most serious incident involved Caroline in October 1975, though authorities are still not sure whether she was the target or not. She was staying with old family friend, Lord Hugh Fraser, in London while she studied art at Sotheby's. As she was preparing for class in the morning—literally just before she and Fraser walked out the door—a bomb that had been planted in Fraser's car exploded. It sat directly in front of their residence. Caroline was knocked down by the concussion, but otherwise uninjured. A pedestrian, cancer specialist Dr. Gordon Hamilton Fairley, was killed instantly as he walked his dogs. Fraser later said that if he had not taken an unexpected phone call "we would all have died." Other times, Caroline's brother John had to cancel plans to attend a tennis camp in Maine and a trip in the Mediterranean because plots were uncovered.

There was also hectoring of them that turned ugly and dangerous. There was a lovesick sailor who would not leave Kathleen alone one year when she was at college. And Caroline was pestered so much by a lovelorn law student that she had to have him arrested.

"It's no big secret that all the Kennedys have been threatened," says Bobby Junior. "I'm not fearful. You can't let it get to you."

That is part of the secret. The Kennedys never look back. "They have not crumbled under the mighty weight of their losses," says a former official in JFK's administration. "As far as I can tell, they have never allowed themselves to ask the fundamental question: Was it all necessary? Nor have they considered the alternative—that they could have said, 'To hell with it! My family has given enough and I'm not going to play this game any more.' They intuitively feel that it was necessary, and they are part of the chain that will carry it on. A psychologist might wonder if that was the healthiest way over the long haul to deal with it, but I don't have any doubts. The Kennedy children are not at all crippled." And they have not retreated an inch.

Theresa Fitzpatrick explains: "They carry no bitterness against anyone. They have been told there will be no moaning and groaning or moping. They absolutely refuse to be put in a position or act in a way where people should feel sorry for them. 'If there is a problem, what is the solution?' That's how they think."

As Kathleen puts it: "It really was an easy way to grow up. We were loved and taken care of. Daddy was around us for sixteen years, and Uncle Ted helped us often. He's been wonderful. People think it's been hard growing up in the public eye, but it's not. It was exciting. It would be a lot harder to be poor and not know where your next meal is coming from."

None of the cousins—not even Bobby in his time of alienation—has ever questioned the basic Kennedy attitudes. Many children of the 1960s and early 1970s were at war with the beliefs and behavior of their parents, but there was no such breach in the Kennedy homes. "My father was on the right side of every issue that made a difference to the young—civil rights, the Vietnam War, the whole youth culture," says Bobby Junior. "There was no reason for us to stand against him or my mother."

For all their power and position, the Kennedy cousins are free of any sense of class superiority. They consider themselves an aristocracy of talent, if not of virtue. Consciously, some of them cultivate reverse snobbery. Bobby Kennedy brags that he is more at home with backwoods Alabamians than high-society New Yorkers. Yet when he wants to chat, say, with Menachem Begin, he just puts in a call and soon has a call back. They know that the world wants to be with them, and they are available.

Kathleen is one of the few to have made an effort to answer the charge that with all her money she could "afford" to be liberal. Her answer: Privilege should not be the province of a few Rockefellers or Kennedys. She admits, however, that privilege does seem to be persistently narrowly based, yet she argues that "everyone can have a sense of responsibility and accountability whether they are wealthy or not." That is as close as she or any of the cousins has come to a political philosophy. The Kennedys believe that the rich can take care of themselves— it is the poor who need their efforts. Unlike many of the other children of means who grew up in the 1960s and early 1970s the cousins never rejected their class or their family's rank. The generation war stopped short of that in their homes. Ethel, of course, has a much more direct approach to the nettlesome questions of how the privileged should relate to their world. Kathleen once asked her mother how to handle someone who would question her hostilely about her politics. "Oh, just throw a glass of water in his face," said Ethel.

Adolescence is a narrow and fragile bridge. Many people never make it to the far side, which accounts for all those 50-year-old babies in the world. The crossing has not been easy for the Kennedys, but just over a dozen of them already have established footholds in the adult world, where they have begun to build personal careers and shape personal identities. Theirs are the most compelling stories of the third wave, and we will now look at them close up.

At the Front

Joe Finds Himself

ONE YOUNG MAN WHO SORELY NEEDED SOME HELP IN 1976 was Joseph Patrick Kennedy II, oldest son of Robert and Ethel and oldest male of the third wave of the family.

Young Joe had a lot of things going for him at 24—all bad. Save for occasional flashes, he simply had not measured up— as a Kennedy, as a son, as a brother, as a citizen. And as a student in a rainbow variety of schools, he had an uphill struggle. He never was tested for a learning disability nor treated for it, but his slow mastery of reading seemed to some family members to confirm it. "I really don't know," Joe says of it when asked. His difficulties in school produced their own trouble, however. To outsiders he was vain, choleric, boneheaded, but those who knew him said he was bashful and easily affected.

Most Americans remember young Joe as a poised youngster gallantly repressing great grief and thanking people for their sympathy as he strode the long train carrying his slain father's body from New York to burial in Arlington. In the public mind, that 1968 event broadcast on network television probably remains Joe's finest hour. He truly was the family's leader and his behavior was exceptional. But after that, it was not so good. In fact it was awful.

First there was school. He hated all of them and the feeling was mutual. "He was constantly under siege," says family friend Tim Haydock, who was an upperclassman selected by Milton Academy to be "big brother" to Joe. "The expectations were so high. He was a very sensitive guy and he was really thrown into a pressure cooker. He was treated with great mental cruelty at Milton by upperclassmen who wanted to see how much he could take—even after his father died. It was not a healthy place for him. They picked on him and he was very insecure and fragile. He never really had a chance to do anything on his own—to find himself."

Friend Andy Cushner put it simply: "Joe just hated classical academic situations. A lot of us did." Among the family there were many hushed, inconclusive discussions, and unpublicized cautionary visits from Uncle Ted—not a great student himself, but at least he finished. "What's the matter with Joe?" was the nagging question at the back of everyone's mind.

Joe's next brush with publicity after his father's funeral turned the public's view of him from noble to reckless—even irresponsible. In the summer of 1968 he made a trip to Spain with Uncle Ted and, despite a total lack of training, chose to fight a bull. Pictures of him with blood streaming down his face after the mercifully slight goring he got raced electronically around the world. Ethel, and everyone else for that matter, was distraught.

After a brief enrollment at the University of California at Berkeley, Joe tried work. In 1973 Mayor Joseph Alioto of San Francisco offered him a federally funded job helping to combat venereal disease and tuberculosis in poor neighborhoods. It was hardly glamorous and paid only $748 a month, but Joe jumped at it. Almost immediately a city supervisor, John Molineri, jumped at him. Molineri charged that Alioto had given Joe the job just because Joe was a Kennedy. "I'm wondering why this particular person was hired," Molineri asked publicly. "Because I was impressed by the young man," Alioto replied. But it was no use. After one attempt at defending his credentials, Joe dispiritedly quit the job and the city four weeks later.

"Sometimes," Joe said to friends, "I wondered if anything was ever going to get any better." Then the bottom fell out.

In the summer of 1973 came the car crash on Nantucket. Fortunately nobody was killed when Joe, driving a group of buddies back from the beach, got into difficulty in clotted traffic. He tried to make an end run and wound up flipping his jeep off the side of the road. Pamela Kelley, a Hyannis Port neighbor, will always be crippled, and Joe's brother David was badly banged up.

Joe was found guilty of negligence and got a strong lecture from Nantucket District Court Judge George Anastas, by coincidence a college classmate of Joe Kennedy, Jr.—Joe's namesake and his father's oldest brother. "You had a great father and have a great mother. Use your illustrious name as an asset instead of coming into court like this," the judge told him.

Ethel sighed, and the family arranged a lifetime settlement for the injured Pamela that could not heal her but that would at least keep her from want.

Nantucket seems to have been the turning point for Joe. Andy Cushner describes Joe's changed attitude this way: "After the accident Joe went down into the well and made a decision. He had a choice. He could refuse the challenge and forget the rest of his life, or he could pull himself together and make a serious life for himself. That's what he did."

Ever since he has been exceptionally solicitous about Pamela's well-being, often calling her, frequently visiting and occasionally supplementing the settlement money. "He has been wonderful and helpful and a great friend," says Pamela. "No one could have asked him to do more for me. He is terrific."

School was still a nightmare, but Joe resolved to get through. The first stop after enrolling at the University of Massachusetts was to work at the Daniel Marr Boys Center in South Boston, where he supervised a group of children, passing out basketballs and playing games with them. It was certainly nothing special— no Kennedy had ever done such scut work—but he refused to miss even one day of it. That summer he passed up the chance to loll around Hyannis Port in favor of teaching some of his working-class gym charges how to sail. He became, in Cushner's words, "superdedicated."

Yet it was not until Uncle Ted tapped him to run his 1976 Senate reelection campaign that Joe, then 24, found any real job satisfaction. There is no overstating the significance of Uncle Ted's act. Joe was delighted. It was vindication from the man who mattered most. "It was the head coach telling him, 'Okay, you're my quarterback,' and it was a powerful vote of confidence," says Cushner.

In the beginning of the campaign he made few friends with his curt ways and rapid-fire decisions. Soon, though, he came to love it—the strategy, the tactics, the combat. He took charge firmly. Jaw thrust forward, hands on hips, he started running the show. "He talked back to Ted," reports another worker in the campaign. "He argued strategy with him. This was no longer a boy dealing with a father figure. This was a politician dealing with a politician."

What is more, he mellowed. "He had a lot of rough edges

at first," recalls Dickie Gallagher, who also worked that campaign. "He went into one of these volunteer meetings and came on like gangbusters, demanding the same kind of effort from them he was putting in himself. I had to remind him a couple of times that his first step should be to appreciate whatever anyone was doing. The second time he addressed the same group he was a different guy."

Joe was beginning to rein in his demons, but even with his uncle's help and the devotion of a growing cadre of friends, he could not have become what he is without Sheila Brewster Rauch. Now 28, she is a lissome brunette from mainline (Villanova) Pennsylvania, has a clickey-click mind, a will of steel, and magnetic femininity. They met at a party in Hyannis Port in 1974—the Harvard grad school whiz and the prep school washout. It is a curious but powerful love story. They have been together ever since.

He has come more and more to rely on her emotional toughness and feminine grace, and she has thrown all her considerable powers into making him feel wanted, secure, comfortable, loved. Sheila is the stabilizer in his life. She tolerated it when he signed his notes "GOD." She stood up to him in his moments of temper. When no one else had faith in Joe, Sheila did. Best of all, she loved the man called Joe, not the name Joe Kennedy. They were married in June 1979 and have produced handsome twin boys, Joseph P. III, and Matthew Rauch, now three years old.

Together, Sheila and the boys have put direction in Joe's life, and that took some doing. Once the tonic of Uncle Ted's 1976 campaign wore off, Joe took a job with the federal Community Services Administration. Again he became disillusioned: "I guess after a year and a half there it seemed to me that the community action agencies were not working the way they were designed and the way men like my father wanted them to run. They were bureaucracies that needed poverty to stay in business. They had really turned into the things they were first designed to attack—institutions that perpetuated poverty."

Joe's irritation came at the same time the country was reeling from the second oil-shortage shock of the 1970s—the oil crisis of 1979, after the revolution in Iran. "I was out at Dick Goodwin's house, and the news came on," Joe relates. "The lead story was about the profits of these oil companies. Goodwin said: 'I wonder what would happen if you set up an oil company that would take those billions and give them back to the people.' That was when the notion started."

The "notion" soon blossomed into Joe's own oil company, which he called Citizens Energy Corporation. Joe and Sheila actually devised the operation on their honeymoon. "We called it that because the purpose was to help citizens, not the corporation," Joe says. "You buy oil at one price, sell the products at a higher price, and even after you figure in the costs, there were still a lot of dollars left over, and you could use those to reduce the cost of heating oil." Those "dollars left over" are what ordinary companies call profit. By shaving profit, Joe could shave prices.

In 1979, shiny new Citizens Energy began selling heating oil to Massachusetts for resale to poor persons selected by a state agency. The price was 57 cents a gallon, compared to the prevailing commercial price of 82 cents. In 1980 Joe's price was 83 cents against an average of $1.01, and last year the figures were, respectively, 89 cents and $1.24.

Yet that was just the beginning. Soon Joe saw how Citizens Energy could be effective in other areas—an innovative refinancing plan, for example, to encourage fuel conservation. The company set aside $450,000 to be used as collateral for loans to qualified landlords picked by the state for installation of insulation and other energy-savers. Typically, a $12,000 yearly heating cost could be rolled back to $8000, and of the $4000 saved one half went to pay back the loan and the other half to hold down rents. Thus the landlord's heating bill would continue at $12,000, but actual oil consumption would decline and eventually both landlord and tenant would painlessly realize substantial savings.

After that, with brother Michael, Joe organized a program all along the eastern seaboard to collect leftover heating oil from families that had switched from oil to natural gas heat. Citizens Energy then sold the collected oil at below market rates to state governments for distribution to the needy. The company's proceeds went to the Robert Kennedy Memorial and to education programs for the poor.

Citizens Energy has probably been most effective and unusual where it might have been least expected to succeed—overseas. It seemed to Joe that a great deal of ill will toward the U.S. had built up in countries that supplied it with crude oil, because, rightly or wrongly, some people in these countries see America as using its technology and capital only for itself. So Joe decided to put Citizens Energy to work "to provide a greater understanding between our countries by taking some of that technology and capital to help other nations start a reinvestment program."

At first the program was the carrot to encourage producing countries to sell CE crude oil. The oil-producing country would be paid prevailing market rates for their crude. As a bonus, Joe's company would also arrange technological and financial assistance to the producing country to help it establish solar, biomass, wind, and other alternative energy ventures for its own people. Most importantly, Citizen's Energy agreed with the supplying country to reinvest about a quarter of the company's profits in the alternative energy projects.

The program quickly expanded to other non-oil-producing third-world nations after Joe decided that it should not be confined just to the countries that could do his firm some good by selling it crude. The first reinvestment project was completed in Jamaica in September 1981—a solar hot water heating system for a hospital in Montego Bay.

By early 1983, projects to convert biomass and waste into energy were under way in Costa Rica, and several other countries had begun negotiations with CE about alternative energy schemes. Although Joe has no objection to making money, he says his decisions on what projects to move ahead on are not based primarily on prospective profits, but rather on relative need, chances of success, and stability of the government involved.

"We're not in this to lose money, but making it is not the primary thing," says Joe.

To those around him and to Joe himself, CE is a vintage Kennedy example of using the family's power to serve others. By happy circumstance it also makes more than a little political hay for Joe in Massachusetts, where the yearning for another Kennedy is palpable.

It was easy at first. Joe had to overcome the strong reservations of most of the family leaders in setting up the firm. Only his mother stood resolutely behind him. The rest believed the odds were overwhelming that he would fail in this seemingly preposterous notion of creating a charitable oil company. Yet Joe, who in many ways resembles a bulldog, marched ahead, using the best thing he had going for him—his name. It is highly improbable that foreign governments would have dealt with this idealistic young man had he not spoken with the weight and backing of his name and family. These opened doors that otherwise would have remained forever sealed.

The company's first purchase of a million barrels of oil from Venezuela, for instance, was made with zero capital. Even Joe now wonders at his own audacity. "Everybody worried about our finances," he recalls. "We didn't own a ship. We didn't own a refinery. We were neophytes. The thing that put us over the top was that we had all the documentation from all the groups that were essential. We had the crude, we had the transportation, we had the financing—all in legal form and heavily backed up." In other words, Joe had learned what he had never learned in school—to do his homework.

Joe now stands as the outstanding third-wave example of the Kennedy ability to triumph over difficulty. He has grown a great deal as a man, too. He has curbed his temper, learned patience, and most of all, has become comfortable with himself. He is delighted with his family and satisfied by his work. Those are the graces of his life. "His outlook on many things has mellowed," says his friend Doug Spooner. "The guy could run for the priesthood now. He won't park in front of a hydrant because he worries there might be a fire. He feels a tremendous amount of responsibility for others."

Friends Andy Cushner and Andy Karsch agree about Joe: If you need cough medicine from the corner druggist, he will give you a hard time if you ask him to get it for you. But if he is in Argentina cinching a deal and a friend calls him with a desperate plea for help, he will be on the friend's doorstep in eight hours. That is actually what he did once in Karsch's case when Karsch became seriously ill with food poisoning. "Joe dropped a lot of important stuff to be at my bedside day after day for many hours," relates Karsch.

Yet a spark of the old Joe glows. One Third World big shot once angled for a bribe to smooth the path for a contract, and Joe had to be restrained from going after him.

The measure of how far Joe has come is also revealed in a story told by another friend, Melissa Ludtke. Joe was interviewing a young woman who had applied to become a babysitter for his children. She was extremely nervous, and at one point stumbled over her words, panicked and stopped, completely tongue-tied. "I have a learning disability," she explained to Joe after she had recovered her composure and was able to go on. "Sometimes I get confused."

"That's okay, we're all a little slow around here," Joe joshed. It was for Ludtke "a moment of stunning tenderness. Joe clearly knew what she was going through, maybe because he'd been there himself." He quickly moved to put her at her ease, and then he gave her the job.

The Virtue of Being Kathleen

IN HER SOPHOMORE YEAR AT RADCLIFFE, KATHLEEN, BROTHER Joe, and some friends spent a weekend at their family's Hyannis Port home. At dusk, when it would have been nice to lay a fire, Kathleen regretted, as she often had, that the fireplace had been blocked off many years before. She kicked through the wall to expose the chimney again.

In the way of such enterprises, the kicking in was easy. It was the rebuilding that was hard. It took several weeks and several trips to the library before the necessary knowledge was acquired. Eventually a new foundation was laid and a hearth built. The chimney drew like a great straw.

"I knew if I kicked in that wall, I'd have to do something about it," says Kathleen. "All those years we didn't have a fireplace were very frustrating. Well, the only way to get rid of frustration is to act on it—do something that forces you to make it right."

Summing up this modest victory over frustration, one of Kathleen's friends says, "She saw things as they should be and asked, Why not?"—an appropriation of the elder Robert Kennedy's favorite Shaw quotation. "That's Kathleen. She will not take no for an answer and she will forge ahead."

Kathleen takes this you-can't-make-an-omelet-without-breaking-eggs position in everything she does. She is every inch her father's daughter, and from the moment of his death she determined that she would be his living legacy, as kid brothers Joe and Bobby also did in their own individual ways.

Perhaps more than either Joe or Bobby, Kathleen burns with her father's flame. His death has shaped her life. Her response to it has been missionary—to bring to the world the virtue she believes he represented.

After the killing, many of Kathleen's friends hated the killer, Sirhan Sirhan, and said so. Yet Kathleen never once showed even anger. "I was trying to comfort her once, and I said two words and burst into tears," her friend Anne Coffey recalls. "There was a whole role reversal—she began to comfort me. Her only reference to the killing was to say once, wonderingly, 'I don't understand why people act that way.' There was great kindness in her tone. She was curious, but not angry."

Kathleen's only public discussion of her feelings confirmed the point. "No, no, no, I just don't think about violence," she told interviewer Barbara Kevles. "I don't put a cause on it and think, who am I mad at? It's happened and I don't think of any ifs. Ifs are just an awful thing to live a life on.

"It's awful and it's horrible [to lose a parent], but you can't live in the past. You'd kill yourself if you did that. For me the important thing was going forward and trying to live by the lessons Daddy taught us. If I didn't keep trying, that would be forgetting everything I've lived for."

The ache was partly dulled, but never erased, by the strength they showed as a family, her friend Anne says. Years after the killing Kathleen would say: "Every moment of the day it becomes more real."

Her friends began to notice changes. Kathleen had always been serious about school, but this had been leavened by a whimsical streak. After RFK's death the lightheartedness vanished.

When she was first at Putney, before her father's death, Kathleen and her "silly preppy" friends were the class larks, according to her roommate Sophie Spurr, challenging the hippie values of the time. "We liked to dress up and we liked to play jokes on the others. Kathleen and I would do these silly skits before morning assembly, like acting out nursery rhymes. We were odd, and people didn't want to associate with us."

That did not matter. They threw parties for the most withdrawn hipsters in the crowd and tried to liven up the place. As Kathleen recalls it: "Sophie and I had parties and made everybody cheery and told them they shouldn't look down at their shoes all day long. We were very self-righteous about it. We were just as creepy as we sound, but we had an awfully good time and, I think, for a while we did change part of the school."

Much of that adolescent brightness dimmed after RFK's death. "Her outlook was very much more mature," says Sophie. "She really had to cope with the most troublesome questions of all. When you lose your father and your uncle you begin to question, 'My God. If there's a God up there, why is this all happening?' She became very unmaterialistic. She wasn't like all the kids who went to prep schools and partied a lot. She is always trying to find the core of things. She became a very intense person to be with."

Immediately after her father's death, Kathleen set the standard for the rest of her siblings by going off to work with Indians—in a Navaho tribe in Globe, Arizona, that her father had known through his work on a Senate committee dealing with Indians. She and Sophie began teaching in a summer school just weeks after the assassination. In addition to the tonic effects of doing good for others, they discovered that one of the great virtues of their work was that it gave Kathleen a reprieve from a prying world.

Sophie: "Our guide would introduce her sometimes as Robert Kennedy's daughter. That summer you would have thought no one would not have heard of Robert Kennedy, but sometimes those shepherds would not know what the guide meant. She never said it, but I thought Kathleen got great relief from that."

Two summers later Sophie and Kathleen went to a Head Start program for preschoolers in Alaska for the same kind of respite.

Kathleen was old enough and independent enough to need no surrogate for her father. However, at Radcliffe she became very attached to social psychologist Robert Coles, and his vision of a just society has strongly informed hers.

Her friends say that many of the traits that attracted her to David Townsend were those that her father possessed, especially David's sensitivity and intellectual curiosity. He was her tutor and mentor. They would stay up late in the night many times talking about reconciling the calcified aspects of their Catholicism with the wonderful life-enhancing aspects of it. They also shared an abiding interest in American literature. He was charmed by her willingness to explore anything at its source, as when they and some friends took a trip down the Mississippi on a homemade raft. They did not get all that far, in part because they did not anticipate a string of minor disasters, but they did accomplish their main purpose—a better understanding of what Mark Twain was writing about.

She was dazzled by David's intellect and his commitment to

justice and learning. After a stint of teaching in New Mexico, David decided to go to Yale Law School, drawn not by visions of a lucrative partnership, but by the hope that the experience would make him a better thinker and writer. "He is a brilliant, really brilliant, guy," says Bobby Kennedy's friend Chris Bartle. "And a rare breed nowadays. He scored amazingly high on every college and graduate test he's ever taken, and he could have written his own ticket in terms of career and salary." Instead, he has settled for a modestly comfortable life in Weston, Massachusetts, a Boston suburb.

They are an utterly complementary couple. "She thinks of herself and David as one," says her sister Kerry. "There was one time when Kathleen was trying to set up a tennis game and she kept saying, 'David and I need a partner. David and I need a partner.' It did not dawn on her that the two of them were a doubles team. They are almost fused."

Kathleen is the iconoclast in a family that reveres its icons. She believes her father wanted her to be the finder of new paths. In bucking the tide, she has become the model for other women of the third wave and for her friends. Even those who do not follow her lead respect her vigor and zeal. "Sometimes," she once said, "when you read what Daddy did, you feel terribly proud and wish you could live up to at least part of what he tried to do. You wish you really were as wonderful as maybe people might think you are."

In her family, most do think highly of her. "I admire her because the difference between us is so great," explains sister Kerry. "She is the kind of person who leads a life you want to try to achieve, but you always wonder whether you'll get there. She has a highly developed moral code."

Developing and applying that code in the political world has been Kathleen's life work. "She is trying to serve all her values— combining the importance of her family with an important public-service role," believes her friend Ruth Kovnat, who taught Kathleen at law school in New Mexico. "Her most dominant characteristic is her intellectual persistence. She takes an idea and pulls it apart until she is the mistress of it. She is the opposite of glib and she is extremely interested in morals and living the right kind of life. And her lodestar is her religion."

During Uncle Ted's losing presidential campaign, Kathleen came to the conviction that "virtue" was dying out in America. The fact that the word itself rings so strangely on so many

American ears she takes as face-value evidence that her assessment is correct. Since the end of that campaign—with time out for tending her family and very successfully helping to manage Ted's 1982 senatorial campaign—she has become consumed with her insight and pursues it evangelically.

"This country is in serious trouble and the crisis, at bottom, is a moral one," she wrote in an article for *Washington Monthly Magazine* in February 1982, entitled "A Rebirth of Virtue." Echoing her father's practice of citing the classics, she argued that Thucydides' explanation of the death of the Greek city-state—it became impossible to distinguish between those who perpetrated crimes and those who prevented them—was becoming a reality in America, because we have "lost something at the core of our national character that once acted to shape our behavior. We've lost our sense of virtue."

Virtue, she argued, is a "habit of mind" that comes from, among other places, religion. Noting the irony, she wrote that liberals had lost touch with that central truth while the New Right has capitalized on it. "Maybe the Moral Majority is onto something. It's onto it too narrowly. But the basic feeling that a spiritual renewal and a repairing of American moral fabric have something to do with each other is not far off the mark."

Robert Kennedy could easily have written that. Always at the center of Kathleen's beliefs stands the memory of her father. Her article noted, quite correctly, that "My father appealed to both rich and poor, black and white, because he took religion seriously. As Cesar Chavez said about my father, 'He could see things through the eyes of the poor.'" She concluded by urging liberals to reclaim the moral roots that had led to the success of the civil rights movement, for example: "I believe liberals can achieve such triumphs again, but only if they open themselves up to their own religious impulses, and like Robert F. Kennedy, reach out to average Americans in a way that touches their souls."

She later wrote in *The New York Times*: "The left must challenge the Moral Majority on its own grounds. In all efforts, we must speak in biblical language. We will dispute the 'morality' that lobbies for a budget penalizing the poor and the meek. We will challenge a foreign policy that finances weapons rather than plowshares. For if we—the true moral majority—do not organize and remain unwilling to speak to the millions of Bible readers in this country, then the religious traditions of an entire nation shall be surrendered to a misnamed faction."

In an unpublished paper, she outlines an even grander vision, "the moral economy," where "the value of labor is measured not only by what we work for, but by what we play for, what we enjoy, and what we wish to create." The way to achieve this just society is through the emulation of "heroes whose lives demonstrate to us the relationship between religion and politics, between morality and economics." The two examples she offers are St. Francis of Assisi and Martin Luther King, Jr.—a typical RFK pairing.

Kathleen thinks people are too selfish, that they should wake up in the morning asking, as she does, "How am I going to help others and help the country today?" She believes that motivated individuals can do important things, and she tirelessly advances this belief. Like Aunt Eunice, she will tell you what to do in an instant. She is very Kennedy. That may be why her father was so supportive of her goals. And it may be why she throws herself so fully into the task.

Kathleen once took a train trip with Sophie Spurr from New Haven to New York. Sophie bought a *Vogue* magazine at the station newsstand and began thumbing through it on the train when she noticed Kathleen's reading matter for the trip—*War and Peace.* "There's so much important material to read and so little time to do it," explained Kathleen. "I really don't want to waste this time."

Steve—He Packs a Wallop

THUMP. THUMP. THUMPTHUMPTHUMP. STEVE SMITH, JR.'S crisp blows beat a leathery tattoo on the sweaty forehead of Norman Mailer, rebounded off his parrying arms, burrowed into his midsection. Steve was not practicing an unusual form of literary criticism. He and the well known writer were sparring at the New York boxing club to which they both belong, called "The Raging Jews" in a play on the nickname of former middleweight champ Jake LaMotta, "The Raging Bull." Steve is there to work out most Saturday mornings.

To look at his cherubic, softly boyish face—it would remind old-time fight fans a little bit of Billy Conn, the Irish heavyweight contender who once lost a memorable battle to Joe Louis—it is hard to believe that Steve Smith is the toughest Kennedy of all. But every now and then those very wide, very blue eyes get his father's Look. When they do—in boxing, this happens when he is snapping a right cross over a path-clearing left jab—his friends know it is time to watch out.

His cousins remember that look from the days at Hyannis Port when the older ones would hold him down and try to humiliate him. On these occasions Steve would never cry. His face would redden, but the vehemence of his protests served only to goad his tormentors. Steve was called "Spitter"—as in your eye.

Now when sides are chosen for any of those heavy physical contests in which Kennedys specialize, such as touch football, everyone picks Steve first. Family historians say his ascendancy came during a ferocious touch-football game several seasons back in which Steve put the shove on mighty young Joe Kennedy himself—besting the oldest male of the third wave. To be sure, there were other players, but at the moment of truth it was Joe and Steve eyeball to eyeball, and it was Joe's turn to blink.

Steve's interest in boxing amazes and concerns his friends, but Steve shrugs and laughs: "It's a great way to stay in shape and it's much more a mental than a physical sport," he insists.

He had done it in college until he broke his hand. One spring evening he and Michael Kennedy were loafing around Cambridge after Harvard classes. They were accosted by three "townies"—locals who traditionally are enemies of the students. This particular group started to harass Steve and Michael, but Steve assured them that his side wasn't looking for trouble.

But the townies would not be placated. One of them kicked at Michael, who dexterously leaped out of the way. Before the offender's foot had regained the pavement, Steve had whipped a six-inch right cross to his chin. His buddies carried the limp figure off into the night. "That's when I broke my hand," says Steve, rubbing the knuckles affectionately.

If Michael is the cunning gazelle of this generation, Steve is the leopard—inventive, consistent, resourceful, powerful. His appearance deceives in a number of ways. Behind that almost-baby face there is a measuring intelligence and a large appetite for life. He has a drive to learn, to achieve, to do. He will stalk an idea for months, years until he has it letter-perfect. His friend Peter Emerson, who worked for a while on the U.S. delegation to the international Law of the Sea Treaty negotiations, was amazed once that Steve had learned of his job and begun study of the issues of the negotiations. "The next time I saw him, he knew more about it than I did," says Emerson. "He never lets go."

When he graduated from Harvard in 1979, Steve was in a typical quandary about what to do next. He started off in Thailand at a resettlement camp bulging with refugees from the Communist takeover in Cambodia and Vietnam. It was hard and frustrating work, the very opposite of glamorous. Steve did it for six months, and turned it into an adventure and an education. He learned Thai and lived modestly on his $300-a-month stipend, first at the YMCA and then in a small home.

Typically, he has a hard time describing what the experience meant to him. Steve is cautious about emotions. But he will give you the benefit of his mind as he details what he saw and learned. "It's a great testament to what the human spirit can overcome," he says. "Many of these people had suffered the loss of their whole families—sometimes they had witnessed it themselves. And yet they somehow found the will to go on and manage very well. They never lost their senses of humor and never quite seemed beaten down."

By the time he returned to the U.S., he had made up his mind about his immediate future. To ground himself in skills that will help him master any public-service role he may seek, he enrolled in Columbia Law School. He isn't all that keen on law school, but sees it as a necessary prelude to more important things.

Family friend Andy Karsch considers Steve one of the brightest of them all: "Steve is very much like his father. He knows that real power is not always visible or apparent. He is extremely willful and he has not yet made up his mind whether the action is in public work or private work. He is always learning and there is always a reason for his pursuits. He knows exactly what he wants."

One of the things he pursues most fervidly is information about his Kennedy past. The reason is obvious, but Steve puts it profoundly: "Because our family is so close, the loss of Uncle Jack and Uncle Bobby was very much like losing our own parents. After Bobby died, especially, I had this powerful sense of the awful possibility that someone very close to me could be taken from my life. When you sense that, it can bring a sense of immediacy to what you do. You make the effort for others that you otherwise might not make, and you become very aware of trying to use your time the best way possible."

At another level, he is most pleased when others who believe in the goodness of the Kennedy past seek him out. In the summer of 1982 he traveled with his brother William to Costa Rica. Whenever their family connections were uncovered, they would be enveloped in an embrace of sympathetic memories of the "Keh-nah-deez." Latin American Catholics will never forget JFK and his family.

"It is impossible to describe the feeling you get hearing about how your family has made a difference to others," Steve says. "It makes you proud, certainly, but that seems too insignificant a way to describe it. Responding to people like that is difficult. There, more than any place else, I realized that I can't think of anything I'd rather do than to try to continue that kind of work. They showed me the best side of politics—the side where people get hope. My uncles created a trust that should not be violated, and the whole atmosphere of our family is dedicated to the things they stood for. That trip brought it into focus."

Even before that, though, Steve made a crucially important pilgrimage—to South Africa in 1977 with friend Peter Kaplan. Steve arranged it himself and tried, as best he could, to duplicate the itinerary of his Uncle Bobby's 1966 visit.

With Francis Wilson, one of the men RFK befriended, as Steve stood on the steps in the center of Capetown University, he tried to imagine how a sea of 150,000 black and white faces cheered the single most important speech Robert Kennedy ever gave. With Colin Eglin, the Labor official who arranged Robert Kennedy's visit, Steve stood on Table Mountain and looked out on one of the world's most magnificent sights—the sparkling junction of the Atlantic and the Pacific oceans and the clouds rolling off the plateau. Off in the distance was the penal colony on Robben Island, where black dissidents are held, and he remembered Ethel telling him how, as the plane carrying Robert departed South Africa, it had been lowered over the island and dipped its wings—a universal gesture of tribute and Kennedy's sign of solidarity with the inmates.

"Those were some of the most morally powerful, beautiful, and important moments of my life," Steve says. "I needed to know about my uncle and the mission that set the stage for the last part of his life. I understood it better and it helped settle choices in my own life, made them easier for me."

Perhaps he had wondered as a youth, after the assassinations, whether public service was good or whether it was just full of pain. He will not say, but who could blame any young man for questioning the worthiness of activities that brought such torment to him and his family? After South Africa, though, the vision and the hope and the goodness of the public arena were brought home to him. It became clear on that mountaintop that the public's business is worthy work, and he committed himself to it.

Somewhere in Steve's belongings is a paper napkin. It was given him by Allard Lowenstein—the liberal activist whose conscience was akin to Robert Kennedy's, and who himself was shot to death by an assassin in 1980. Steve and Lowenstein had been in a bar in New Hampshire during Ted's 1980 campaign when Lowenstein was seized with the need to show Steve one of the last things Robert Kennedy had given him before his murder.

Lowenstein wrote on the napkin exactly what RFK had scribbled to him on a scrap of paper as they rode on a bus in the frenzied days of the 1968 campaign. Typically, it was from Ralph Waldo Emerson: "If a single man plant himself indomitably on his instincts and there abide, the huge world will come round to him." It has become Steve's personal motto.

John—Prince Disarming

"WE WOULD NEVER HAVE NAMED JOHN AFTER HIS FATHER IF we had known what was going to happen," Jackie said years later, referring to the steam bath of attention that engulfed young John Kennedy following JFK's assassination. Wherever and whenever possible, which was most of the time, Jackie threw cold water on the publicity seekers, producing the fog that has shielded John from at least some of the prying.

As a result, John Kennedy has grown up normal—"disgustingly normal," says one cousin with maybe a tinge of envy.

Certainly the temptations have been great. At 22 he is astonishingly good-looking, reminding at least one gawker of the Greek athletes sculpted by Praxiteles. Girls have literally camped on his doorstep eagerly, but in vain. He could easily have followed Oscar Wilde's advice that "The only way to get rid of temptation is to yield to it." Instead John has followed Thomas More: "Men must live where men will not be tempted."

"Everyone in the world would probably like to have John Kennedy's dance card," says family friend Linda Semans. "It's full. The special thing about John is that he will not take advantage of that or abuse it."

John apparently is a respectable amateur actor, and he has been offered any number of fat movie and television opportunities that would have allowed him to work his way up from the top. Again, he has resisted temptation and has enlisted his Uncle Ted in holding at bay the endless requests.

For his tranquility, John credits Jackie, who once summed up her parental goal this way: "I want them to know about how the rest of the world lives, but also I want to be able to give them some kind of sanctuary when they need it, someplace to

take them into when things happen to them that do not necessarily happen to other children."

Although he could easily have become the Todd Lincoln of
his day, devastated by his father's ghost, thanks to Jackie, he
has not. Those close to him say he is determined to do good
in his life and he has begun preparing seriously for the role,
after an undistinguished adolescent scholastic life.

He remembers little of his three years in the White House
and, presumably, nothing directly of his father. Only the emp-
tiness, the negative image, is there, but that can be painful.
Before he was ten, for example, Jackie once arranged an entertainment for him at her mother's place in Newport. Jackie's
stepfather, Hugh Auchincloss, had captured John's fancy with
stories of pirates harrowing the coastal areas for the vast treasure
Captain Kidd reputedly had buried somewhere in New England
in Colonial times. Somewhere right around Newport, Auchincloss suggested to John, possibly on the property of Ham-
mersmith Farm, the Auchincloss home.

The elderly man and the little boy would pace the property
together, heads down, looking for likely hiding places. Eventually possibility became certainty.

Jackie arranged with the local Coast Guard station to borrow
a longboat one evening and convinced a handful of men to dress
up as pirates. The family party was interrupted by a sudden
howl that seemed to come from the beach, and then a boat
drew up on the shore, from which a half dozen of the "pirates,"
wearing eye patches and wielding swords, disembarked amid
shouts and alarums.

All the young boys at the party, including John, were supplied
with wooden swords and urged to drive off the intruders, most
of whom were their own fathers. This was accomplished with
dispatch, and as punishment one of the captured pirates—Secret
Serviceman Jack Walsh—was sentenced to walk the plank.

At the moment before he plunged into the sea, John recognized Walsh and realized it was a prank. But he feared the
game had gone too far and that Walsh would actually die. He
burst into tears and raced over to the agent, gripping him by
the leg. "You can't die!" he shouted. "You can't die!" Many of
the others there also began to cry, and the game ended more
in sorrow than in joy.

Walsh was one of the good men in John's life who helped
his mother steer him through—men like Robert and Edward

Kennedy, Robert McNamara, Maurice Tempelsman, and, when the going got rough in school, psychiatrist Ted Becker. He also had wise-beyond-his-years Tim Shriver to provide friendship and emotional ballast. They were inseparable for many years in activities ranging from diving in the South Pacific to examining sunken ships and working in Guatemala in 1976 to help in a Peace Corps rebuilding program following a crushing earthquake.

John also got a good deal of emotional support from his stepfather, Aristotle Onassis. Unlike Caroline, who did remember her own father and resented another man in her mother's life and in her own, John and Onassis actually became pals, and would go to ballgames together. Dick Gallagher, a friend, remembers once when he went fishing with John and Onassis, and Ari gave John two hundred-dollar bills to buy some bait. "They were really quite close," says Gallagher.

Like his cousin Joe, John hated school and did badly in it, first at Collegiate School and then at rigorous Phillips Academy (Andover). He was neither natively very adept nor, like Caroline, determinedly studious, and he bridled at the scholastic regimen altogether. Yet he enjoyed the friends he made at school and they kept him happily occupied. Because he is a Kennedy he could probably have gone to Harvard if he chose, but he picked Brown instead and it appears to have been a wise move. At Brown he has blossomed on three fronts—athletically, artistically, and intellectually.

John is probably the least competitive Kennedy, which also seems a consequence of maternal influence. Jackie would not let him into the arena when he was little, and he has in the main avoided it as he has grown older. In the past two years, though, John has sprouted impressively. He began to lift weights, and he has become increasingly interested in contact sport. Perhaps because of Tim's influence, he began to play rugby at Brown University and no longer waves off efforts to enlist him in family contests. He also has a normal interest in swimming and skiing. Still, he is emphatically no jock.

"I think Jackie took a look at Ethel's house and decided all this competition wasn't the healthiest thing in the world," one family observer believes. "John is totally free of any urge to prove himself on the playing fields. He can take it or leave it. The thing that has changed since he got to college was that he takes it more often now than he ever did."

John's passion is the theater. He discovered it at Andover, where he gained a reputation as a gifted raconteur and has pursued it seriously at Brown. Though his mother worries about the exposure this gives him, she is quite proud of him and thinks that at least this interest is consonant with her own passion for the arts. For years he was hostile to that side of her upbringing, but he has now swung fully around. His acting skills make him a delightful companion—for those whom he allows to get close—because he will frequently break into renditions of his favorite scenes or act out elaborate stories.

Latterly he has developed a strong interest in his father's life and career. "John has suddenly learned there really is such a thing as the family legacy, and he has decided it is worth pursuing," says a cousin. "He used to sit quietly while the rest of the family devoured the subject, but now he's in the thick of things."

The most important element of his intellectual development is his interest in South Africa. He traveled to the land of apartheid, with the help of Jackie's friend Tempelsman, and it galvanized his interest in racial and foreign policy questions. He met with most of the major players in the racial drama in South Africa and Namibia, worked for a while in a mining camp in Johannesburg, and has been a passionate follower of news from the region. Together with some friends he organized a group at Brown to pursue those issues, arranging for speakers to come to campus and for discussion groups when important developments occur in the region. In the way of such things, John's interest has broadened to other foreign policy questions as well. "John is a living example of the notion that reflection breeds reflection," says a family friend. "He has come out of his shell."

John has also emerged as a willing worker. In 1981 he spent a summer apprenticing at the Center for Democratic Studies in Washington, a party-policy think tank. He did everything there from answering phones to filing to writing letters. When he chafed a bit at the menial work, his boss, Ted Van Dyke, speedily enlisted him in fund-raising appearances for the financially struggling organization. In the old days John would have balked at making publicized personal appearances even for the most worthy of causes—or Jackie would have insisted that he turn them down. However, he did it for Van Dyke and was appreciative, if somewhat in awe, of the attention he received.

Back at Brown, he continued the affiliation, organizing disarmament forums on New England campuses and getting deeply involved in some elements of campus politics.

He graduated from Brown in June with a degree in American studies and is thinking now about taking a little time off for himself before making the big decision about whether to go to law school or not. Still, the thing about him that impresses others so much is his untarnished modesty. "He has not let this John Kennedy, Jr. stuff go to his head," says Andy Karsch. "You would think that he would be a hardened 'I've-seen-it-all' kind of guy, but he isn't. He is a very, very normal young man who wants to make a life of consequence for himself."

After his junior year at Andover, John spent a month in the Outward Bound survival program, which included rugged sailing and a three-day test in which he was left to get by on a gallon of water, no food and a book on edible plants. When he returned to civilization, he described his ordeal—the deprivation, the uncertainty, the fear.

"You must have learned a lot about yourself," offered Linda Semans, a friend, when he told his tale. "You must know a lot about John Kennedy—the man."

With an actor's flair, John slowly explained the real significance of the adventure to her. "I'll tell you what I learned," he said, and then drew out every word, milking each for maximum effect: "I . . . learned . . . I'll . . . never . . . allow . . . myself . . . to . . . be . . . that . . . hungry . . . again."

David in Exile

THERE WERE TIMES, ADMITTEDLY NOT OFTEN, WHEN ROBERT Kennedy had difficulty interesting his children in being with him. "Who wants to come to the office?" he would shout some weekend mornings, and the response was silence. After all, with the pool, the football games, the horses, and the general possibilities for fun at Hickory Hill, the office wasn't much of a draw.

David, though, would always go.

He did everything he could with his father, whether it was dull or not. And Robert understood why. He had been a third son, too, and it isn't easy, especially in a Kennedy family. It made Robert Kennedy especially sensitive to David's needs. He allowed David, alone, to get candy and pocket money that others did not get and he made special efforts to give the boy the extra care he obviously needed.

Despite his inferior rank, David had gifts. He was a graceful athlete and has a quick mind. He might easily have grown up safely under his father's guiding hand. Instead, Robert's death sent him into a 15-year slide.

After seeing his father shot on television David was inconsolable—"dripping pain," recalls a family friend. For months after the murder he would walk the hedgerows that border Hickory Hill or along the beach at Hyannis Port alone. They were all bereft, of course, but David seems to have been the only child who would not cry. The day his tears finally came, family friend John Glenn, the astronaut and now presidential aspirant, urged those who rushed to comfort David to let him cry. He had to do it, Glenn said, for his own good.

But David never got relief. Overnight his personality switched from shyness to combativeness. He flashed unprovoked anger, picked fights that he could not win and sulked when bested. He ran for a time with brother Bobby's pack when it was on rampage—and when it did him nothing but harm. Without defenses, he needed affection badly, but was not able to accept it.

"Where have you been all these years?" Pamela Kelley asked him when they were in the hospital together after the Nantucket car crash. The Kelleys and the RFKs were very close, but Pamela could not remember seeing David much or knowing him at all.

"I've been around," she recalls David answering, "but I haven't been around with the rest of the family. I've been more by myself. That's just the way it is."

The crash, which left Pamela with partial permanent paralysis, also injured David's back, and the consequent pain led to painkilling drugs, which perhaps marked the beginning of an involvement with drugs that was to turn the next decade of his life into a long torture for himself and those who loved him.

"We would spend long hours together at the hospital, just rapping," said Pam Kelley. "He was very concerned about me and very upset when a lot of people would be around for any period of time. We had a very strong bond. Both of us had problems and we talked and talked about them. He was trying to come out from the shadow of his older brothers and he was trying to figure out how he should move ahead in his life. He was so very sensitive. The accident just made him more so."

His drug problems intensified when he went to Harvard in the fall of that same year, 1973. Psychologist Robert Coles, who had known several of Robert Kennedy's children, spotted looming trouble and urged the family to get him out of the Harvard-Boston environment where he was overshadowed by other Kennedys, especially Bobby. Michael, Caroline, and Steve Smith all were close by, too, and Joe, John, Courtney, and Chris Lawford were not far off. "There was a lot of talent, drive, and frustration under one tent," as one old friend of RFK puts it. "That was certainly not the best thing for David." Possibly this contributed to David's misuse of the Percodan, Dilaudid, and Quaaludes that had been prescribed for his pain and his depression by a psychiatrist.

It was also at Harvard where some of his distressing behavior became glaringly evident. He was intentionally slovenly, especially when he had to be presentable. He used his sardonic humor as a cutting weapon—except that he'd often get cut up in the fights it provoked. There was, for instance, the time he sassed cousin Steve Smith once too often and suffered a one-punch knockdown. They made up—quickly—but David was unchastened.

"It was a classic case," says a friend. "He hated almost everything connected with his family, but he wanted them to acknowledge his life." He stopped skiing for a long time, for instance, even though he was one of the best, and perhaps the most graceful. He also quit playing touch football. Instead, he turned to drugs and "looked wasted all the time," as one contemporary puts it. His older brother Joe, who became the principal disciplinarian for David, agonized over his decline. "Look at him," he said one day to a companion as David lay in a stupor. "He was a varsity halfback as a sophomore [in high school]—something none of the rest of us could do. He was terrific. And now he can barely put one leg in front of the other."

The next few years of David's life were a blur of health problems related to drugs. In March 1976 he was admitted to Massachusetts General Hospital, suffering from "pneumonia." He ended up in intensive care, perilously close to death.

He returned to Harvard for the fall semester, but one day just drifted off and never came back. He said he wanted to write, but never got around to it. Bobby, no Shakespeare by several miles, had just published his book about federal judge Frank Johnson. David's only real interest seemed to be making the scene—or making a scene—at Manhattan's steamy discotheques with a succession of beautiful young women.

Yet he displayed "a wonderful sense of humor and was always very merry," says his onetime girl friend, actress Rachel Ward. Back at Harvard, he became increasingly hostile. Several cousins finally alerted uncles Ted and Steve, and a family flying squad led by the senator, brother Joe, and Dick Goodwin swooped down and whisked David off to Massachusetts General Hospital for detoxification.

That did not take, however, and the next news of David came when an anonymous caller tipped off New York City police that a white man was being beaten in a hotel in Harlem. It turned out to be David, and the place turned out to be a notorious drug "shooting gallery" on West 116th Street near Eighth Avenue. When police arrived they found David, bleeding profusely, in the lobby and they later found a 25-deck stash of heroin in one of the hotel rooms. Though David claimed that he innocently had pulled his sports car over to the curb when two men beckoned him and then followed them into the building, there were reports that he had been there to buy heroin.

The family swooped again, but three days later David again gave them the slip. A general council of Kennedys was called to deal with the matter when he surrendered, penniless and desperate. By the time they got him into treatment, he was suffering from bacterial endocarditis, an inflammation of the heart lining and valves that is frequently associated with drug abuse.

Family leaders, including Joe and Bobby, chose a program called Aquarian Effort because its leader, Donald Juhl, had been highly recommended. Earlier therapies had all failed—including one by a European specialist who attached David to a mysterious black box that emitted electric charges. It was a measure of the family's desperation.

David, at first, angrily opposed the new regimen, too, denouncing it as a way to get him "out of the picture" so that he would not be an embarrassment to Uncle Teddy's presidential campaign. He was extremely suspicious of the whole family and thought virtually every important person in his life was conspiring against him. Eventually he yielded and went off to Juhl in California because, a friend says: "His alternative was further degradation and death in a few short months. He was a sick, sick young man. I think that was the thing that made up his mind. He knew that he was not far from an ignominious and frightful death."

Juhl's treatment is reported to be prodigiously expensive, up to $50,000 a year, some say, and David is said still to be paying for it out of his inheritance. Nevertheless, it succeeded. After several slips back, he has beaten his drug habit and tried to right his life. It took an 18-month exile from the family, but it worked.

David no longer feels betrayed by Kennedys, although he is still suspicious of what they think of him. At one family function during his recovery he watched the eyes watching him and sneered to a friend: "They're all looking at the junkie. That's what I am to them."

Yet he is endearing in a quirky way, and he manages to ingratiate almost despite himself. Chris Lawford, who was in mortal combat with David for years, has asked him to be best man at his wedding. "He is a great, great guy," says Chris. Adds another brother: "He has shown more courage than any of the rest of us. Something in him wants to live and come back. It's just that he has had such a hard, hard time."

He has become the conscience of the family, and is a brutal unstuffer of shirts. He is also a vocal critic of anyone he even suspects might be trying to trade on his father's name. He can be withering about the shortfalls he sees in others and he has near clairvoyance in seeing through their high-sounding explanations for their actions. He still picks confrontations with others, but now he is usually right and his penetrating, raw intelligence is his weapon.

He is on the mend, for now. He completed a six-month internship at the *Atlantic Monthly*. But he is determined to show the doubters that he can make it. When a friend wondered if going back to Harvard was a bit much for him because of the memories it could revive, David said firmly that he wanted to finish what he had started and Harvard was the place.

The pain of Robert's death is still a daily torment to him, which is why he is the only cousin who has dared to challenge the family's loyalty to its earliest commitments. David does not think his father should have run for the presidency because he knew the misery it would bring.

The Mellowing of Chris

"I WAS NEAR THE END. NOTHING. CHECKING OUT. I MEAN, my heart almost stopped beating. Something had to change and I knew it."

Chris Lawford was in a Boston hospital early in 1980, very close to death from pneumonia and a collapsed lung. The underlying cause was the plain dumb behavior that had driven him from his home and into the use of the drugs that had wasted his body.

Like many of his generation, Chris grew up angry, cynical, and rebellious. He was already the child of a broken home when the two other male models in his life, uncles John and Robert Kennedy, were snatched away. Robert's death affected Chris almost exactly as it did David, and he too turned to drugs as an escape and refuge. He went to the edge of the cliff, but he has come all the way back to a full and responsible life.

In Christopher Kennedy Lawford, the glamour of Hollywood clashed with the celebrity of Kennedy politics. It has left him with feeling that "I'm a little bit different from some of my cousins in that my father has a recognizable name. I'm not jumbled in with them all."

For the first ten years of his life it was the Hollywood side that controlled. He lived with his family in Santa Monica, a coast away from the rest of his cousins, and his father's success as an actor was if anything more influential to him than his uncles' in politics. From his father came also Chris's dark good looks.

Yet before Chris was ten the perfect match between his parents fell apart, and the Hollywood side of Chris went into remission for many years. His mother Pat moved back East with her children, and suddenly Chris found himself competing with all those burly Kennedy boys.

"I went through a period in my teens and early twenties when I would say, 'I want out. I wish I could go off and be somebody else.' " he explains. At his most bitter points he would appropriate his Uncle Bobby's comments about wealth and poverty, hurling them at his mother to make her justify their attendance at an ornate Catholic church on Park Avenue. Soon he had rejected the faith as well as the edifice, and has never gone back. But his dislike of the church has softened, and he has come to appreciate the meaning of religion to others in the family.

Chris also mirrored his generation's cynicism about politics and government in the era of Vietnam, the Nixon presidency and Watergate. He even saw Uncle Teddy as part of a cursed "establishment." One step further, he also agreed with many of his contemporaries that school was not "relevant."

Worst of all, friends and family kept beating him with the sticks of Jack and Bobby. "Uncle Jack said this. Uncle Bobby did that." To Chris, "Sometimes it was just too much."

So enter the drugs. "I grew up in a generation that experimented a lot with drugs," he says now. "At first for me they were recreational and then they became a friend, in the sense that they took away whatever hurt inside me. You have reasons for taking drugs but those reasons don't matter after a while because you have to take them. For me they helped alleviate the pain of my deficiencies and my hurts. The chemicals killed the pain."

In his own eyes he was always falling short of the high expectations others had for him. He lived in young Bobby Kennedy's shadow, especially in competing for Lem Billings' attention, and that hurt too.

Yet Chris plodded through school and outside activities avoiding—but only narrowly—David Kennedy's complete alienation. Still, there were great similarities between them. When David was beaten up purportedly attempting to buy drugs, Chris joked that he would never be that dumb. Not long after, Chris was arrested for attempting to buy heroin. Later he was accused in another incident of trying to forge a prescription for drugs in Aspen. Many in the family gave up on him, figuring that his own sense of inferiority, his near emotional paralysis out of fear of failing, and his drugs would do him in.

Unlike cousin Joe, Chris says there was no single dramatic

incident that compelled him to change his life radically. Rather, he says his recovery was more like coming to a delta of a great river. Some of the tributaries led nowhere, others took him forward. If there was a turning point, it was the pneumonia. It frightened him, and after that, rehabilitation was cumulative.

"I struggled and I worked at changing the way things were going," he says. "A certain amount of it is that you grow up. If you have sense enough and you have help—and sense enough to seek that help—then you'll be okay."

Ramsey Clark helped. Chris worked in his Senate campaign in New York in 1976, and Clark gently nudged him toward law school and stilled his doubts that he could succeed there. Father Richard McSorley, the peace activist and helper at the RFKs', shaped Chris' commitment to work within the political system rather than despair of it. And Father Philip Berrigan counseled him too.

As with Joe, real salvation came for Chris through a strong woman and loyal friends. The woman is Jeannie Olsson, with luminous smile and dark features that echo both her father's Sweden and her mother's Korea. Like Chris, she is a child of divorced parents. That was how they connected. "We missed the same things when we were growing up," Chris says.

The change Jeannie sparked in him came from her unflinching determination to see things to their conclusion—no matter the cost. Jeannie demanded that Chris live by the same standard. "Instead of allowing me to walk out the door, she would force me to deal with whatever it was—be it the biggest or the littlest thing," Chris says. "I learned better how to cope."

Chris' friend Jack Weeks adds that Jeannie "put discipline into his life. She was the one who told him, 'Sure, you can have anything you want and then go on to other things when you get tired. But is that really worth it? Sticking with things, through good and bad, is the only real test of who you are.' "

Another mentor, psychologist Robert Coles, urged Chris not to think of himself as all alone. "It's okay to ask for help," Coles told him. Eventually, Chris exorcised the ghosts that had possessed him: "One of the struggles is to come to grips with your capabilities, your strengths, your weaknesses. Not everybody can be John Kennedy. Not everybody can be Robert Kennedy. Not everybody can be Peter Lawford. But when you're growing up you're thinking along those lines. One of the things you can do when that point comes is say, 'There's no way I can compete with my uncles or my father or my grandfather. So I'm going to give up.' On the other hand, you can come to a point and say, 'Who is Chris Lawford? What is he going to do?' And then you look at it from a different perspective. You don't have to compare yourself to these figures in your life who have been important. That brings a certain peace of mind."

It also was comforting to know that life was not entirely sanguine even for the heroes of the family, either. Of all the things he did for all the family, that was perhaps the great lesson Lem Billings brought to this generation of Kennedys, according to Chris. He told them the stories—the real human-textured stories—about the family icons. They were fun stories, most of them, but they also bore a critically important message to Chris:

"One of the things he said to me was how much difficulty big Bobby had deciding what to do when he got out of law school. He was really confused for a while. That made me feel like I wasn't competing against some kind of god. They guy was a human being, and he struggled and he had trouble in his life, and it wasn't all perfect for him. That gave me a lot more hope than if I had been competing against a monument." Just as importantly, Lem was a passionate companion—"a father, a brother, and a friend." He was reliable and forgiving.

Uncle Teddy helped to humanize the monuments, as well, by telling Chris of his own false starts and errors. Chris now sees his uncle as a kindred soul: "He's somebody who really had to come to grips with who he was. I can talk with him about things, and he is full of incredible insights."

All that remains to be resolved, it seems, is the Kennedy-Lawford split in his life. He thinks the two worlds can be welded, perhaps by his becoming a lawyer in the entertainment industry. In recent years, Chris and his father have begun to spend some time together and tried to sort out the past. They are now closer, says Chris, more like friends, actually, than father and son.

To a degree that has helped him try to bridge the Kennedy and Lawford strains in him. "All of us want to work for change," Chris says. "You can't grow up in this family without feeling that you have to make a difference. That can come through the communications industry as well as through politics, so I'm not looking at politics now. Maybe I will down the line."

Chris is unique in the family for exploring what he calls "the emotional self." "It's difficult for the Kennedys to show emotion," he believes, "because our emotions have run from the highest—election as President—to the lowest—assassination. Who could handle that? So you have to mask it, and I wonder how good that has been for us."

He has spent considerable time pondering such matters, and that has been the key to his salvation. Introspective, still struggling, Chris is sure he will make more mistakes—a daring admission for a Kennedy. It makes him an appealing and likable figure.

He has finally grasped the significance of the notion that his mother and Aunt Eunice had tried to pound into his thick teenage skull—that family was the ultimate refuge, the source of abiding comfort and support. "It was there all the time," he says now, shaking his head at his own past blindness. "I just didn't see it."

RFK Junior Awaits the Call

WHEN IT BECAME CLEAR TO THE ELDER ROBERT KENNEDY that his clever second son, Bobby, seemed interested only in the care and raising of animals and might not wish to go in for politics, the father said to the boy one day, "It's all right. Be a vet, if that's what you want. Be the best damned vet that there ever was."

So Bobby started a serious study of animals—filled his home with them and even wrote once that he liked animals more than he liked a lot of people. He enjoyed animals so much he began to write a book about them. It was 75 pages long, with a few stories, a few drawings and some biological descriptions of the beasts that most captivated him. It was neatly typed by his father's staff, and lay among his family's papers, awaiting some final touches—an impressive work for a 12-year-old.

Just before he began his fated presidential campaign, RFK gave Bobby his favorite book, Tennyson's *Ulysses*. Only the last passage was underlined, which Bobby found strange because his father usually marked up his books heavily. To this day, Bobby struggles with the message he thought his father was trying to convey because it contradicted his earlier prompting that Bobby be a veterinarian.

Some nights he will sit, as his father did, with a friend or acquaintance and try to explain what the passage from Tennyson means and what his father meant him to draw from it. Then Bobby will begin to read at the point where the aging Ulysses urges his crewmen on to one more great voyage:

The lights begin to twinkle from the rocks:
The long day wanes: the slow moon climbs: the deep
Moans round with many voices.

"Maybe to my father that was Jack, or Grandpa or the many people he wanted to reach in his life."

> Come, my friends,
> 'Tis not too late to seek a newer world.

"I think my father was trying to speak to me and to all of us about what he was doing and why." The lines gave Robert Kennedy the title of his last book, *To Seek a Newer World.*

> Push off, and sitting well in order smite
> The sounding furrows; for my purpose holds
> To sail beyond the sunset, and the baths
> Of all the western stars, until I die.

In the thrall of his father's spirit, Bobby's voice chokes a bit, but he presses on: "He really was trying to leave us a message— it was to carry on—to take up the mantle. He knew the pressures were going to be on me."

What a load for a youngster to bear, especially as he tried again and again to decipher the meaning after his father's death. During most of adolescence he was just trying to get his bearings. There were staggering mood and behavior swings. Some teachers praised him, others damned him. Bobby truly had one foot in heaven and the other in hell. So many questions were— and never could be—answered.

Two years after his father's death, Bobby, then 16, planned to run away from Hyannis Port with John Kelley, of the neighboring Kelley family that figured so prominently in the growing up of the third wave. Bobby wrote the following note to Mrs. Kelley:

John and I are seated in your abandoned automobile, contemplating our next move. It is 9:00 [P.M.] and we take off for our destination presently. We feel rejected because of your apparent 'blaze' [sic; blasé] attitude to the news we gave you last night of our departure. We do not know what to attribute this negative attitude to, but John feels that it is due to lack of care for him. . . . And I am forced to accompany him as a nursemaid. There is adventure in the air, and the high seas offer quite an enigma for our unsatisfied minds.

Bobby

The running away never took place—that time. But Ethel threw Bobby out of the house a year later, launching him on the first episode in an extraordinary Odyssey of his own that has seen him rollicking through uncharted whitewater reaches of South America, living off the land in the jungles of Central America, dodging bullets in the middle of a coup in Chile, riding bulls in backwoods Alabama, marching safari in Africa, living for a half year with the Aymar Indians in the Peruvian Andes, and riding the rails, hobo style, through the American West.

Like his father, Bobby is a fascinatingly complex character. He is one of those rare individuals who dominate their environment. His high spirits and sociability have drawn even the retiring among his friends into perilous pursuits. His call to action is intoxicatingly alluring. Always, he is in the center of a crowd. He cannot bear to be alone.

He was the central figure in his generation of cousins while they were growing up. He dominated by wits, shrewdness, and strength his own group of males and set the example for the younger ones. Sometimes it was exemplary, other times questionable. But inevitably, everywhere Bobby Kennedy Jr. was the standout figure.

He has lived as full and adventurous a life as anyone of his age. He has published a book, trained falcons and hawks, played polo, has already appeared on more talk shows than most celebrities, and supped with the most important persons of the age. As his father wished, he has been in the center of the arena. Unceasingly, his life has been full of movement and action at a breakneck pace, torn between his past and his future.

One of those who tried to help was Lem Billings, who was John Kennedy's roommate at Choate and later became a full-time friend to most younger Kennedys. In many ways, Billings was the fifth Kennedy brother. The family trusted him as they did no other outsider. He managed the trust fund for the children until his death in 1980, and was a completely reliable confidante to all. Most important, he was a more ardent and explicit Kennedy cheerleader than many family members were themselves.

He embraced Bobby wholeheartedly and never let go. At Lem's encouragement, Bobby began to focus on his father's legacy. After that he was pulled in two directions—and still is. His interest in animals competed against his father's will, as he understood the Ulysses passage. The choice he faced was between public life and all its demands and his animals and the idyllic self-fulfilling life they represented.

In one ear Lem, his closest friend, was whispering that Bobby was the heir apparent and he, Lem, would manage his ascent to power. In the other ear he heard the call of the wild.

The summer after his pot bust Bobby got into another row with the Hyannis Port police. He was arrested for loitering after a run-in with a cop who charged that Bobby mouthed off to him and spat ice cream. Bobby denied the accusation, but spent the night in jail after refusing to call home. On the advice of another prisoner, he pleaded "no contest" to the charge because "it seemed to be the smart thing to do." It was not.

Scores of reporters awaited him when he was released and Ethel boiled over. She bounced Bobby out of the house. After several days of sleeping on neighbors' porches, he collected $600 from his savings, bought a beat up Ford Falcon and headed west with two friends. One dropped off in Minnesota and the other, Conrad Lowery, continued to California, where the car broke down. They sold it in Fresno for $400.

Then began the real adventure. From there they hitchhiked and rode freight trains throughout the West, at times subsisting on Vienna sausage and cheap wine. Usually they were in pursuit of Kim Kelley, a sister in the ubiquitous Kelley clan and Bobby's girl friend. She was also out west, but never seemed to be near where the trains took them. On one leg of the trip they mistakenly got aboard an express fruit train from Los Angeles to San Antonio that did not stop for three days. "I thought we were going to die of thirst," Bobby said. "We were completely black by the time we got off the train because we'd been riding on the piggyback cars that were exposed to the air."

Even though they stayed in the meanest and cheapest places they could find, the money soon ran out. At times they panhandled or got odd jobs (once Bobby was a lumberjack near Seattle). At times they stayed in runaway homes. A scion of America's best-known family literally lived as a hobo for four months of his young life. At the end, the prodigal son was allowed home.

It was not much later, though, that he took off again for a half-year sojourn in the Peruvian Andes to study the Aymar Indians for his high school thesis. He has never quite exhausted his bent for adventure.

Some years later, Bobby looked back at that period and said: "I was a kid, just curious. I was trying to find some direction."

Settling down began at Harvard, where he learned to appreciate the stimulation of books and ideas and started to seek out his past. The most significant intellectual journey came as he researched an honors thesis on George Wallace, the Alabama governor who was a political foe of his father's. Bobby eventually turned the project into a study of Judge Frank Johnson, a path-breaking federal civil-rights jurist. The thesis was well received, and the Kennedy imprimatur helped turn it into a modest commercial success.

His close friend Peter Kaplan traces Bobby's personal interest in politics to a visit the two made to the Alabama Legislature when Bobby was researching his thesis. It was not long before Kennedy's presence was noted. Word spread quickly through the chamber, and politicians of all sorts rushed to meet him and exchange reminiscences about his father.

"To me that was the day of Bobby's coming of age," says Kaplan. "He had real rapport with them and he loved it. It was a completely political moment, and he saw what it was like to stand for something and be recognized for it. He was happy responding to the task of being a public person."

Of all the cousins he is the one most adept in a crowd. He is a gifted spinner of yarns, complete with Southern exaggerations, arm gyrations, and a folksiness that calls to mind Gary Cooper. He is at home in the backwoods of Alabama and the tenements of Bedford-Stuyvesant and the jungles of South America. He will walk into the seediest bar in the seediest neighborhood and instantly start swapping stories with the gang. He delights in sauntering through a jungle village charming children with his magic tricks. No matter where he is, Bobby is Pan leading the flock.

Still, he is plagued with ambivalence about his public role. In fact, he explains much of his contradictory behavior, which others love to find offensive and presumptuous—as his way of fending off the inevitable tug of his ancestry.

"I take a lot of risks with my life," he concedes, "saying things and doing things that I know I shouldn't do or will come to regret." Indeed, after one relatively brief sailing excursion with him, one shaken and none too pleased woman told a friend of Bobby's: "I don't know how much more of this I can take. Bobby is not happy unless he risks his life twice a day."

"I think that is a way of exposing myself to the possibility of cutting off the alternative—politics," Bobby says. "It is my way of putting my hand between history and me. That's why I have a strong affinity for Uncle Teddy. Both he and I are doing things we 'have' to do."

His sprinter's pace has been slowed a bit by his marriage to Emily Ruth Black, a beauty with husky voice and endless patience for Bobby's adventures. She has brought Bobby a stability that not even his closest friendships had been able to produce.

Yet there is still that chorus of voices whispering, "Run, Bobby, run." Lem was the leader of the chant while he was alive. His death in 1980, an emotionally devastating event to Bobby, did not silence the refrain. "People are always going to be recommending him and urging him to do it," says Kaplan. "He gets calls offering him a crack at politics the way the rest of us get calls offering life insurance."

His gravitation to politics has been tempered by his work in Manhattan District Attorney Robert Morgenthau's office, which he truly loves. The issues he faces there have sharpened his sense of the division of the world into good guys and bad guys and, just like his father, he has become fervent about stopping the bad guys.

New York City has been tough on him. His every move has made headlines—for instance, his failure, by one point, to pass the New York bar exam the first time he took it in 1982.

He is plainly still trying to make up his mind. The pull of politics seems to be growing stronger all the time, and it would be a natural decision for him to make. But few around him—much less Bobby himself—say he has finally bade goodbye to the peaceable, if wild, kingdom his animals represent.

Bobby Shriver Makes Up His Mind — for Now

ON THE DAY IN 1971 WHEN HE WAS ARRESTED ALONG WITH cousin Bobby Kennedy for smoking marijuana, Bobby Shriver phoned his father and did not quite know what to expect. Rage would have been appropriate, but that's not normally Sargent Shriver's way.

The elder Shriver flew up to Hyannis Port and sat his son down. "You were set up," he said, after he had heard Bobby's story about Andy the "taxi driver." Then he added: "But this is not good at all. Now, what are you going to do about it?"

To the boy, his father's action was stunningly compassionate. Only later, after he had studied family history in some detail, did Bobby Shriver realize that his father had handled the crisis exactly the way Grandpa Joe would have.

Even so, Bobby was angry with himself and frightened. The police officer appearing at his door one evening had paralyzed him. He had been dumb—really dumb, hurting himself and his family in the silliest possible teenage way. He was a teenager, of course, but he really was not silly, and now he had called public attention to himself and his family in a shameful way. That was the worst thing. He immediately saw that his behavior had far greater consequences than personal misery. No, it was not good, not good at all. Nothing like that would ever happen again, he and his parents resolved. It has not.

"They yanked his chain back a bit after the drug bust," one of Bobby's cousins remembers, "they" being his parents. "It really brought the whole Shriver family closer together and they worked and worked at making things good in their home. If you could pick a model of how two parents should behave in a crisis, the Shrivers would be the ones. They showed Bobby that they loved him and they helped him over the roughest spots. He knew he was never alone."

There was nothing surprising in how the Shrivers reacted. The only surprise was that Bobby had gotten into trouble at all. He was highly motivated and an excellent student. "He stood out in every way," recalls a lifelong friend, Neal Nordlinger, offering in evidence a sixth-grade anecdote. The science teacher had asked for volunteers for a noncredit extra project. "This kid with the glasses was the first one to raise his hand, and he was the only one who could decipher the workbook," says Nordlinger. "He was gregarious. His personality was electric, and he was very attractive. I remember others used to stand around watching him because he was so engaging."

This does not sound like the kind of boy who would get mixed up with cousin Bobby Kennedy and the "Hyannis Port Terrors" on such a stupid, dangerous outside project as dope—but Bobby Kennedy has an electric personality, too, and few teenagers of the late 'sixties and early 'seventies managed to escape all contact with drugs.

Bobby Shriver is a quick learner, though, and thereafter his chief contact with the law has been in studying it to become a lawyer. He is determined to achieve. "Bobby has been told from the beginning that he was put on this earth for a purpose and that eventually his maker is going to ask him if he did well by the gifts he was given," says Nordlinger. Bobby agrees: "I believe you have to justify yourself—otherwise there would be no point to it all."

For all his considerable gifts, Bobby probably feels more keenly than any of the other cousins a need to succeed. Those nearest him wonder if he will ever be satisfied with his own performance. "He has the most complete and seemingly satisfying life of any of us, but there is always an undercurrent of doubt in him whether he stacks up well," notes one of his closest relatives.

It is hard to see how he could have done better—or want more. Like cousin Bobby Kennedy, his natural peer and intrafamilial competitor, Bobby Shriver is a magnetic personality, full of brash good humor and a sure sense of his attractiveness to others. He cuts a dashing figure—tall, dark, and handsome, with a very engaging manner. He has his father's peripheral vision for spotting wallflowers and drawing them into his orbit.

He is comfortable to be around and comforting to those around him.

Like his father, he went to Yale, where he became fascinated with his Grandfather Kennedy's life—and not only with Joe's business dealings, but also the family environment he created. "How could it be," Bobby Shriver asks now, "that my grandfather arranged it so that none—absolutely none—of his children were interested in his work and did not even think about making money? Every child is interested in his father's job, yet he insulated that part of himself very thoroughly. They really never knew if he struggled with it, loved it, hated it." Despite his study, plus long discussions with his parents about the phenomenon, Bobby is still baffled by it—and loyal enough not to suggest that therein lies the source of the streak of financial illiteracy running through the family.

Young Shriver greatly admires the unswerving devotion that Grandpa Joe inspired in all his children. Many children from rich families renounce their backgrounds, but no Kennedy ever would have dreamed of doing so. What was Grandpa Joe's secret? Ignoring money within the family circle obviously was part of it, but Bobby Shriver still wrestles, inconclusively, with the problem.

After Yale, Bobby Shriver (the family name is an Anglicization of the German *Schreiber*, which means "writer") began a career as a reporter on a small newspaper in Annapolis, Maryland, but soon moved on to Chicago. He is still shocked by the attitude of his editor to a story he covered in those first days— the killing of a man in a slum district during a family quarrel. "It's a cheapie," the boss told him, instructing him to dismiss it in a couple of paragraphs.

Later Bobby moved on to the *Chicago Daily News,* and after that to the *Los Angeles Herald-Examiner.* He was always a general-assignment reporter, the backbone of any newspaper, although the work is often not very glamorous. He worked the overnight "lobster" shift in Chicago, freezing his joints at dead-of-winter fires on the North Side and broiling on midsummer hostage stakeouts. And he lived in a no-star hotel on his $125 a week salary.

Although he capitalizes on his star's magnetism, Shriver is a very hard worker according to Mary Ann Dolan, who was his editor at the *Herald Examiner* and is a diehard friend. "He is a wise guy—in both senses of the word," says Dolan. "The first time I met him he was a seventeen-year-old kid tagging along on a luncheon date. He had an expensive modish jacket and he spoke French to the waiter with a great gaudy flair. He is a wonderful, wandering collector of artifacts. The most important thing of all to him was that he always be learning. He has a fire in him to find out what is going on and what it is all about."

Despite the importance of the role, it is rare that a reporter will dominate a newsroom, but by all accounts that is exactly what Bobby did in Los Angeles. He was right out of *The Front Page*. His loud, imploring voice could be heard at every corner of the city room, begging for more information from a reluctant source on one phone while shouting directions to a street photographer on another, balanced with precarious symmetry on the opposite shoulder. Then it would be off to drink till dawn with his colleagues, regaling them with his great store of tall tales.

Because he was so good, he got many plum assignments, such as covering the Rolling Stones when their tour took them to L.A. "I kept him wandering the streets as much as I could, because he was the best at spotting things and making stories out of them," says Dolan. "He has a very sure eye, and he will ask anyone about anything if he's interested."

Still, in the end he could not accept being only a spectator, which is the reporter's doom. He could taste the political life as strongly as any of his cousins, and that was the main thing pulling him away from journalism.

"I began looking around me in Chicago and tried to see my future," he says now. "I just didn't see all that many 40-year-old reporters who still had the fire. I didn't know that I would ever be that angry or stay that angry to make my work worth while. The only one I saw who kept it up was Mike Royko, a *Chicago Sun-Times* columnist, and I did not have the anger he did. The only real way to make a difference, I guessed, was to run the place.

"That was the other thing. Good reporters, if they stay good, are so angry that they cannot be in the the power circle. I was brought up in the power circle. People would invite me to their parties and to ski in Aspen because of who I was. Mike Royko should get the same invitations because he has a lot more to say than I do, but he never will because of what he feels. That is what makes him the king of reporters, and I just didn't see myself able to do that."

On the day he left the *Herald-Examiner* for law school, another reporter commented to Mary Ann Dolan, "What are we going to do without Bobby? It's so quiet around here."

But his obvious choice was to follow the ordained Kennedy path to law school. That was also the problem. He did not want to be just another Kennedy going to law school. Yet law school was clearly the best preparation for public service. What to do? In the end he decided that law school it had to be.

"Education was a mess when I was an undergraduate," he explains. "It was unfocused and coming out of the struggle of the 'sixties. When I looked at the writing of really learned people, I realized how much I had shortchanged myself. Yale was set up so that anyone who was sufficiently glib could get through and do well. I was angry at the whole system and at myself for being so behind, and it seemed to me that law school was the best way to work my mind into shape. It wasn't until I got to law school that I figured out that there is a struggle involved in this business of learning."

Another impetus toward law school was an experience with the law when Bobby was working for the *Herald-Examiner*. One of his license plates was stolen, but the reporter didn't report it to the authorities. Two weeks later, the police called him in for questioning. A car carrying his license plate had been involved in a hit-run death. He was able to establish fairly easily that he was not involved, yet the incident showed him how even the most benign interrogation can be frightening.

Bobby Shriver is an array of contradictions. He is dazzled by celebrity, yet reticent about being a celebrity. Making money intrigues him, and he has announced a determination to do so, yet he is scrupulous about serving the less fortunate.

He has dated a number of beautiful young women, including a good many celebrities and socialites, but says he has no marriage plans. He seems content to be at the center of any stage he happens to be on, yet wants to create his own stage.

His life to date contrasts most markedly with Bobby Kennedy's—especially after the drug bust, when their paths diverged. Bobby Shriver moved back into the circle of his family and concentrated on achievement. Bobby Kennedy set out on a years-long course of rebellion against established patterns, familial and educational. Now they are totally different person-alities. An admirer of both characterizes Shriver as "lawyerly, thoughtful, serious, purposeful and careful," and Kennedy as "earthy, emotional, and fearless—he acts on his gut."

Bobby Shriver has also thought about the distinctions: "I am much more tentative and questioning. Bobby Kennedy does things instinctively. He is sure he can do things he has never tried. It is a powerful trait. It is the same as they say about good banks. Banks that have no bad loans are not good banks because they are not aggressive enough. Well, I don't have many bad loans, and Bobby Kennedy has many more bad loans. He has dared to do so much more than I have. It has gotten him into more trouble, but it is the thing that makes him unique. He will never back down."

Although he's made his big decision, self-doubt still gnaws Bobby Shriver. He misses writing, although he decided he could never be a Royko or a V. S. Naipaul, a novelist whose work he also admires. But he sees no sure achievement in law: "The lawyers in my father's day were the cutting edge," he says, "but it is not that way anymore. Lawyers more often stand in the way now."

So Bobby Shriver continues the search. He sees it as an analogy with tennis, his big sport, and what he learned from watching the best players: "They had a little extra something. Some people work their way to that point, others are born with it. That is what I am looking for—the thing where I am the one who has 'it.' "

Reluctant Princess Caroline

INNOCENT AND UNKNOWING, CAROLINE KENNEDY HAD A vision almost from the time she began to think about her life—that important period between ages eight and ten when memory and reason start coming into focus. Her dream was that somehow it would all end, the curiosity and the intrusions. She believed, she told select friends, that she would reach a magic day when she could be free of it.

The dream died hard. And when it became clear how futile it was, she wondered aloud to her intimates like Andy Karsch: "Why? I haven't written a book. I haven't sung a song. I haven't acted a part. I haven't run a race. I haven't done anything. I'm just famous for my name and they won't leave me alone."

With regret, she made her adjustments.

In 1977, when she was working at the New York *Daily News*, a young man took Caroline to see a Broadway musical. In the cab he noticed that she was growing perturbed.

"What's the matter?" he finally asked.

"I really hate to be indoors," she confessed. "You don't know what will happen to you and you have so little control. I don't know who'll sit next to me or who will recognize me, and the feeling is confining."

They got out of the cab several blocks before the theater, timing their arrival as the lights went down. Then, at the intermission, she bolted from her seat before the lights went up, explaining hurriedly: "I'm going to hide in the bathroom until after."

Even with those precautions, the man behind her date grabbed his shoulder as intermission began and exclaimed: "Hey! Isn't that Caroline Kennedy you're with?" He laughed it off: "Nah. But doesn't she look just like Caroline?"

That is one side of Caroline Kennedy, the nation's unwilling princess. She is always leaving through the back door. But there is another side—lively, charming, disarming, even serene. Richard Licata, who worked alongside Caroline at the *Daily News*, also in 1977, recalls that once he was checking out a tip that a certain adult home in the Bronx was riddled with abuses. He told this to Caroline, and she was intrigued with the idea of helping. One night they drove in her BMW to the home. They passed quietly over fences and through guarded doors, and were able to get some clandestine interviews with staff and residents, confirming bad management and wretched conditions.

Caroline loved the undercover work, and was pleased with the results—prominent play of the story under Licata's byline that prompted a shutdown of the facility.

Ironically, the place was the Joseph P. Kennedy Adult Home— but not officially connected in any way with the family. That delighted Caroline too.

Caroline Kennedy's life has been shouted through a megaphone. No gesture is too insignificant, nor is any event too trifling to avoid consuming interest. She snaps a few photos and she is the next Margaret Bourke White. She writes for the college paper and she is Mary McGrory or Flora Lewis. She goes on a date and she is engaged. Nothing is real because everything is overdone.

She once told some friends, including Maura Moynihan, that she sensed that many of those around her at Harvard hoped she would fail. There was much talk behind her back and, though it pained her, she realized she simply had to live with it. "There eventually came a point when she got a grip on the notion that she could do nothing about the gossips," says Moynihan. "It is marvelous the way she ignores it now. She has a very strong constitution."

The discovery of this was difficult, though, and it distorted some of Caroline's wishes. She really was interested in photography and journalism when she first started mulling her career choices. Yet every time she stuck her nose outside the door the mob sent her into reverse.

Journalist Pete Hamill, who briefly dated Jackie, tried to help Caroline's writing career. He took Caroline to Nashville with him to help him cover Elvis Presley's funeral. She was the only reporter allowed into Presley's home, and she feverishly canvassed the mourners for their reactions. At first she was not recognized, but when she was, that was the end of the reporting. Wherever she is, she becomes the story.

Her father, of course, had toyed with being a journalist, and her mother had been a newspaper photographer. Still, it is hard to believe she thought she could have worked as a reporter without seeing the irony that it would make her a working part of the publicity machine—especially at a scene like the Presley funeral—and that this was what she had spent her life fleeing.

In her fitful efforts in the news business, before she got it out of her system, she also traveled to Appalachia and the Middle East with television film crews covering the life of Arab tycoon Adnan Khashoggi (who billed himself as another "Onassis") and even signed up for a cub reporter's job next to cousin Bobby Shriver for the *Los Angeles Herald-Examiner* before backing out when other reporters got all over the story and drove her away.

She came to feel that her only choice was retreat, and so she has retreated, settling fairly comfortably into the special projects section of New York's Metropolitan Museum of Art, handling television and other media presentations of the museum's works. It is quiet and unobtrusive and indulges her passion for art and art history.

"She is very loyal, witty, intelligent, fun, and warm," says Maura Moynihan. "Her greatest wish is to lead a private life like an ordinary person, working nine-to-five, watching television, eating popcorn and making no big deal about things. She is a model to a lot of her friends—a very impressive young woman."

Equally important, she has become involved with a man who represents a new direction for her, Edwin Schlossberg, a middle-aged cultural historian with eclectic interests ranging from art to the history of science. He has written, for instance, a fictional account about a conversation between Albert Einstein and Samuel Beckett, devised children's museum exhibits and a popular book about computers. Caroline's romance with him has separated her from long-standing friends of her own age and background. "It is a bit of a rebellion," says an old friend who has not seen much of her since she met Schlossberg. "It is a way of getting out from under the family boot." That is a reference to the extended family, not her nuclear family. Jackie seems to like Schlossberg, perhaps because he is not at all athletic.

At some cost, Caroline seems to have achieved some serenity

about her notoriety. Licata recalls one day when they were out for a walk. A deranged man spotted and shouted. "They should have shot your whole family."

Licata was shocked, but Caroline just passed it off with "Oh, I get that all the time. There are just as many people who tell me how wonderful my father was, and that makes up for it."

"There was something very soulful about her," Licata says. "She was in touch with things that would drive the rest of us mad. She always looked at the bright side and tended to slough the worst of it off. There was no sense of urgency in her and a great kind of self-control. She had to be a politician to negotiate things in everyday life—who to be with, who to turn down, where to go and where to avoid. And she was very adept at it."

Another side of her is impulsive and spontaneous. She loves to take off and explore different parts of the city with friends and will occasionally insist—with a jarring phone call—that they do it with her at 4 A.M.

She is very considerate of friends, sending flowers and candy all over the world when she has heard good news about someone or if she knows they need a boost. Steve Smith was spending Christmas 1981 alone because he had law school exams while his family was off skiing. She called to invite him for dinner and had Jackie and John buy presents to ease his loneliness.

She can be whimsical. On more than one occasion she has asked a male friend out, then told him she would tip off the *New York Post* about it so that he would get a big play as her new true love.

She is not above a little adventure, either. Like many of her cousins, she experimented with marijuana in the days when it was as common on campus as illiteracy. One time a date dropped her home after a roaring party where she was as tooted as anyone else. Instead of chewing her date out, Jackie told the young man: "Next time you have a party that's so much fun, I want to be invited."

Caroline, like all Kennedys, voices few regrets. "I've met the movie stars I liked," she says, "and I've met kings and queens and heads of state. It's been fun. There are advantages." She also relishes the history behind it, too. "It was uncanny how you'd begin a story and she'd know all about it—even the most obscure anecdotes," an older friend of Jack Kennedy remembers. "She'd ask questions about everything—from the biggest policy events like the Cuban missile crisis to stories from the campaign trail. Nothing was too trivial."

Many years later, when she worked as an intern in Ted Kennedy's Senate office, Caroline made a pilgrimage to the house on N Street in Georgetown where her family lived before they moved to the White House. She made several passes back and forth in front of it and later told a friend: "I just went back home. It was very strange. I remembered a lot more than I thought I would."

From the time of her father's murder, her initial responses to any new circumstance or person was guarded. John Seigenthaler characterizes it as "a very healthy cynicism of the world on the one side and on the other a human trustfulness of the people who contributed to what her father and her uncle were all about."

What she always has wished for most fervently she never can have—escape from the consequences of her notoriety. Theresa Fitzpatrick remembers the first time she met Caroline. She said, "Nice to meet you," and thought no more about it. But when Caroline was leaving, she thanked Theresa. "For what?" Theresa asked, puzzled. "You didn't say, 'So you're the President's daughter,' " Caroline replied.

Maria—Beauty at the Crossroads

"SHE STARTED TO SING AS SHE TACKLED THE THING THAT couldn't be done—and she did it."

Maria Shriver is always doing unusual things, as these lines from the opening of her undergraduate thesis suggest. She is making a career in television, a first in the family. And she has a Republican body-builder boyfriend, a very large first.

The thesis, about Jack Kennedy's presidential campaign, originally had as its premise that Jack's Catholic faith was not a political liability, but in fact, in a secularized America, something of an asset. Catholics were aching to have "one of their own" elected, and the Protestant majority was so ashamed of its previous bigotry that Kennedy would actually benefit from a backlash of tolerance. At least, that is how Maria saw it—at first.

It soon became apparent, though, that she had been wrong. The evidence suggested that anti-Catholic feeling still had been powerful. The question became how to retreat gracefully.

"Although I am optimistic, ambitious and daring, I am not foolish," Maria says. "Realistically, there were too many facts going against my belief that JFK's religion had been an asset. Yet a quitter I am not."

So she modified her arguments, hung onto as much of the original material as she could and wrote an honors-graded thesis.

As youngsters, when the Kennedy cousins staged a show, Maria was inevitably the star. In *The Wizard of Oz* she was Dorothy. In *Cinderella* she got the title role. It helped, of course, that she did much of the script-writing, assisted in the costume-making, and directed the others—whether they thought they needed it or not.

She is Eunice's daughter as well as her close friend. Her first concern about anything is: Will it fly in the family? She has never taken a drug, does not drink, and is rhapsodic about her parents: "My parents did the most incredible thing of all—they raised five children who are best friends."

This has not stopped Maria from going her own way with a determination to succeed that is the equal of any Kennedy male. She is not to be crossed, because she has the strongest will of any of the cousins. "I had a famous grandfather, a famous father and mother, five famous uncles, and 28 famous cousins," she explains. "There comes a time for everyone when they have to decide if they are just going to fit in the niche or whether they are going to go out on their own. I wanted to do something that nobody else had done—apart from law school, apart from politics."

She has parlayed her drive, her name and her dark, Sophia Loren-like beauty into a successful television broadcasting career. It was an interest that derived, she says, from her study of her Uncle Jack's presidential victory, which in great measure was attributable to his astute exploitation of television. Her work in Uncle Ted's 1980 campaign clinched her belief that television "is the power in politics now."

Television was a natural medium for her, as well. The way of life of broadcasters closely parallels that of politicians—the back-room maneuvering, the Gypsy-like traveling, the groupies, the need to communicate. Maria learned early how important it is to get the message across. Also, television is glamorous, and so is Maria.

After college she signed up for a Westinghouse television production training course, beginning off camera in places such as Baltimore and Philadelphia. Eventually she worked her way on camera as a hostess of the network's *PM Magazine.*

Colleagues attribute her success to hard work and professional refinement. She took extensive voice and dramatic lessons to master the art of informal chatter, and she dieted away some excess weight with remarkable architectural results. After a year off for her Uncle Ted's presidential campaign, she settled in Hollywood, again with *PM Magazine.* She reports mainly on celebrity doings in the movie capital—hardly the moral center of the universe, especially for a Shriver—but she hopes to get into documentaries.

"I wanted something beyond the things that people associated with the family," she says, and resents the whispers that she is trading on that connection.

Her answer was to work harder. "She would literally work three days in a row without sleep," reports Baltimore colleague Oprah Winfrey. "It was an obsession with her that people respect her effort and her work. Everybody else was living on pills and anything that would keep them going, but Maria did it on sheer grit."

There was also the reverse discrimination. Skeptics who thought she had used her name to get where she was did not hesitate to ask her to use it for their own ends, chiefly in getting celebrities she might know onto the show. She refused.

Her obsession with achievement consumed every ounce of her energy, however, and she eventually saw that it was cutting into other things she thought were equally as precious. "It ended up being harmful, because I lost touch with the world beyond my work," she says—including the family.

Not for long, though, do the Shrivers allow one of their own to stray, and they didn't let Maria. She also got encouragement from iron-pumper Arnold Schwarzenegger, "Mr. Everything" and now prosperous actor and business tycoon. They met at a Kennedy tennis tournament and waged a bicoastal romance for several years until Maria got the Los Angeles television slot. Their biggest problem now is meshing two careers, but at least they are now in the same part of the world.

Many people thought of Schwarzenegger as just a sometime fling, but Maria is not a sometime woman. This is serious business, and she and the Austrian expatriate—he arrived in the United States only with the money he had on his person—have been deeply attached for six years. Arnold's stout Republicanism makes it more piquant.

Maria has told others that the difference in their backgrounds is the thing that makes their relationship work. She is in awe of what Arnold has done. "Look at all this," she told a friend once as they walked around his mansion. "He did it all himself. He had nothing and he has built this in a few years. It's so different from what I knew. I had all this to start."

Schwarzenegger also is emotionally strong and, according to Maria's friends, one of the few men in her life ever able to assert himself. For him it was much the same. He needed no wilting flower, and Maria is not that. Moreover, he has passed the crucial Shriver tests. After initial suspicions were eased he has become a favorite at the Shriver home. He won the ultimate compliment from Sargent when he was given a dog named

Conan after the barbarian character Schwarzenegger played in a hit movie. "Sarge loves his dogs nearly as much as his kids, so that means he thinks pretty highly of Arnold," notes one of Maria's friends. Arnold is similarly close to Bobby Shriver, another must in the tight-knit family.

The younger Shrivers and many of Maria's cousins are in awe of what one of them called "the perfect catch." Even to a family of doers, Arnold has big muscles, fiscally as well as physically. Beginning with body-building, he has built a fortune on prudent investments, and he is a charming companion with lively intelligence and humor. He and Maria and Ted Kennedy's press secretary Bob Shrum were walking through the streets of Georgetown one recent summer day when a pedestrian approached them and asked, "Hey, aren't you Arnold Schwarzenegger?" Without missing a beat, Schwarzenegger pointed at Shrum, who in his heyday weighed about as much as the muscleman but in far different proportion, and said, "No. He is."

Marriage? Family? Maria hungers for these with an appetite that is almost visible. She is at a crossroads in her life: Career and family? Career or family?

Michael — the Pointman

A COUPLE OF YEARS AGO, A HOT-DOG SKIER CARELESSLY BAR-
reling down one of the tougher trails at Aspen sliced across the
ski tips of an older woman and flashed on without even an
"Excuse me." He probably did not hear the shout, "Get him,
Michael," but he certainly felt the effect when a furious bundle
of energy overtook him and slammed into him from a racer's
crouch, knocking him down. The hot dog rose for revenge, but
just as he was drawing back his ski pole to slash Michael, he
was hit from behind by another attacker, Ethel, who grabbed
him by the throat and, along with Michael, completed the rout
of the hot dog. Ethel, of course, had been the woman offended
at the beginning of the adventure.

That is what happens when you tussle with the Kennedys.

Michael Kennedy will challenge anybody or anything. Nothing seems to perturb Robert and Ethel's middle son. Everyone
seems to have a favorite Michael story, and they are mainly
admiring. Bobby and Stevie Smith are both excellent skiers,
too, but when it comes to the sheer drop of Harvey's Rock at
Aspen, they will stand back with the others to watch Michael
soar from the precipice and swish away under the chair lift,
cutting a neat slipstream through the powder.

"The rest of us could do that," says Bobby, "But it is such a
beautiful thing to see him do it that we would not want to follow
and blemish his path. We are all proud of him."

"He's the only person I've ever seen who can be completely
calm suspended in midair 70 feet off the ground," adds Bobby,
only slightly exaggerating. Sometimes he thinks Michael has a
death wish, but Steve Smith thinks its just Michael's "way of
achieving distinction in the family. It's crazy, but there's nothing
sinister to it."

Everyone still talks about the time when, as a young teenager, Michael jumped from a 75-foot cliff during a raft trip down the treacherous Snake River in Wyoming at a point where it was not clear how much water was beneath him. "He landed almost flat on his stomach and nearly broke his whole body," Steve says. "There were huge welts all over him, but it didn't faze him in the least."

Was it foolhardy? Admirable? Dumb? Courageous? No one knows, but if Michael did it, it is okay with the Kennedys, and they never ask why. So someone else did. "Because I like to," he replied.

Michael's daring and buoyancy set him apart as field marshal in a family of generals. Every time they go on rafting expeditions, Michael commands the lead raft, guiding the others through the rapids. "He's never tipped a boat," says brother Bobby with both pride and envy.

Also, it was Michael who set up the obstacle course for special occasions at Hickory Hill—such as the annual pet show. He would deliberately design it to such an Olympian standard, says younger brother Chris, that only he of all the family could complete it, the rope climbs just so high, the swings just so far apart. Even professional athletes such as Washington Redskins quarterback Joe Theisman were humbled by Michael.

Despite his daring, Michael is a straight arrow—good student, good athlete, good sport, good citizen. His academic route from St. Paul's School to Harvard to the University of Virginia Law School has largely duplicated the standard family march. Still unformed, his career plans seem to be pointing toward a standard legal apprenticeship followed by public service and perhaps a judicial post.

Like other third-wave Kennedys, Michael early on developed a lasting attachment to a woman—Victoria Gifford, attractive daughter of football star Frank. They were married in 1981 and Michael LeMoyne Kennedy, Jr., was born early in 1983. Michael and Vicky's romance is almost a carbon copy of RFK's and Ethel's. Close friends say that Vicki is another determined woman who saw what she wanted and never relaxed until he saw it too.

To many of Robert Kennedy's contemporaries, Michael is a living memory of his father, in looks as well as mannerisms—the full head of tawny hair, all those teeth, the wiry frame, the delivery, even the voice. In a family of fighters, he is the conciliator, charming everyone. He was the one, for instance, who remained close to David throughout his ordeal and tried to patch things up between David and others in the family who had tangled with him.

His college roommate Lorenzo di Bonaventura tells of the time he and Michael, on a school project, found themselves on New York's Bowery in the dead of winter. They came upon a derelict passed out in a doorway. Michael got him a pair of shoes to replace the rags he had on his feet, and, as Lorenzo tells it, "I was so repulsed I couldn't touch his feet, but Michael knelt over him for several minutes, cleaning his feet and putting the shoes on."

Michael is one of the serious students of family history and he did it for a purpose. "At Harvard I always felt I should know all the criticisms of my Uncle Jack's administration," he says. "There were a lot. People would say his administration was reckless and prone to brinksmanship—because at Harvard revisionism was popular. So I took it upon myself to learn everything I could about that period. I felt I had to defend him, not by getting the hairs up on the back of my neck, but in a scholarly way. The more I studied, the more I believed in what he did. I think I was independent enough that if I really disagreed with him I would have said so, but I never found a case where I disagreed with him."

That is a typically Michael-like formulation—thoughtful, discreet, and protective. He is the careful one among those in the RFK home when it comes to upholding the family honor. He is a toned-down, perhaps shrewder version of his older brother Bobby.

Possibly because he has so securely notched a high rank in the family, Michael is completely serene. Juan Cameron, his close friend, recalls a long conversation with Michael in the summer of 1982 during which Michael rhapsodized about his past, his marriage, the baby on its way. What great fortune he had in his life! His family and friends—they were of the kind every person should have. For the undemonstrative Kennedys, it was an unusual exposure of emotion.

"I felt like he wanted to hug me," says Juan. "He had taken stock of his life and he wanted to share his discovery that it really was good."

Tim in Search of Anonymity

ON JULY 4, 1981, ONE OF WASHINGTON'S LARGEST DEPART-
ment stores took out a full-page newspaper ad to reprint the
Declaration of Independence. Tim Shriver clipped it and took
it next day to the high school equivalency class he taught at
Lorton Prison.

"Most of them knew nothing about it," he says, referring to
his students. "They'd never heard of it and never seen it. They
had no perception that we had once been colonies and we fought
for principles to become independent. They didn't know that
the city of Washington got its name from the general who won
the war and then became President. They didn't know about
'all men being created equal.' Their eyes just popped out. They
all asked for copies of the thing to post in their classrooms. It
was a stunning experience."

Equally stunning—and pleasant to Tim—was that the students did not know who he was, either. That was fine with Tim.
Tim Shriver has set out on an unusual journey for a Kennedy—
destination anonymity.

He completely embraces the family dedication to service—
with a vengeance. He just does not think any fuss should be
made about it. When bureaucracy derailed his chance to work
full time at Lorton, he shrugged and went back to New Haven—
like most Shriver men, he's a Yalie—where he landed two plum
jobs, one with an agency helping sexually abused children, the
other lifting academic standards for gifted poor children. Tim's
combined pay is $20,000 a year, on which he lives. The Park
Agency, the Kennedy family's private bank, pays the taxes,
however.

To this day some people, in the family and out, do not believe
he is serious about this way of life, but he is. Tim is happy to

be apart from the mainline family scene in New York, Boston, Hyannis Port, and Washington, and he has no interest in going to law school, tantamount to heresy for Kennedy males. He likes what he is doing and where he is doing it:

"I love New Haven. I have a tendency to look for things that aren't conventional because everybody else is in New York going to these big parties and doing glamorous things. That's sort of dumb to me. I end up sounding wonderful, and I don't mean to sound that way, because it's not some sort of altruistic thing I'm doing here. I just would much rather meet normal people and do normal things here in New Haven."

Some of Tim's maverick independence could be traced to the notion that he is a younger son in a family where the older is a star. Both his father and older brother Bobby were big byliners on the *Yale Daily News*, for instance. Tim says he just did not think he could measure up.

At another level, though, his life so far offers a splendid example of the proposition that you can be a Kennedy and not be a lawyer, a politician, a star athlete, a publicity hound, or even rich—and still be quite happy. He has something the other cousins talk about a lot, somewhat wistfully, but would most probably never accept: a life apart. "I wanted fulfillment on a personal level rather than in a family setting where people think I've traded on my name," he explains. "I wouldn't want people to make a big thing out of me because of my last name. It's important to do things on my own. It was regurgitated around our house: You're so lucky and that's why more is expected of you. I guess that's the part I'm trying to live up to."

Yet he would challenge those who think he is something special. "I don't consider my work some kind of great sacrificial act," he insists. "Yes, I like the job, but I'm not going to heaven. I'm not justified by my position. I don't feel that in any sense, social or otherwise. There is a simplistic view that, 'Oh Timmy, he does good things and the rest us do normal things.' "

The cousins and his friends call him The Priest. Although they say it good-naturedly, Tim takes it seriously, and hasn't ruled out the possibility. His home, car, and office are stocked with religious effects and decorated with quotes from the Bible. "He thinks about his religion as it applies to every aspect of his life, and he is intent on carrying out its prescriptions," says his friend, Linda Potter. "His theology is very Catholic. You love God and you love each other. He exudes those beliefs."

Tim, on his religion: "I enjoy it. I've learned a lot. It helps me grow and have faith. I don't see it as anything special. Those who don't practice their faith as much as I are just as much a part of the divine plan as I am. We all have callings. It's just that some are called in different ways. I'm no saint, for sure, but I like the mass and I enjoy going to it."

Tim is no dour bluenose. Darkly handsome and built like an oak, he loves parties and is a true Kennedy in his love of bone-crunching sport, in his case rugby. Nor does he mind a few beers afterward.

Tim is content to be a teacher and counselor. His friend Bob Brown says Tim has a firm, disciplined hand with those he helps. "He is not a bleeding-heart liberal," notes Brown. "He believes you have to be willing to carry the ball yourself. He will help you, but, ultimately, he thinks everybody should take responsibility for his own life."

So when Tim's charges trashed a dormitory in which they were living for a summer education program, he came down heavily on them. And when cousin John Kennedy—for whom Tim has been a brother and dear friend—was slacking off a bit in his own counseling duties one year when they worked together, Tim laid the law down to him too, and a quick adjustment was made. The other cousins loved it because Tim lives by a solidly conceived set of rules. But he also fights determinedly for those he thinks can make it, even if they do not quite live up to all his rules. Brown remembers his working extra hours and making extra house calls for one youth who was flunking the program, but had great potential that was never realized. Despite Tim's best efforts the young man left New Haven for a relative's home and then was able to cope with his school work. "The issue died hard with Tim," says Brown. "He really wanted that boy to make it here and it was tough for him to see that the boy just could not do it. Tim is a very special young man—full of love and idealism. He is the hardest worker I know and, heaven knows, he doesn't have to be here."

Tim wants to extract from the world the small victories that, in their way, are as satisfying as the big victories his Kennedy kindred have achieved. He positively enthuses over a program he developed in 1982 to get parents from poor families more involved in their children's school work. Brown notes that it was Tim's infectious idealism that convinced those in his social service agency to try the once-discarded idea of parent support groups to show sometimes struggling families they are not the only ones battling with their children, and there are ways to solve discipline and homework problems.

He had to convince a major insurance company to give his agency a grant to fund some extra programs he had conceived, and he did it—through channels, never using his name. He says he did throw his weight around once, though. That was when the handyman in his apartment building asked if Tim knew of a full-time job that had complete health and pension benefits. "I tried pretty hard for him and we ended up getting him a place," says Tim. "Do I think that was wrong? I don't know, really, but I'd do it over again." Tim truly works at being effacing, the only problem being that people tend to think he is grand and he does not want to be seen that way.

Tim's quest for independence is summed up in a small but revealing story he tells about his decision to lobby a Connecticut congressman for help with his social service agency. "I think obviously he knew my name and therefore my family and that's too bad," he said. "I wouldn't want it that way. I think I can do more on my own." He got the assistance he sought.

Kara — the Making of a Woman

"ONE LOOK IN THOSE EYES AND I KNEW," SAYS LINDA SEMANS of the day she first met Kara Kennedy, "this was a kid who knew how to have fun." That was in the eighth grade at the Cathedral School in Washington eight years ago. Linda and Kara are still best friends, and the glint is still there in those great green eyes.

Yet when Linda first saw Kara, Kara must have been wondering what the words "having fun" meant. Most of her young life had been taken up with the consequences of crisis. As much as children can, she had suffered the consequences of the killings of her two uncles. In between those shocks, her own father had nearly been killed in a plane crash in 1964. Five years later, his character and career had been smirched by Chappaquiddick, when she was nine. Her youngest brother, Patrick, suffered perpetually from aggravated asthma, and the older one, Teddy, was threatened with death when he lost a leg to cancer. The last trauma was the longest and in many ways the worst—her mother was drinking her life away.

Kara does not talk about the emotional effects of all this, but the impact was powerful. Physically she was the healthiest person in her very unhealthy home. Emotionally, she was very troubled for a while, as any child would be under such circumstance. Still, in coping with these problems, she grew up most appealingly. "Kara's story is the nicest in the family," insists her friend Linda. "She could have absolutely been crushed, but instead she grew."

The story begins in the middle with Teddy's illness. The impact of his cancer operation and fretful recovery was dramatic. Kara began it in mortal fear. The 13-year-old girl assumed she could contract the same dreaded cancer, and she had terrifying nightmares about her own death. It was a relatively short period of a few months, but the effect lingered. Her only salvation—as well as Teddy's—was to concentrate on helping him get well. That was what her father encouraged her to do. "Teddy needs us now and you can't let him down," he would say. It had just the right impact, for she soon threw her energy into Teddy's recuperation and thought less of her own worries. First, she learned to cry. Then she learned to laugh, in part to encourage Teddy. And most of all, she became very maternal toward both her younger brothers, perhaps because Joan was not well enough to be so.

"She was very mature about it and very protective of them," says her friend Cindy O'Brien. "Kind of a mother hen, but in a helpful way. She was always available to them and looking out for them. Teddy's operation really drew them together."

In addition to Teddy's operation the children were trying to cope with their mother's disease. They do not talk about it now, but the mosaic of their lives pieced together by outsiders is a classic one for children of alcoholics. Contemporaries of their parents remember them as deeply troubled and confused. Their peers suspect they were embarrassed. Like many children of alcoholics they had some moments of resentment and other moments when they wondered if they or their father were to blame. Their self-criticism was hard and penetrating.

It was a portrait in futility. Every so often the children would organize searches of the house or enlist the help of the staff to find what they thought were their mother's hidden bottles, believing that if they destroyed them or confronted their mother with them that somehow she would see the light. The efforts sometimes produced evidence, but they were utterly fruitless in result. Their frustration did not end until they came to grips with the essential notion that their mother was sick—in her own way as sick as Teddy had been with cancer.

Joan responded to her drinking problem with a multitude of therapies that tried to combat the "reason" for her drinking, rather than the drinking itself. For years she was in and out of rehabilitation centers that never worked. She would be sober for a few days or even weeks, then she would slip back. Outside intrusions always threatened, like the time some members in one of her group-therapy programs sold their version of her supposedly confidential revelations to one of the grocery store tabloids.

Her children rode an emotional roller coaster during the period, delighted with each indication of progress, distraught at every defeat. Through the worst of it their father counseled patience. "There was no rancor in him," said a former aide. "He just wanted the children not to fall to pieces after it became clear that she was not going to stop drinking quickly. 'Be patient,' he told them. 'Be patient with your mother.' "

As Joan revealed in a celebrated magazine interview: "It doesn't happen overnight; it just creeps up little by little. But it is so insidious that you don't really think about it as it is happening. For the moment, it blots out reality. It blots out a lot of things that you don't really want to look at."

Her salvation came when she left the hotbed of Washington for the relative serenity of Boston. In the summer of 1977 she joined Alcoholics Anonymous, accepted the bedrock assertion that her life had become unmanageable because of alcohol, and took the pledge.

Many who are close to the family credit all the children, but Kara especially, for support and devotion after Joan went to live by herself and joined A.A. When Kara was in Boston she would go regularly to A.A. meetings with Joan and at least once stood up to tell her own "story" about dealing with her mother's problem. It is said to have been loving, candid, even funny.

"She was the first to take an active interest and show real concern for her mother. Once she understood that it was critical for the whole family to become involved she was very committed to helping her mother any way she could," says an admiring friend. "She was her mother's chief emotional supporter." For her father, she stitched a wall hanging of the A.A. "serenity prayer"—one of the foundations of the program and a reminder that alcoholics and their families are urged to repeat when the going gets tough: GOD GRANT ME THE SERENITY TO ACCEPT THE THINGS I CANNOT CHANGE, THE COURAGE TO CHANGE THE THINGS I CAN, AND THE WISDOM TO KNOW THE DIFFERENCE.

It hangs on the wall of Ted Kennedy's Senate office.

Eventually the other children too took an active part in their mother's recovery. They worked, along with their father, in a private family program that was devised for them in part because they could never be sure when they went to meetings of A.A. or Al-Anon (the support group of A.A. relatives) that their anonymity would be preserved.

"They rallied round her and loved her and supported her during the most trying times," Father James English recalls.

One other major problem for Kara was the miserable public perception of who she was. As a former boyfriend and still friend, John Florescu, tells it, "She was a composite of a few stories about her that portrayed her as a confused, neglected, and errant child. When I met her, the person underneath the image was composed, not terribly self-assured, and completely lacking in vengeance."

She had been portrayed as a chronic runaway and a drug abuser, but had never been either. The one time she "ran away" came after a tiff with governess Theresa Fitzpatrick over the standard "I'm going to a party"—"Oh no, you're not" battles. Her escape lasted until 1 A.M. the following morning—not even overnight—when she called home to be picked up from a friend's house.

The drug question concerned Ted Kennedy more. Family members and friends say Kara was never in trouble with drugs, nor was she anything more than an infrequent recreational user of marijuana. Still, her father worried that she might get into trouble and that her use of pot, no matter how light, stemmed from other problems. So he tried in his way to shepherd her through the toughest period and at times arranged for her to see others when he sensed she could not tell him everything that was troubling her. "He agonized over Kara and knew the pressures that were on her as the woman of the house," said one associate. "He tried to make it clear that he wanted to fight at her side, but he realized she needed something different from that at times."

Ted Kennedy's campaign loss in 1980 set his children's lives on a wholly different course. It helped them mature and it liberated them. Actually, the process had begun before the campaign started when the senator sounded out alcoholism experts about his wife's prognosis. He was told that the whole family had to become more involved in supporting her and dealing with their own reactions to her drinking. That was when the family program was set up and everyone started to do what Kara had been doing for some time—confronting the problem.

It was during this precampaign period that the children began to probe their parents' relationship in delicate ways. Their father sensed what they were asking and, for the first time, explored with them what had happened. He loved their mother, he said, and he was sorry they were not all together as a family. He conceded that it hurt him and he said he knew it hurt them and if he could wave all the pain away he would. Their best hope was to love and support their mother and pray for the best.

The campaign united them strongly one last time, but it also was the catalyst for their dissolution. Joan gained enough strength and self-esteem from it to begin her own exploration of the future. When she and the senator finally discussed their marriage, after many years of avoiding the issue, they decided rather quickly that the best thing was to split up.

Since then, despite the separation and divorce, they have blossomed as a family. "Things were closed off for a while between us, but it has been great since the campaign," says Patrick. Of his mother: "She has really come back and made a great recovery. We really have been getting to know each other in a way that I couldn't when things were worse. Now it's just like the old days.

"We've caught up on a lot. We took a trip to the Holy Land [in December, 1982], just the two of us, and that was the best time we have ever spent together. You know, when you have little hassles, like losing your luggage or getting stuck in traffic jams, you just learn a lot about the people you are with. My mother and I kind of discovered each other on that trip. We shared a lot together."

They are quite giddy at times about their mother's recovery, says one friend of the children. "Hey, you guys, look at my mother!" they seem to be saying to all. "That's the mother we remember."

Patrick, too, has started to come out of his shell. He has largely overcome the wasting asthma and has shown a good deal of Kennedy "vigah." In the autumn of 1982 he played football for his school, the Fessenden School in Boston, and won the Fessenden trophy for being the "most spirited" on the team. In addition, he has thumbed his nose at his doctors in typical Kennedy fashion and started on the wrestling team in the 105-pound-weight class.

"Teddy will pull me aside sometimes and point at Patrick and say, 'Can you believe it? That's Patrick doing that! He's growing up,' " reports Teddy's friend Adam Randolph.

But the most noticeable change is in Kara. She and her mother have become friends, and Kara has developed a strong quality of empathy. Linda Semans offers an example:

"My mother and I had a huge fight over nothing one day. At the time it seemed like the biggest deal in the world. I ran out of the house and immediately headed to Kara's. That was the refuge. I poured this whole thing out on Kara and was frantic about the entire mess and she stood there just crying and crying. She just understood what I was going through. She was not patronizing or even being sympathetic. It was complete empathy. It's the most marvelous quality she has."

Florescu: "Kara loves to do things for others. People are forever doing things for the Kennedys, so much so that they would never have to exert themselves in their lives if they chose. The thing that is so impressive about her is the happiness she gets when others let her do them small favors."

Kara, who has enjoyed studying public affairs at Tufts, sees herself somehow working in that area, perhaps in international diplomacy. Joan strongly urges her to do what she wants and not to step aside for any man in doing it, Kennedy or not. Kara smiles. "It doesn't have to be politics," she says. But that glint is still in her eyes.

Teddy Junior — A Most Uncommon Man

WITH TEDDY AT THE WHEEL OF HIS JEEP, HE AND KIEVY Goldsman, his Wesleyan College roommate, were flying down a country road at a speed far in excess of the posted limit. Kievy tried to conceal his alarm, but apparently not too successfully. "You know why I drive so fast?" Teddy explained. "After you lug this thing around all your life, you have to go fast at something."

The "thing" was Teddy's prosthetic leg. He really has lugged it around for much of his life and it is a story of great human triumph.

He had met the issue head-on. It began in November 1973, when he was 12. His governess, Theresa Fitzpatrick, noticed a bump on his leg just below the knee and reported it. It was some days before the diagnosis was final. His father remembers watching his graceful son—fastest runner in his class—play during that interval and wondering, "Will I ever see him run again?" The senator still winces at the memory.

After the diagnosis was final—chondrosarcoma, a fast-growing cancer of the cartilage—Ted had to tell his son, and he had to be careful: "The brain can only take so much, and the heart can only stand so much," he says. "I'd never have forgiven myself if I had handled it badly." After delicately leading up to the question the father could no longer avoid it. He found it extrordinarily difficult to look at his son.

"You're going to lose part of your leg," he said finally.

"How much? Are they just going to shave a little bit?"

"No, they'll have to take your leg above the knee."

Looking back, young Teddy now remembers, "I guess I feared it was cancer all along after a certain point. I felt pretty bad, and I got pretty bummed out. Luckily the operation was the next day, so I didn't have much time to think about it."

Neither did his father. All he could manage was to exclaim to his old friend Claude Hooton, "My God, have we done the right thing?" before he had to rush off. The next day was his niece Kathleen's wedding day as well as the day of Teddy's operation. The cancer could not wait, and the wedding had been set months before. Who had time to think? From telling Teddy what had to be done, the senator went straight to the wedding rehearsal and dinner, just as his brother Robert would have done had he been alive. "He sang his heart out and joked around," Kathleen recalls. "He was wonderful."

Next morning, as soon as the senator was sure that the operation was successful and without complication, he hurried from Georgetown University Hospital home to McLean, Virginia, to dress for the wedding. "Theresa," he called to the governess, who was laying out his suit as he emerged dripping from the shower with only a skimpy towel covering him, "unless you want the sight of your life, you'd better leave."

Theresa still laughs when she tells about it: "Even at the worst of times, the Kennedys wanted something to lift their spirits," she says.

Shortly afterward, a beaming Uncle Ted delivered his niece Kathleen to a nervous but very happy David Townsend. Then he raced back to the hospital, arriving shortly after Teddy had been brought into the recovery room. The family priest, James English, was with him. Here is how he remembers what happened next:

"The boy was struggling to come out of the anesthesia, and his father just bowed down and put his forehead on his son's chest. The boy just instinctively put his arms around his head, and he just held on, and held on, and held on. It was the most beautiful thing I've ever seen."

Teddy was home for Christmas, full of determination and high spirits. "He became a man in 24 hours," declares the governess, who is not the impressionable sort. Rick Burke, one of the senator's former assistants, recalls the boy's unflagging good spirits and the delight with which he'd ask everyone to look at his stump: "I think he knew it would be tough for some of us to do that. It was his way of having fun with us," says Burke. "It was also his way of showing us that he was all right."

Teddy was undaunted by his ordeal. He wanted to know that

his leg had been used somehow for research "so that other kids wouldn't have to go through what he did," Hooton remembers. He made an elaborate Christmas card in the form of an eight-panel cartoon to send to Dr. George Hyatt, the surgeon who operated on him:

In panel 1, the surgeon, reading a medical chart, stands over "T.K." In the background, crutches lean ominously against the wall. "What!!!!!" cries Teddy in panel 2, jumping from his chair. "Teddy, just take it easy," Dr. H. says soothingly in panel 3, whereupon Teddy socks Dr. H right in the nose in panel 4 and the doctor sees stars. Laid out on an X-ray table in panel 5, Dr. Hyatt hears the recommended treatment for his damaged proboscis—"Amputation of the Nose." The sorry spectacle of Hyatt's operation is chronicled in panel 6, and in panel 7 noseless Dr. H. is fuming—literally—at Teddy, smoke pouring from his ears. Panel 8 ends with Teddy's Christmas greetings: "Just getting you back," the youngster signed off. "Merry Christmas!"

Right after Christmas, his father told him that an old colleague, Sen. Hubert Humphrey, had been hospitalized with cancer, which would eventually take his life. And Teddy's sturdy spirit shone through again. He wrote to Humphrey: "Dear Sen. Humphrey, I'm sorry to hear you are in the hospital. Once you are out of the %#&!$* hospital you'll be fine, believe me. Love, Teddy Kennedy, Jr."

He always did things with a smile, even when it hurt. During the operation, a cast had been taken of the diseased limb, from which a temporary and later a final prosthesis were shaped. Within a few days Teddy was walking with the aid of therapists, parallel bars, and the encouragement of his family. The final, sophisticated prosthesis was fastened to his leg by suction and by a belt secured to his waist. "Just a few days after I began to walk, Kara and Patrick were making bets with each other as to how far I'd go before I'd fall. It was a relief that they were not going to treat me differently. But you can't help some resentment. You feel that life has done you wrong."

A remarkable initial recovery ensued, and within four months Teddy was struggling down ski slopes with one ski on his remaining leg and two small skis attached to his poles.

Then came the worst part of all—chemotherapy, designed to prevent recurrence. Teddy remembers those 18 months as being very close to hell. His father saw him through it all the way. Every third weekend they would go together to Boston Children's Hospital for the massive, painful injections of the anticancer drug called methotrexate, so highly toxic itself that it is accompanied by other injections of an antidote called a citrovorum factor.

"The drugs make you so sick that I'd begin to vomit as I walked in the door," Teddy remembers. Before they even arrived at the hospital after their plane flight, Teddy would begin to feel ill, and as soon as he saw the *Citgo* sign over Kenmore Square, he knew that the hospital was only six minutes away, and his stomach would start to churn. "I really hated Boston for a while," he says, "because I'd only go there to get sick. They'd start about 6 P.M. Friday and the drug went in for six hours. They make you so nauseous that they give you other drugs to knock you out. You are basically incoherent until the next day at 6 P.M. You vomit incessantly until you can't vomit any more. There are times of real despair—I didn't get them as much as others I've heard about—where you think it would be better to live with the disease than to go through one more session. In the midst of them you think to yourself, 'I'd rather die.' But that's when my father and my friends were so important. They were always there, and that presence was enough to get me through."

Often the senator would sleep in a chair in his son's room, giving him the doses of antidote every five hours and holding young Teddy's head while he vomited through the night. The father learned how to give the antidote injections, which spanned three days, so that he could take Teddy back home on Sunday instead of Monday or Tuesday. That, too, became a family joke: "Here comes the mad scientist," Kara or Patrick would yell as their father headed for his son's room with the hypodermic. It may have been this long shared ordeal that produced the astonishing physical similarities between father and son. Teddy replicates his father's mannerisms to perfection: the same grin, the same gestures, the same shaggy heartiness.

Friends like Sam Medalie and Adam Randolph and Joey Gargan were also critically important to Teddy's recovery. They sat for hours with him, often helping him to vomit when he was awake or just perched at his side while he slept.

Unyielding realism and unremitting insistence on normality were the ingredients of the family's reaction. "We used the word 'cancer' from day one, just as we used the word 'stump,' " says governess Fitzpatrick. "Even a horrid word loses some of its terror if it is used often enough. I was always tough with Teddy right after he came home. I said, 'Teddy, Kara got the paper last week and Patrick did it the week before, so it's your turn now. And don't complain. When I was your age I had to milk twelve cows before I did anything else in the day. Get on with it.' "

Father English: "His recovery was strictly a 'Kennedy' thing. First, there was enormous support and love inside the family. The senator, for an unemotional man, gave enormous tactile love. They just hugged at critical times. The other part of it was the heritage and the training. Teddy was aware of it all—you're a Kennedy and we Kennedys overcome everything that happens to us. So don't expect any sympathy. Get right up now and do the next big thing. And the next big thing for you is to get on with your life on one leg."

It was all harrowing for Joan, who later revealed that she simply could not cope with her son's cancer nor help much in his recovery. She stopped drinking during the period before and just after his operation, but then, she says, "I fell to pieces" and began drinking heavily. "Ted carried the whole burden by himself," says a former aide. "It was an incredible performance. The thing he talked about most, though, was how the other kids were doing."

The spirit with which he bore his affliction, the determination he showed in conquering it and the great publicity he received all encouraged Teddy to begin a virtual career of helping others who faced the same thing. It started when he was asked to counsel another boy who was the same age and who needed the same operation. "Teddy didn't hesitate a moment," says English. "It was like two old ladies talking about their illnesses." Teddy showed him how his new leg worked: "Have you ever shoved your finger in a Coke bottle and then been able to pick it up? That's how my leg stays in place." It was immeasurably comforting to the other boy and he got through his operation and recovery very well.

Teddy has become tirelessly dedicated about helping the handicapped. He has worked in hospital wards, answered untold letters from those seeking moral support or just a kind word. His friend Sam Medalie mentions how once Teddy talked a terrified youth into having an operation, and that the young man now tells his own friends that if it weren't for Teddy Kennedy he would have died.

"I'm in a position where very little effort on my part can make a lot of difference to others," Teddy says. "People remember that. My letters usually say, 'Look, things are going to probably get worse for you, but that's not the end. You have it in you to fight on and make a difference. You have to take what you have and work with it.' One of the best handicapped skiers in the world came up to me recently and told me that he'd never thought of skiing until he saw a picture of me skiing. It's that type of thing that makes me feel good."

Now he carries his message of hope wherever he goes. "I've used sports because they are important to me. I've tried to tell handicapped people that sports can make them feel independent and make them feel good about themselves. There is nothing worse than feeling that others have to do little favors for you. Well, in sports, you do it or nobody does it. No one will swim 20 laps or ski downhill for you. I told one guy once who loved fencing and was afraid to do it again that he should try because it was the thing he really wanted to do. You are the same person you were before your disability and the key is to show that to the world. The way you look at it affects the way everyone around you looks at it."

Teddy's passion is skiing. He raced in competitions for handicapped skiers in the winter of 1982-83, and has begun promoting a "Kennedy Cup" for skiers with disabilities. Proceeds will go to help the handicapped—and the U.S. Olympic Ski Team.

"People give me much too much credit," he insists. "Many have had to do more than I have. Everything is sensationalized. To me it was something very simple. I had a disease and I had to lose my leg. I went through my chemotherapy, learned how to walk again and that's that. Plus my family could afford the best doctors and best treatments. I had a lot of opportunities, and one of the reasons I'm getting involved in speaking is that I want to repay some of that debt. It takes so little from me to make others feel better about themselves, it would be unthinkable not to make the effort."

He is completely uninhibited about his leg. The first time his roommate Akiva Goldsman met him, Teddy was doing acrobatics on a rope high above a swimming reservoir. Kievy thought to himself, "My God! This guy's insane the way he's jumping and swinging around. His leg is going to fall off or he's going to kill himself." Teddy also makes no attempt to conceal his prosthesis. "We were at a party once," says Kievy, "and Ted was wearing his very brief shorts, and this woman just could not take her eyes off his leg. Teddy decided to help her relax about it. He grabbed a piece of cheese and a knife and started slicing the cheese on his leg. 'See,' he said. 'It makes a great chopping board.' "

As his friend Adam Randolph suggests, "Teddy has extracted every ounce of wisdom from his experience."

No one in the family knows better than Teddy how to have a good time. He loves to act, and did so professionally one summer in *The Petrified Forest* at the Berkshire Playhouse. He loves to treat his friends well and loves a lark. He also loves to love. His mother now cautions photographers to arrange family pictures so that Teddy's current girl friend is at one of the ends. It is easier that way to crop her out when Teddy moves on, as he seems always to do. So far.

The archetypical Teddy Kennedy tale took place one sultry summer's afternoon when he and Adam Randolph and Linda Semans decided to sail from Cape Cod out to Nantucket despite dead air and forecasts of fog. A trip that would normally take about three hours meandered its way into its eighth hour before nightfall—and fog.

Finally they dropped anchor, they had no idea where. They had plenty to eat and drink, but were unable to see beyond the prow, and worried that the ferry that services Nantucket might cut them in two. Another boat full of revelers passed, but they decided after less-than-coherent exchanges that neither boat knew where they were. To get out of the traffic they pulled anchor in the pitch black and within two minutes had run aground. "I can't get my leg wet," deadpanned Teddy. "You guys get out and push." So they did until the boat was off the sandbar. As dawn broke and the fog burned off, they awoke to find they had spent the night about 300 yards from the entrance to the harbor.

"See, you guys, you're always okay when you're with me," Teddy proclaimed.

His father certainly thinks so. "The whole experience has made our relationship grow and get much richer," says the senator of the cancer and its aftermath. "It has developed a bond that has been extraordinary. He is my friend, my son, and my colleague—a combination of them all."

On Teddy's 21st birthday—in September 1982—Kara organized a weekend party on Nantucket for about 20 of Teddy's friends. They rented a cottage and on the birthday evening itself took over a large portion of a local restaurant. Ted Kennedy was master of ceremonies for a night of organized celebration at which many of the guests performed. The toasts to Teddy and the family were elaborate and full of Irish mirth and mawkishness.

Everyone remembers Patrick's toast: "You might say Teddy is a great partier . . . and it's true. And you might say Teddy is a great lover . . . and it's true. And you might say Teddy is a brave guy . . . and it's true. But I know something better than any of you. He's the greatest brother that ever was." As usual, Patrick could barely get out the final words because he was in tears as he remembered what his older brother means to him.

"The Dads" finished the evening with an elaborate tour de family: that Kara was the most beautiful and kindest of the lot . . . that Patrick was the nicest teenager who ever lived . . . and that he and Teddy had shared hard times, good times, bad times and come through them together. No friends had been through more, and they had seen it through and become closer for it. The celebrants had barely put their handkerchiefs away after Patrick's toast than they were moistened again for Edward Kennedy's. As they tried to regain control, the celebrants heard applause coming from the other side of the partition in the restaurant. When some peeked around the corner, they saw a roomful of diners standing and cheering them.

An End and a Beginning

THEY MET ON THE DAY AFTER THANKSGIVING 1982, IN JACKIE Onassis' bungalow in the compound—the "President's House," where Bobby Junior and the rest of the Hyannis Port Terrors had gathered sometimes on summer nights past to hatch their plots after sneaking past Ethel or Jean or Ted or Eunice or other parental watchdogs.

On this day, Ted Junior, Kara, and Patrick were there to analyze quite a different kind of plan. Together with young Joe, Kathleen, and Steve Smith, Jr., plus Steve Senior, his wife Jean, and Pat Lawford, they had come to help Ted Kennedy make the final decision as to whether he would run again for the presidency. On generational lines, the council was weighted six to four for youth, and their voices carried at least equal weight in the deliberations, particularly with the senator.

"The dream will never die," Kennedy had declared in the peroration to his eulogy of brothers Jack and Bobby at the Kennedy Library dedication in 1979, and the fact is that Kennedys do seem to roll along with a powerful inertial force, like the sun, generating heat. So, although Kennedy's sure-thing run for the presidency, or at least the Democratic nomination, had fallen short in 1980, by the middle of 1982 he was ready to go after Ronald Reagan—an even more inviting target than Jimmy Carter had been.

Despite the final collapse in the interim of Ted's marriage to Joan, the auguries were surprisingly good. They had been in '79, too, only this time, it seemed, even more so. There was not high inflation any longer; it was deep recession, with 10 percent unemployment as a national norm, and interest rates even higher. This time Kennedy was sure the gods—at least the liberal wing of the Democratic Party—were with him.

But this time his children were not. The family had been wrestling with the issue for months, while out sailing, at the dinner table, after the touch football games, in quiet encounters at EMK's house on Squaw Island off Hyannis Port—as Kennedy looked beyond his certain reelection to the Senate to the next stage, if any, of his career.

Larry Horowitz, a key adviser, distributed a report that strongly supported another bid by his boss. Poll data from Patrick Caddell, for example, showed that the TV ads backing Kennedy's Senate race had been somewhat successful in responding to the character issues that had derailed his primary run against Carter two years before. One of the dramatic ads featured Kathleen telling how her uncle, standing in as always for his murdered brother Robert, had given her away on her wedding day only hours after Teddy Junior had lost his right leg to cancer.

Although the results did not take into account the effect of the impending divorce, the turnabout had been impressive, Horowitz pointed out: among voters who saw the ads, the percentage who considered Ted to be a moral person had leaped from 35 percent to 52 percent, and he'd posted a similar jump in trustworthiness. Although more people than not still thought he would panic in crises, he had picked up 17 points on reliability too. Voters clearly were beginning to feel much more comfortable with Ted Kennedy.

Other signs were cautionary, though. Exit poll data from Massachusetts—the heart of Kennedy turf—showed that fully a third of the electorate felt he should not run for the presidency. The feeling was broad among Kennedy-haters and Kennedy-lovers, Republicans and Democrats, persons who thought he was a good man, and persons who thought he was the devil himself. Some people simply thought he was unfit for the job, others thought it was an open question, and still others, though they believed he was a fine legislator, said they simply could not vote for him as an executive. Polls in New Hampshire showed that the ads, as good as they were, had not budged this group at all.

It would be a considerable handicap to begin a contest with that much sentiment against him. Although it was not a highlight issue of the meeting, the participants knew that the coming divorce would not improve this situation and that Kennedy had no appealing alternative—he could not possibly run as a bachelor, and a quick remarriage at the beginning of the campaign would not have put him in a much better position. In addition, another Chappaquiddick book, billed as containing sensational new information, was soon expected.

Before they had hashed it through, Teddy Junior abruptly cut Horowitz off in midsentence: "I don't really care about the numbers," he said, turning to his father. "I care about what is best for the family and what I think is best for you. As we learned in 1980, polls don't mean a hell of a lot. We haven't seen my father much since that time," he added, now to the whole group. The unspoken implication was that, with Joan gone and yet another campaign to wage, family life would simply be annihilated.

The group chewed these matters over for a while, the younger members reporting how they had recoiled with fright and anger from the virulent personal attacks made on Ted about Chappaquiddick and about his marriage during the 1980 primaries. They weren't especially anxious to go through that again, ads or no ads.

The strain of an anticipated campaign was already showing on some. Young Teddy had succumbed to an uncharacteristic flash of anger during a Philadelphia Democratic conclave early in the summer at a reception given by his father. He overheard a wellfed delegate mocking his family. "These Kennedys will do anything for votes," the man joked as he helped himself to a lobster freshly flown from Maine. Enraged, Teddy reached over several shoulders to snatch the lobster. "If that's the way you think, then get outta here! Beat it!" he cried.

The other cousins had similar misgivings, and like the trusted counselors they now were, Joe and Kathleen and Steve Junior spoke thoughtfully and objectively about the pitfalls any new campaign would bring. Patrick, lounging in front of an aging couch, let his thoughts be known with unhindered body language, scowling at anything suggesting that his father run. And his teeth sparkled in a grin when his big brother weighed in with the strong emotional plea against another campaign. Teddy, in fact, was speaking more for Patrick than anyone else. The two had discussed Patrick's misgivings about the race, and the big brother, as he always had, was standing up for Patrick's position. All the cousins obviously influenced EMK at least as heavily as their elders.

In great anxiety, the senator adjourned the meeting so that he could talk again privately with all three of his children. The discussions went on during the rest of the weekend. The children were unanimous and adamant—almost strident—in insisting that he not run. They had done it his way in 1980. Now it was his turn to do it their way, and his safety was still the dominant, if unmentioned, concern. Patrick, 15, held the trump card. He was literally terrified by the prospect.

It was a tug of war between the power of the children and the power of the staff, armed with their persuasive polls and persuasive ads and, as they viewed it, the country's paramount need. It was no contest to Ted Kennedy. His children held all the cards, and their judgment also coincided with political reality. Finally, after Kennedy had heard all the staff arguments for a race, he told them of his children's concerns, and cut the staff off with a brusque "Nothing will change my mind."

Quickly a statement was drafted and on the following Wednesday morning Kennedy announced that he would not run, citing all the reasons that had been extracted by that exhausting weekend, and not even trying to duck the painful one of his disintegrated marriage. He said: "For the members of my family the 1980 campaign was sometimes a difficult experience and it is very soon to ask them to go through it again. In addition, the decision Joan and I have made about our marriage has been painful for our children as well as ourselves. For these reasons I believe that my first and overriding obligation now is to Patrick and Kara and Teddy."

In firmly closing the door on 1984, however, EMK left a latchstring out suggesting no lack of interest in the White House later: "Actually, I enjoyed campaigning in Iowa in 1980, and so I may do it again," he said—and he had included that teaser over Patrick's tearful insistence the night before that he delete it. For, as Teddy Junior had reminded the family caucus, his father was still a young man and events might yet prove propitious for him. Besides, there would certainly come a time when family emotions would subside. With the Kennedys, there is always another day—or at the very least, another Kennedy.

Young Ted summed it up: "Circumstances are different now, especially for Patrick, who is young and been through enough as it is with the divorce. The consensus was that it is not a now-or-never thing for my father. He didn't rule out doing it sometime in the future. I'm sure I'll feel differently and my sister and brother will feel differently then."

So, just as Robert Kennedy's children had taken affairs into their own hands when they demanded and won from their mother an end to the public memorial masses for Robert, now EMK's children had used their power. They wanted a chance to assimilate the dreadful and dizzying events in their young lives, to be alone with themselves and their father, family, and friends.

It was not a new desire. Right after the 1980 campaign, young Teddy had rejected an attempt by the senator's staff to have him cooperate with a television effort to dramatize his struggle with cancer: "This is a time I want for me," he insisted. "Kara and I deserve a chance to have a few years to ourselves." The veto was sustained.

The real message the Kennedys sent to the nation with Ted's statement following the Thanksgiving conclave was that they were rethinking strategy and regrouping forces for another engagement at another time, probably on the same field and possibly with the same leader.

Yet at the same time, many of the younger Kennedys had been savoring those salutory aspects of life that, because they were Kennedys, had largely been foreign to them—things like quiet weekends with loved ones, marriages and children, families of one's own, and careers not even linked indirectly to politics and the grueling drudgery of campaigning. Eric Breindel, a friend of Bobby Junior's, recently introduced his mother to Bobby and his new wife Emily. "My mother was very struck," Briendel reports, "that Bobby was constantly referring to 'my wife's feeling,' or 'my wife thinks,' or 'We have to do this or that.' It was a whole new facet of life that he was discovering, and he was rather enchanted by it."

Similarly, Anne Coffey, a friend of Kathleen Townsend's, has noticed how preoccupied Kathleen has become with her own family and its concerns. "It is clearly the center of her life," Coffey says.

Even combative Joe has discovered, according to brother Bobby, that "You don't have to back-slap your way around politics in order to get something meaningful done. It's changed his beliefs about what is important and how it's best to get it done. Politics isn't everything, anymore."

Many, too, were just now, as young adults, evaluating for the first time their father's and uncle's roles in great events of the recent past. "We studied the Cuban missile crisis," says Kara, "and it was hard to hear the criticism that 'President Kennedy used a macho style.' You want to be protective of the family.

It's almost a sense of caring too much and loving him too much that makes it hard to study him now."

Politics remains the measure of the Kennedys, though. The public expects it and the family feeds upon it and dynastically encourages it. As Jack Kennedy once had inscribed on a cigarette case he gave to brother Bob: "Where I end why don't you begin?" Or as Ted Kennedy joked in Ames, Iowa, one wintry night in 1980: "I'd like to introduce my son, Patrick Joseph Kennedy. He told me last night he had decided he loves campaigning—and just may do a little of it on his own. I said, 'Not yet.' But you can expect to see Patrick out here running in the Iowa caucuses in 2004. That's the first time he'll be old enough to run for President. I'll be with him giving him a helping hand."

When the younger Kennedys do finally enter politics—and it clearly is a matter of when and not if—they will find an atmosphere vastly different from the one in which their parents moved. Certainly it will be less adoring and less prone to swallowing the Camelot script whole. Doug Spooner, a friend of the cousins, is correct when he suggests that Kennedys will still get a "bye" into the finals—that is, they will not have to slug their way in low-level political battles before they are considered ready for top jobs. The name still pulls in those thousands upon thousands of homes across the country where a framed picture of Jack hangs right alongside the oleograph of Jesus or the photo of Martin Luther King, Jr. And Robert Kennedy is still almost daily invoked somewhere as the great liberal martyr.

Even so, it is now wholly apparent that the competition in the finals will be stiff. There will be no victories by default, and certainly no automatic succession. Jackie's marriage to Aristotle Onassis; the Chappaquiddick affair and the breakdown of Ted's marriage; posthumous scandalous revelations, true or not, about Jack Kennedy's boudoir diplomacy; and finally Ted's failed 1980 campaign—all these have been astringent correctives of the family image.

The Kennedys are no longer seen as gods in a new pantheon, but as highly favored human beings with the faults that privilege almost invariably magnifies. And privilege dies hard. The Kennedys have a tendency to think that other people will just get out of their way if they want to move where another stands. Young Joe was rather taken aback, for example, when his suggestion that he might run for state treasurer in Massachusetts in 1978 was greeted without acclamation by the state's Democratic leaders.

Similarly, Bobby Junior, still in law school, was approached by New York City political figures—and he had emissaries talking to them—in late 1979 and early 1980 to see if maybe he could run for Congress somewhere in Manhattan, Staten Island, or Brooklyn. Again, wiser counsel prevailed. When similar entreaties were made to Bobby in 1982, he turned them down flat, agreeing with friends that he had to prove himself in some way before he accepted the chalice. Still, the massive self-assurance that seems to come with Kennedy genes is still alive.

They know that their time will come, and they believe they will win. The lesson to be learned from Jack and RFK is not merely that they offered the world a new and liberal vision of human potential—but that they had won. Beyond their money and their sex appeal, the Kennedys have the will and the training to succeed.

"One must never be defeated," Grandma Rose kept repeating to herself as she paced outside Georgetown Hospital while young Teddy was having his cancer operation. "I must never be vanquished."

Neither, almost certainly, will the younger Kennedys. The only real questions are, Who will be first? and When? There is no dearth of prospects. All the older cousins are potential and promotable candidates. Kathleen, the oldest, although intensely devoted to her family, has invested enormous energy in politics already, and is adept at formulating and arguing issues, having shown herself to great effect in managing Uncle Ted's 1982 senatorial campaign. Her family obligations are preeminent for the immediate future, though, so the family is looking to others.

The first to make a tentative stab at politics, young Joe, probably still draws the greatest attention as the oldest male. His Citizens Energy oil company could come to grief as oil prices plummet. The higher the price of oil, the greater the profit margin and the easier it is for Joe to trim his prices below market and still not lose money. The lower crude prices prevailing nowadays will strip him of at least some of this margin of safety. Yet CE is a neat piece of political invention, and has achieved a precisely targeted strategic effect.

As much as, if not more than any of his brothers or sisters

or cousins, Joe has found great satisfactions in being a husband and father. He is on his own. He has done well and he feels much less pressure now to get into the public arena than he did a short while ago. But he is still, of course, Joe Kennedy and the prospects for a Kennedy in Massachusetts are usually very good.

If Joe and Kathleen are at the moment somewhat reluctant candidates, the two most eager are Bobby Junior and Steve Smith, Jr. They both have natural presence, Bobby perhaps slightly more confident, but Steve being the more thorough. What would happen should they both decide to go for the same thing, or even different things at the same time? They both, after all, live in Manhattan. "I told him I wouldn't stand in his way," Bobby says. "He was just kidding around," Steve replies. When the time comes, the issue will be resolved and everyone will get behind the nominee. There is something to be said for going with a Kennedy who is not quite a Kennedy—that is, who carries a different name—although memories of Sargent Shriver's vice-presidential dunking on the McGovern ticket still smart, not to mention the bath he took on his own in the 1976 presidential race.

Of all the cousins, Michael, at 24, is the embodiment of what the Kennedys would like the world to think of when they think about the young Kennedys. He is a fine athlete and a good student. Less flamboyant than some of the others, he is still purposeful and decisive. He is quite respectable on all counts. If the older siblings or cousins do not make a move soon, they will have to get out of Michael's way.

But if romance still rules the Kennedy heart, then young John must have his chance—if he wants it, that is. To date he has not shown much inclination, but he has become a serious student of politics and public issues and it is a certainty he wants to move in important public service circles when his education is done. Young Ted gets that look in his eyes when the subject comes up. He wants to get into public service in some way, and would bring to it the formidable skills he has developed while promoting the cause of the handicapped. He, too, wants to—needs to—take a while off after college and then move on to professional school. But on the horizon there is another Ted Kennedy coming.

Bobby Shriver and Chris Lawford, both lawyers, are equally resolved to live by the family standard that enjoins all members to "make a difference." Both speak about politics in the distant future of their lives—Chris after he has proved himself on legal battlefields and Bobby after he has ripened his fortune and conquered numerous other horizons. Bobby has the greater yen for it and, like his father, is a serious and eclectic thinker. In a meritocracy Bobby Shriver would rise to the head of his generation.

In the end, though, there will be fewer opportunities for a larger number of Kennedys. "How many tightrope walkers can one family take?" asks Bobby Kennedy's friend Chris Bartle. There is a subtle competition that is unfolding now inside the family that is aimed at confronting that very problem. None of the tightrope walkers is trying to knock the others off, but it is clear that some are moving quickly in an attempt to be the first to the other side.

It was only after he got out of law school that Bobby Shriver began to study his uncle Bobby Kennedy's life, and he came away amazed at how hierarchically RFK's generation had been arranged—especially that someone as accomplished as Robert Kennedy should have spent so much of his life being what amounted to a spear carrier for his brother Jack. "His duty had been to protect Uncle Jack's interests," says Bobby. "It was only in his final years that he was forced to go on his own. There are no such protectors in my generation, in the sense Uncle Bobby was—acting always on behalf of an older relative.

"To me, the great tragedy of Uncle Bobby's death is that it threatened to cheapen his life. The assumption is that he just had what it took to be great. If he had lived, he would have conveyed to us that it just didn't fall into his lap, that a tremendous amount of work went into making him the great man he became."

The lesson has had its effect. Bobby Shriver now tells anyone who wants to know that the price of glory is sweat. "Not many of us have paid our dues," is how another cousin puts it, "and nothing we do will have much meaning or impact until we do."

By tradition with the Kennedys, it is oldest first, and young Bobby Kennedy, for one, adheres to that position. Therefore, he insists, "I would not do anything without first talking to Kathleen and Joe," his older siblings. But there are also younger brother Michael and cousin Teddy and Steve Smith, Jr., and the older Shrivers. They all have shown resolve to pay such dues as might be extracted, and they too might have wishes and could easily become dominant figures.

Wishes aside, American history reveals no great appetite for dynasties, although the Kennedys are arguably the most noteworthy one since the Adamses in the early years of the republic. The very fact of the geometric expansion in Kennedy numbers, however, carries with it a dilution of effect. It was relatively easy for Jack, Bobby, and Ted to make plans together. It is far harder for twenty-nine cousins, no matter how well bred, to avoid one another's toes. Moreover, the Video Age, which, for political purposes, Jack introduced and exploited, has a short memory, and always craves new images and new names. The Kennedys, despite their youth and the uniqueness of their individual lives, might be old hat—getting stale. In this Me Generation, so might be their doctrine of service. "I wonder whether their commitment to politics isn't a great white whale now," muses a friend of young Joe Kennedy's. "They spend a lot of time thinking about it, so much so that it would be awful if one or some of them tried it and failed. It is a true love-hate situation. They are fascinated by it and repelled by it at the same time. I think the thing that gives Joe the most pause is the prospect that it could come crashing down around him. Senator Kennedy's presidential loss took the pressure off a bit, but it is still there in themselves, in the family and in the public."

Still, several elements of the Kennedy story separate them from failed dynasties of the past, the most important being their uncommon ability to ride out disaster, which requires a special and enviable grace. They also have the unusual capacity to attract and retain talented and loyal assistants with diverse and complementary abilities: "With the Kennedys, everything was a kind of huge magnetic grid, everybody in touch with everybody," one of the aides, Fred Dutton, told journalist Burton Hersh. Moreover, they are passionately loyal to one another, living examples of Grandpa Joe's belief that a united family has a head start in any undertaking.

Many in the family argue, however, that it is too constricting to think of success only in terms of political victory. It is a family that has a singular capacity to create success in almost any area. The Shrivers, all by themselves, through the Special Olympics and the Joseph P. Kennedy Foundation, have altered the way the world looks at the handicapped, and Sargent Shriver's work to build up the Peace Corps and the Job Corps and the Legal

Services Corporation are vintage examples of imaginative social work. Arguably, Robert Kennedy's greatest success came from channels outside of government—the Bedford-Stuyvesant Corporation, which brought economic life to an arid ghetto. Kennedys are good at institution-building.

One way or another, they have an imperative need to play a role in the nation's future. They are summoned to service by those Kennedy voices, living and dead, that can never be stilled for long. Kara's friend Linda Semans describes a scene at Hyannis Port: "Teddy and John and two more of us played a game called Password practically through the night and had a terrific time. It was fun and goofy and very pleasant at this big house at the beach where we didn't have a care in the world. When the game was over, at about 4 A.M., John just turned to Teddy and said, 'You know, we should really see more of each other.' I thought, My God. That's John Kennedy talking to Ted Kennedy—only this time it is the juniors. John seemed to be saying that they really had something very deeply in common—bound to each other by a force no other humans could share. All of them hate the stuff about 'the torch being passed'—and I think it's romantic nonsense. But it is hard to express the meaning of that moment without reference to that feeling."

The drama that began with old Joe Kennedy piling up a great fortune and using it to catapult his family to the center of the world's stage seems, therefore, far from ended. Had they followed the usual course of empire, the family would have gone from celebrity (Honey Fitz) to society (Joseph P.) to aristocracy (JFK, RFK, and EMK), and then to hell. They have not. Through the regenerative power of the family, the cousins have been very carefully programmed, and they are willing and able to carry on. With allowances for the lens of a new age, they see things pretty much through their parents' eyes, and what they see is an unbroken line of achievement to which they are determined to add. It is the only acceptable way in which they can assure their parents and themselves that the past and the sacrifices of their dead do have a meaning, and that, come what may, they will be worthy of their heritage and their name.

Index